A-Z BLACK[BURN]

C000282094

Key to Maps

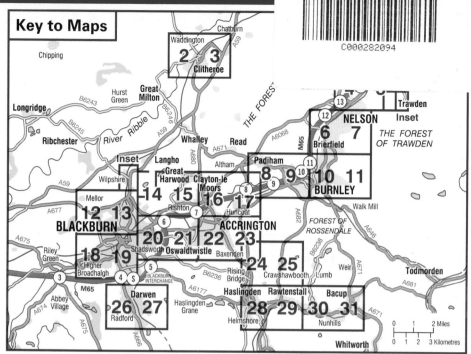

Reference

Motorway	M65
A Road	A679
Proposed	
B Road	B6234
Dual Carriageway	
One-way Street Traffic flow on A Roads is indicated by a heavy line on the driver's left.	→
Restricted Access	
Pedestrianized Road	
Track & Footpath	
Residential Walkway	
Railway Station / Heritage Station / Level Crossing / Tunnel	

Built-up Area	RYDAL RD.
Local Authority Boundary	
Postcode Boundary	
Map Continuation	12
Car Park (Selected)	P
Church or Chapel	†
Fire Station	■
House Numbers (A & B Roads Only)	246 213
Hospital	H
Information Centre	i
National Grid Reference	345

Police Station	▲
Post Office	★
Toilet with facilities for the Disabled	▽
Viewpoint	※
Educational Establishment	
Hospital or Hospice	
Industrial Building	
Leisure or Recreational Facility	
Place of Interest	
Public Building	
Shopping Centre or Market	
Other Selected Buildings	

Scale 1:19,000

3⅓ inches (8.47 cm) to 1 mile
5.26 cm to 1 kilometre

Copyright of Geographers' A-Z Map Company Limited

Fairfield Road, Borough Green, Sevenoaks, Kent TN15 8PP
Telephone: 01732 781000 (Enquiries & Trade Sales)
01732 783422 (Retail Sales)
www.a-zmaps.co.uk
Copyright © Geographers' A-Z Map Co. Ltd.

Ordnance Survey® This product includes mapping data licensed from Ordnance Survey® with the permission of the Controller of Her Majesty's Stationery Office.
© Crown Copyright 2003. All rights reserved. Licence number 100017302
Edition 2 2000, Edition 2A* (Part Revision) 2003

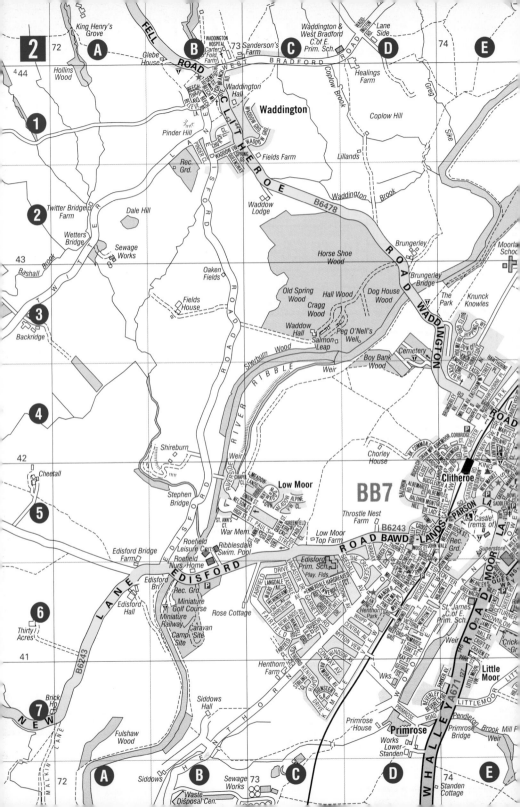

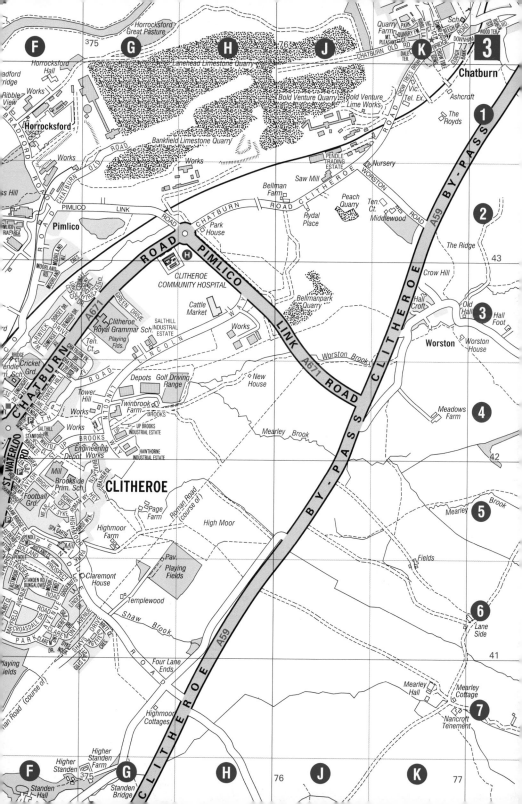

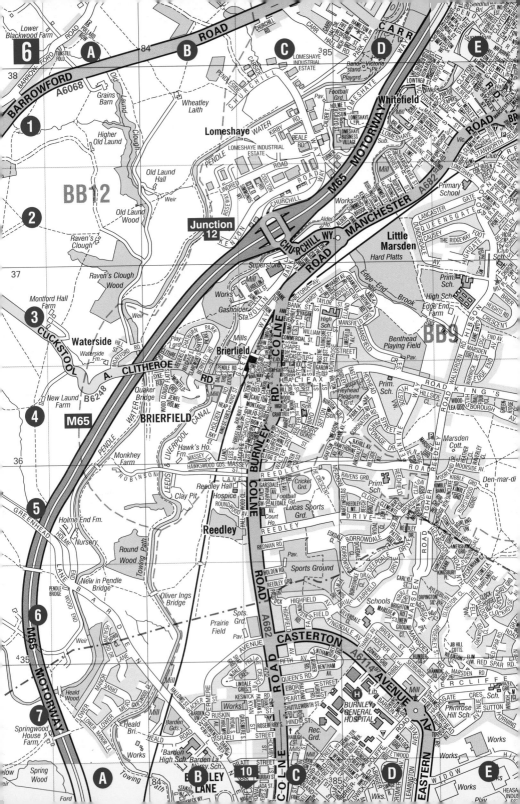

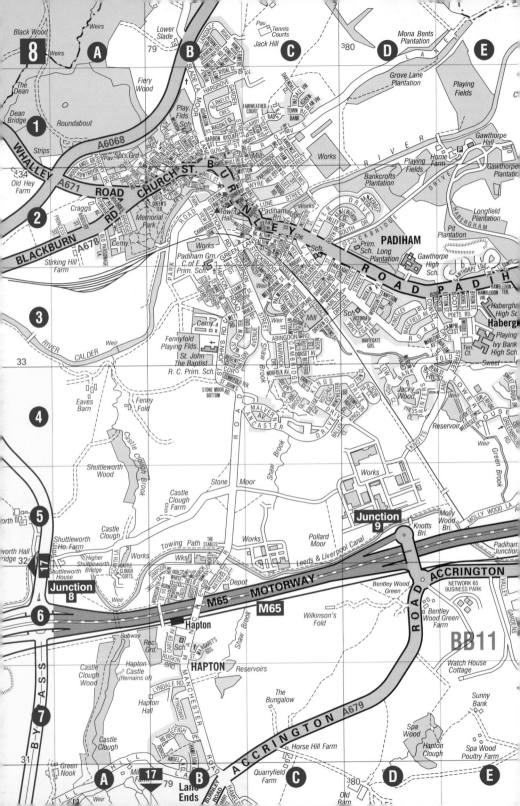

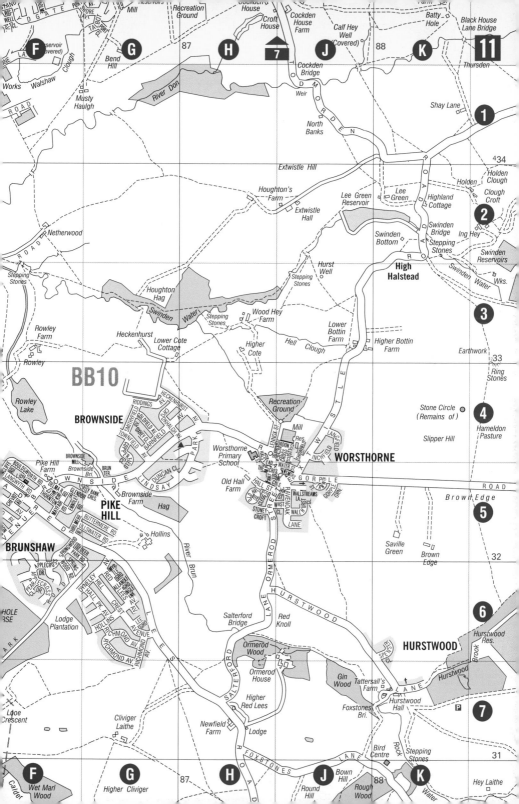

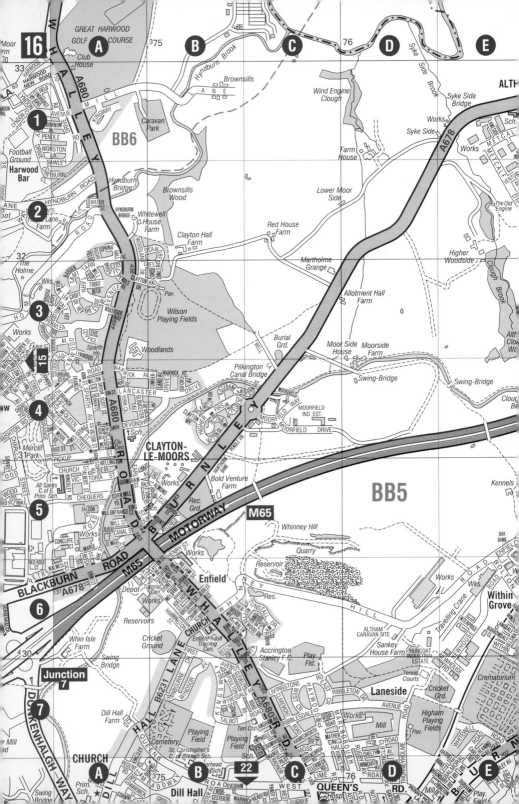

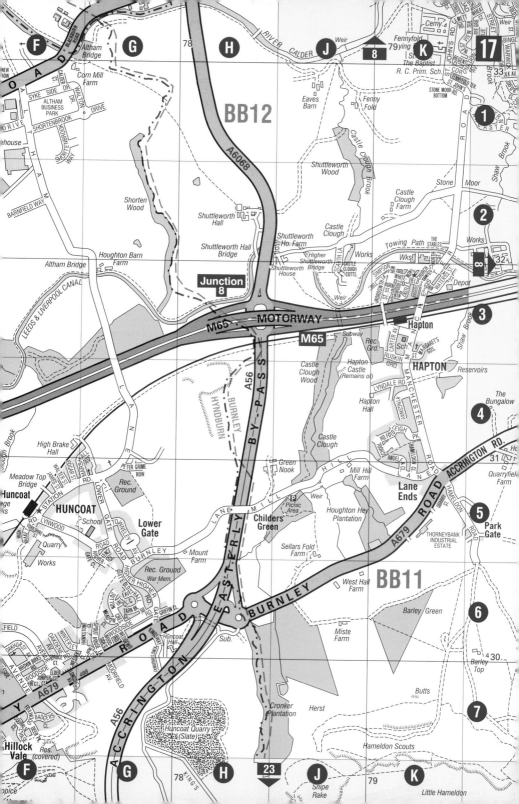

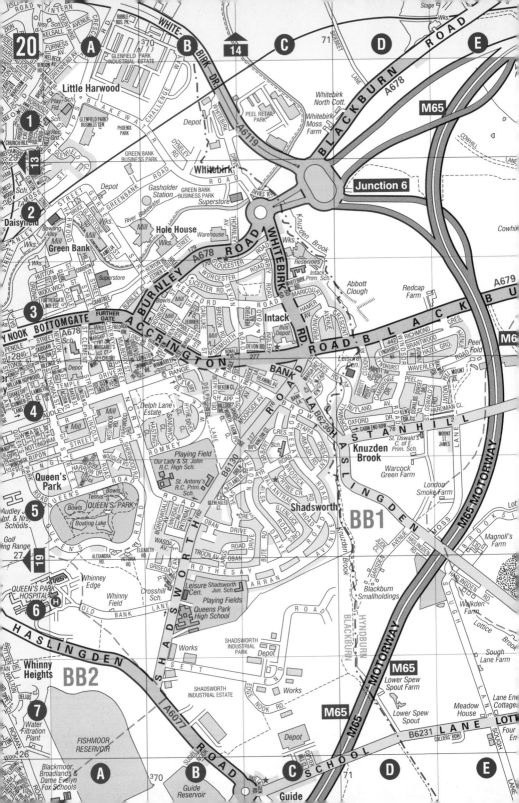

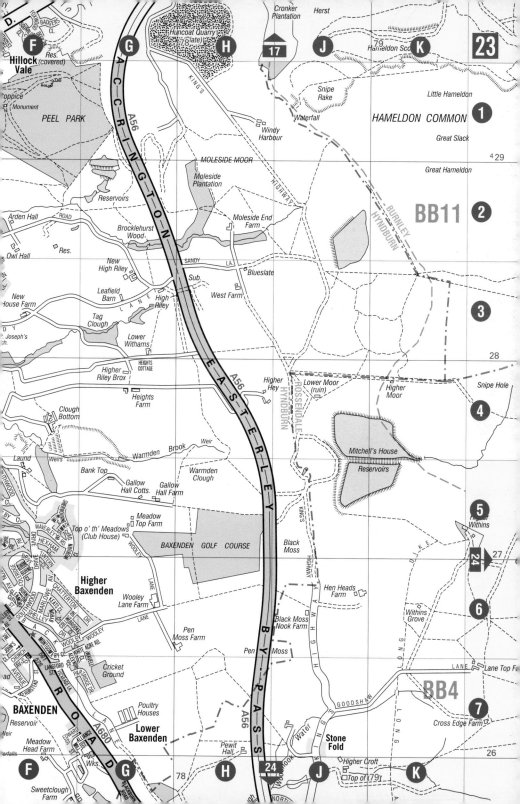

F **G** **H** **17** **J** **K**

Hillock Vale
Res. (covered)

Badgers Cl.

Coppice

Monument

PEEL PARK

Huncoat Quarry (slate)

KINGS

Cronker Plantation

Herst

79

Hameldon Scout

Little Hameldon

Snipe Rake

Waterfall

Windy Harbour

HAMELDON COMMON

Great Slack

1

MOLESIDE MOOR

4 29

Great Hamaldon

Moleside Plantation

BB11

2

Arden Hall

ROAD

Reservoirs

Brocklehurst Wood

Moleside End Farm

Blueslate

Res.

Owl Hall

New High Riley

SANDY LA

BURNLEY

HYNDBURN

New House Farm

Leafield Barn

High Riley

Sub.

West Farm

3

St. Joseph's ch.

Tag Clough

Lower Withams

28

Higher Riley Brox

HEIGHTS COTTAGE

Higher Hey

Lower Moor (ruin)

Higher Moor

Snipe Hole

4

Heights Farm

HYNDBURN

ROSSENDALE

Clough Bottom

A56

Laund

Weirs

Warmden   Brook

Weir

Mitchell's House Reservoirs

Bank Top

Warmden Clough

Gallow Hall Cotts.

Gallow Hall Farm

Withins

5

24

27

Meadow Top Farm

Top o' th' Meadows (Club House)

WOOLEY

BAXENDEN GOLF COURSE

Black Moss

KING'S

HIGHWAY

DYKE

Higher Baxenden

Wooley Lane Farm

LANE

Hen Heads Farm

Withins Grove

6

HEXHAM

WAVERLEY

Pen Moss Farm

Black Moss Nook Farm

Pen Moss

LANE TOP Fa

LONG

Cricket Ground

LANGFORD

BAXENDEN

Reservoir

Poultry Houses

Lower Baxenden

BB4

GOODSHAW

HIGHWAY

7

Cross Edge Farm

Meadow Head Farm

A680

ALLIANCE

A56

BY-PASS

EASTERLEY

ACCRINGTON

KINGS

Water

Stone Fold

Higher Croft

Top of 79

26

F **G** 78 **H** **24** **J** **K**

Sweetclough Farm

Pewit Hall

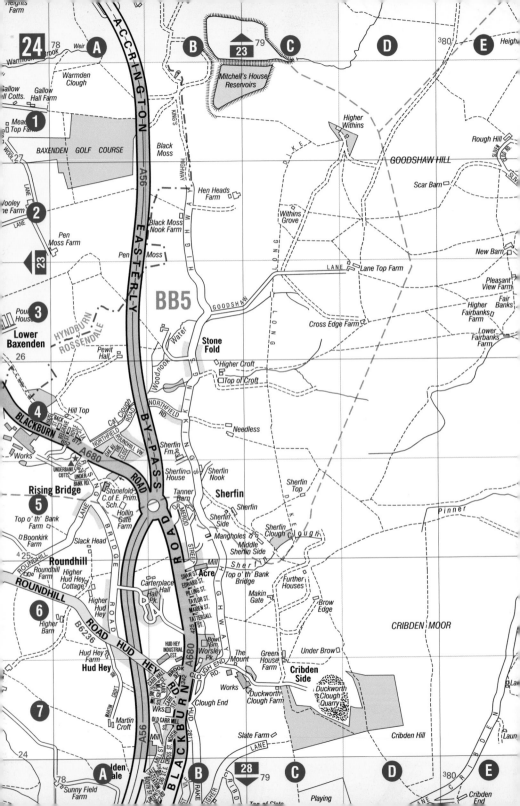

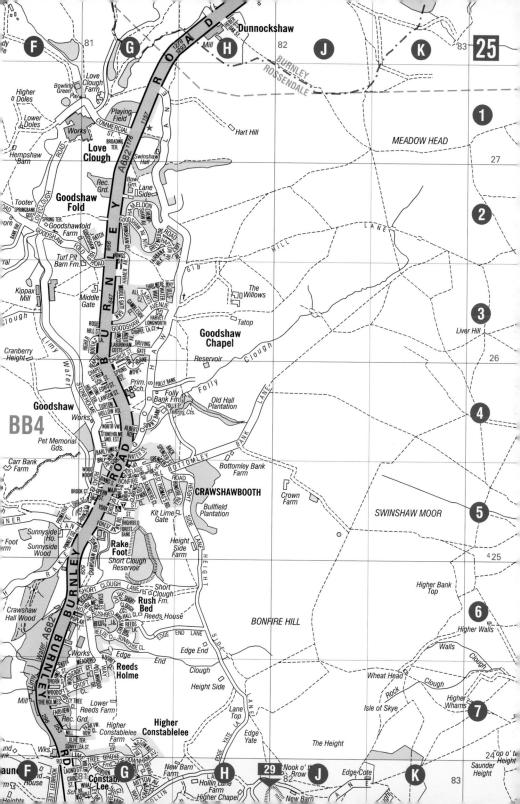

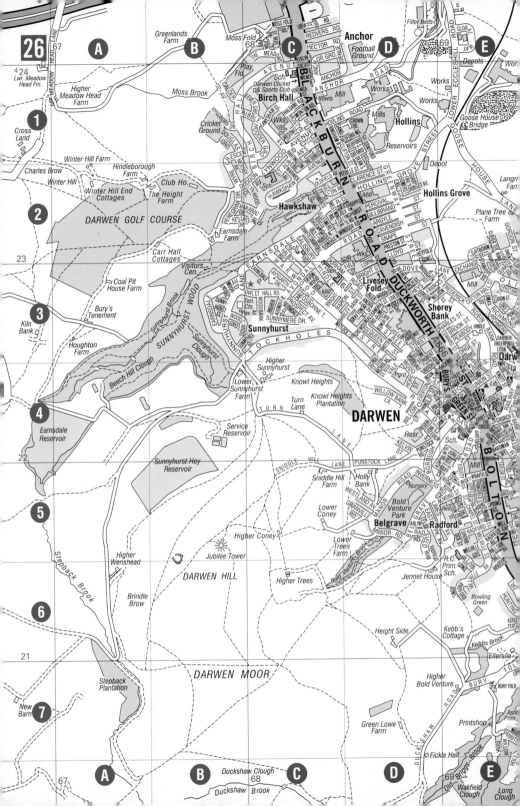

F
G
H
J
K
Bank Fold
Sniddleholme Farm
Bank Fold Lane
Lower Grimshaw Farm
New Waterside Paper Mill
Higher Grimshaw
Pleasant View
NURSERY NOOK
Davy Field
Flash Brook
370
71
72
24
Holme Fold
Dryster Fold
Hole House
1
Dick Bridge
Pickup Bank Res.
Ooze Castle Wood
Quaker Fold
2
Owlet Hall
Mill Barn
Mill Cottages
Garsden's Fold
Shorrock Fold
23
Pickup Bank
3
Lwr. Scholes Farm
Stock Clough
Mills
Hoddlesden
4
Holker Ho. Fm.
LONG HEY LANE
Langshaw Head
22
SUNNYFIELD LANE
Sunnyfield Fm.
5
Far Scotland Farm
Middle Scotland Farm
Near Scotland Farm
6
Scotland Res.
21
HODDLESDEN MOSS
7
Cuckoldmans
Far Hillock
Hillock
Hoddlesden Moss Brook
Scotland Clough
Stand Hill
Stand
JOHNSON ROAD
JOHNSON NEW ROAD
Waterside Brook
Luddington
Weir
Reservoir
Grave Yard
CLIFTON TER.
ST. PAUL'S TER.
Hoddlesden Hall
Sch.
QUEEN ST.
CARUS AV.
CHAPMAN ROAD
GLENSHIELS AVENUE
GLENCOE
RANKIN DR.
GLENCARRON CL.
GLENEAGLES AV.
ALPINE CL.
EARLS DR.
DUKES DR.
KINGS DR.
ROMAN RD.
ECCLESHILL COTTS.
Manor House Farm
ECCLES HILL
Pottery
Eccleshill Fold
Shaw Fold
The Bungalow
ECCLESHILL GDNS.
Bent Farm
Barnes Holme
Two Bridges
Lower Waterside Farm
VICTORIA BLDGS.
Waterside
Works
WATERSIDE TER.
LEONARD T.
Harwood Fold
Pot House
DANDY ROW
POT HOUSE LA.
THIRLMERE DR.
CONISTON DRIVE
AMBLESIDE DR.
HAWTHORN AV.
Playing Field
Darwen Moorland High Sch.
Sports Ground
Chapels
Beehive Mill
HOLDEN FOLD
Brocklehead Farm
BB3
FOLD LANE
T. ELLISON
Works
Sett End Playing Fields
Harwood's Farm
HARWOOD'S LANE
HODDLESDEN ROAD
Marsh House
Marsh Ho. Hostel
Tower Vw. Adult Train. Cen.
AVALLON WAY
MARSHAM GRO.
Princes
MARSH HOUSE LANE
Reservoir (covered)
Play-ground
BLACKSNAPE ROAD
Marsh House Mill
Stork Street
PRIORY DRIVE
CLOISTER DRIVE
Turncroft
St. Peter's C.of E. Prim. Sch.
CHAPTER CRESCENT
Blacksnape Playing Fields
Wks.
THORNCLIFFE DR.
MOOR CL.
BOSLEY CL.
RUDYARD
HEYS LANE
Blacksnape
Manor House Farm
Taylor's Green
SPRING MEADOWS
Hatton Hollow
ROMAN ROAD
Works
Rosehill
PICKUP FOLD RD.
Spring Vale
Sough
Works
Sough Tunnel
St. James C.of E. Prim. Sch.
Mill
GRIMSHAW STREET
SPRING VALE RD.
CRANBERRY LANE
Wks.
Spring Vale Garden Village
Mill
Kirkhams
Lower Barn Farm
Baron's Fold
Blacksnape Reservoir
Rushton's Height
Pinnacle Nook
Haddocks
Drummer Stoops
Plantation Cottage
Moss Side
Day Eye
Gorton Well
Cranberry Bottoms
Cranleigh
LANE
Jacks Key Clough
Sch.
ROAD CEMETERY RD.
Darwen Cemetery
KNOWLESLY
370
71
72

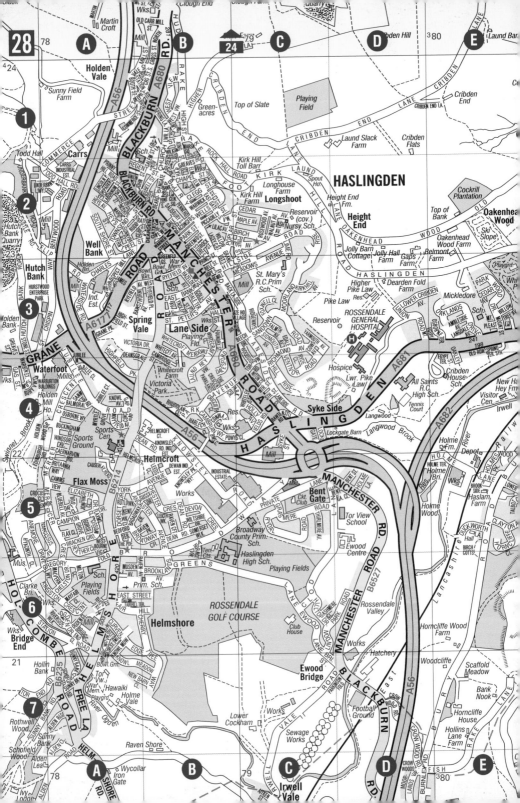

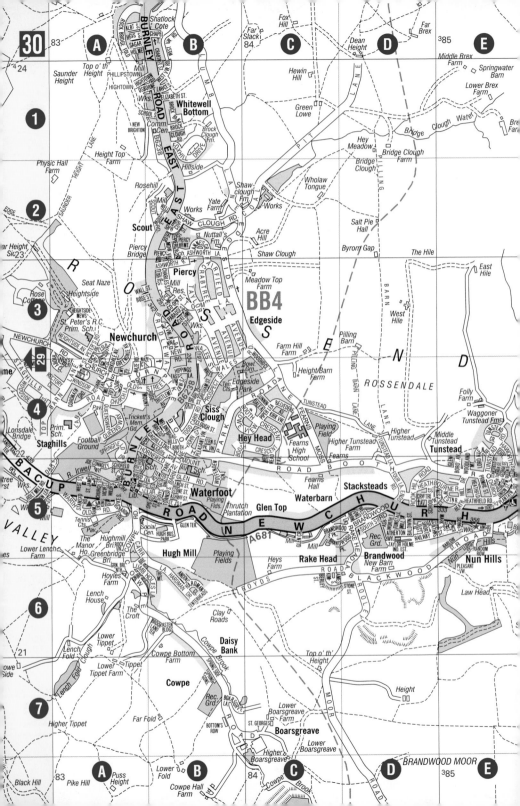

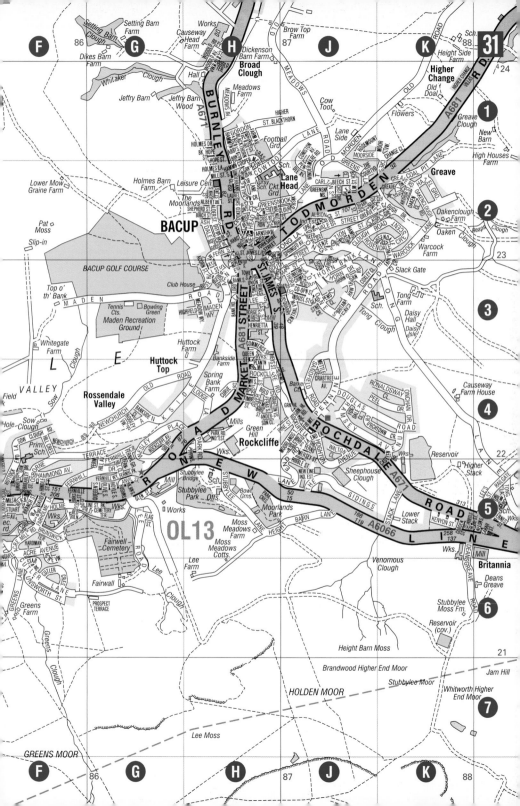

INDEX

Including Streets, Industrial Estates, Selected Subsidiary Addresses
and Selected Places of Interest.

HOW TO USE THIS INDEX

1. Each street name is followed by its Posttown or Postal Locality and then by its map reference; e.g. Abbey Cres. *Dar* —5G **27** is in the Nottingham Posttown and is to be found in square 5G on page **27**. The page number being shown in bold type. A strict alphabetical order is followed in which Av., Rd., St., etc. (though abbreviated) are read in full and as part of the street name; e.g. Alderford Clo. appears after Alder Bank. but before Alder St.

2. Streets and a selection of Subsidiary names not shown on the Maps, appear in the index in *italics* with the thoroughfare to which it is connected shown in brackets; e.g. *Abbeyfield. Burn —6C **10** (off Oxford Rd.)*

3. An example of a selected place of interest is Bacup Golf Course —3F **31**

GENERAL ABBREVIATIONS

All : Alley	Ct : Court	Lit : Little	Rd : Road
App : Approach	Cres : Crescent	Lwr : Lower	Shop : Shopping
Arc : Arcade	Cft : Croft	Mc : Mac	S : South
Av : Avenue	Dri : Drive	Mnr : Manor	Sq : Square
Bk : Back	E : East	Mans : Mansions	Sta : Station
Boulevd : Boulevard	Embkmt : Embankment	Mkt : Market	St : Street
Bri : Bridge	Est : Estate	Mdw : Meadow	Ter : Terrace
B'way : Broadway	Fld : Field	M : Mews	Trad : Trading
Bldgs : Buildings	Gdns : Gardens	Mt : Mount	Up : Upper
Bus : Business	Gth : Garth	Mus : Museum	Va : Vale
Cvn : Caravan	Ga : Gate	N : North	Vw : View
Cen : Centre	Gt : Great	Pal : Palace	Vs : Villas
Chu : Church	Grn : Green	Pde : Parade	Vis : Visitors
Chyd : Churchyard	Gro : Grove	Pk : Park	Wlk : Walk
Circ : Circle	Ho : House	Pas : Passage	W : West
Cir : Circus	Ind : Industrial	Pl : Place	Yd : Yard
Clo : Close	Info : Information	Quad : Quadrant	
Comn : Common	Junct : Junction	Res : Residential	
Cotts : Cottages	La : Lane	Ri : Rise	

POSTTOWN AND POSTAL LOCALITY ABBREVIATIONS

Acc : Accrington	*Clough* : Cloughfold	Love : Loveclough	*Sam* : Samlesbury
Alt : Altham	*Col* : Colne	*Lwr D* : Lower Darwen	*S'stne* : Simonstone
Alt W : Altham West	*Craw* : Crawshawbooth	*Mel* : Mellor	*Stac* : Stacksteads
Bacup : Bacup	*Dar* : Darwen	*Mel B* : Mellor Brook	*S'fld* : Southfield
Barfd : Barrowford	*Dunn* : Dunnockshaw	*Nels* : Nelson	*Stone* : Stonefold
Bas E : Bashall Eaves	*E'hill* : Eccleshill	*Newc* : Newchurch	*Traw* : Trawden
Bax : Baxenden	*Fence* : Fence	*New H* : New Hall Hey	*Tow F* : Townsend Fold
B'rron : Blackburn	*Fen* : Feniscowles	*Osw* : Oswaldtwistle	*Wadd* : Waddington
Black : Blacko	*Good* : Goodshaw	*Pad* : Padiham	*Waterf* : Waterfoot
Brclf : Briercliffe	*Gt Har* : Great Harwood	*Pick B* : Pickup Bank	*Waters* : Waterside
Brier : Brierfield	*Guide* : Guide	*Pleas* : Pleasington	*W Brad* : West Bradford
Burn T : Burnham Trad. Pk.	*Hap* : Hapton	*Ram* : Ramsbottom	*Whal* : Whalley
Burn : Burnley	*Has* : Haslingden	*Rams* : Ramsgreave	*Whi I* : Whitebirk Ind. Est.
Chat : Chatburn	*Helm* : Helmshore	*Raw* : Rawtenstall	*Whit I* : Whitewalls Ind. Est.
Cher T : Cherry Tree	*Hodd* : Hoddlesden	*Read* : Read	*Whit B* : Whitewell Bottom
Chu : Church	*Holc* : Holcombe	*Reed* : Reedsholme	*Wilp* : Wilpshire
Clay D : Clayton le Dale	*Hun* : Huncoat	*Rish* : Rishton	*W'gill* : Withgill
Clay M : Clayton le Moors	*Hun I* : Huncoat Ind. Est.	*Ris B* : Rising Bridge	*Wors* : Worsthorne
Clith : Clitheroe	*Int* : Intack	*Ross* : Rossendale	
Cliv : Cliviger	*Live* : Livesey	*Sale* : Salesbury	

A

	Accrington & District Golf Course.	Addison St. *Acc* 1D **22**	Alan Haigh Ct. *Col* 2G **5**
	. . . . .1H **21**	Addison St. *B'brn* 7F **13**	Alan Ramsbottom Way.
	Accrington Easterley By-Pass.	(in two parts)	*Gt Har* 3J **15**
Abbey Cres. *Dar* 5G **27**	*Acc* 7G **17**	Adelaide La. *Acc* 3D **22**	Alaska St. *B'brn* 3H **19**
Abbeyfield. Burn 6C **10**	Accrington Rd. *B'brn* 3A **20**	Adelaide St. *Acc* 3D **22**	Albany Rd. *B'brn* 6E **12**
(off Oxford Rd.)	Accrington Rd. *Burn & Hap* . . .5K **17**	Adelaide St. *Burn* 4J **9**	Albemarle Ct. *Clith* 5D **2**
Abbeyfield Ho. Burn 5K **9**	Accrington Stanley F.C.	Adelaide St. *Clay M* 6B **16**	Albemarle St. *Clith* 5D **2**
(off Harriet St.)	(Crown Ground)	Adelaide St. *Ross* 5G **25**	Alberta Clo. *B'brn* 4E **12**
Abbey Pl. *Dar* 5G **27**	Acorn Av. *Osw* 5A **22**	Adelaide Ter. *B'brn* 7F **13**	Albert Pl. *Lwr D* 6J **19**
Abbey St. *Acc* 2D **22**	Acorn St. *Bacup* 3H **31**	Adelphi St. *Burn* 3B **10**	Albert Rd. *Col* 4F **5**
Abbey St. *Bacup* 1H **31**	Acorn St. *B'brn* 4A **20**	Adlington St. *Burn* 4B **10**	Albert Rd. *Ross* 4G **25**
Abbots Clo. *Ross* 1G **29**	Acre Av. *Bacup* 5F **31**	Admiral St. *Burn* 5C **10**	Albert St. *Acc* 3D **22**
Abbots Clough Av. *B'brn* 4D **20**	Acrefield. *B'brn* 5D **12**	Agate St. *B'brn* 3J **13**	Albert St. *B'brn* 3F **19**
Abbotsford Av. *B'brn* 4G **19**	Acrefield. *Pad* 1B **8**	Agnes St. *B'brn* 2F **19**	Albert St. *Brier* 4C **6**
Abbott Brow. *Mel* 1A **12**	Acre Mill Rd. *Bacup* 5F **31**	Ailsa Rd. *B'brn* 5C **20**	Albert St. *Burn* 4C **10**
Abbott Clough Clo.	Acresfield. *Col* 3K **5**	Ainsdale Av. *Burn* 4D **6**	Albert St. *Chu* 2K **21**
B'brn 4D **20**	Acre St. *Brclf* 6H **7**	Ainsdale Dri. *Dar* 7F **27**	Albert St. *Clay M* 5A **16**
Abbot Wlk. *Clith* 5F **3**	Acre St. *B'brn* 1C **10**	Ainslie Clo. *Gt Har* 2G **15**	Albert St. *Dar* 7F **27**
Abel St. *Burn* 1B **10**	Acre Vw. *Bacup* 5F **31**	Ainslie St. *Burn* 4H **9**	Albert St. *Gt Har* 3J **15**
Aberdare Clo. *B'brn* 5H **13**	Active Way. *Burn* 4A **10**	Ainsworth Mall. *B'brn* 7H **13**	Albert St. *Hodd* 4K **27**
Aberdeen Dri. *B'brn* 1K **19**	Adamson St. *Burn* 4H **9**	(off Ainsworth St.)	Albert St. *Nels* 1E **6**
Abingdon Rd. *Pad* 3C **8**	Adamson St. *Pad* 1B **8**	Ainsworth St. *B'brn* 7H **13**	Albert St. *Osw* 4K **21**
Abinger St. *Burn* 1D **10**	Ada St. *B'brn* 7F **13**	Aintree Dri. *Lwr D* 6K **19**	Albert St. *Pad* 2B **8**
Abraham St. *Acc* 3C **22**	Ada St. *Burn* 1C **10**	Aintree Cres. *Burn* 6J **9**	Albert St. *Rish* 6G **15**
Abraham St. *B'brn* 3H **19**	Ada St. *Nels* 3F **7**	Airey St. *Acc* 5E **22**	Albert St. *Ross* 1A **30**
Acacia Wlk. *B'brn* 3A **20**	Addington St. *B'brn* 7K **13**	Aitken St. *Acc* 1D **22**	Albert Ter. *Bacup* 2H **31**
(off Longton St.)	Addison Clo. *B'brn* 7F **13**	Aitken St. *Ram* 7C **28**	Albert Ter. *Barfd* 5A **4**

Albert Ter. *Clough* 3H 29
Albion Ct. *Burn* 6K 9
Albion Rd. *B'brn* 4G 19
Albion St. *Acc* 2C 22
Albion St. *Bacup* 2J 31
Albion St. *B'brn* 4F 19
Albion St. *Brier* 4C 6
Albion St. *Burn* 6K 9
Albion St. *Clith* 5F 3
Albion St. *Nels* 1E 6
Albion St. *Pad* 3C 8
Albion St. *Stac* 5E 30
Albion Ter. *Burn* 5A 10
  (off Albion St.)
Alden Clo. *Helm* 7A 28
Alden Ri. *Ross* 7A 28
Alden Rd. *Ross* 7A 28
Alder Av. *Ross* 3H 29
Alder Bank. *B'brn* 1E 18
Alder Bank. *Nels* 2D 6
Alder Bank. *Ross* 2G 29
Alderford Clo. *Clith* 6C 2
Alder Gro. *Acc* 5F 17
Alderney Clo. *B'brn* 4E 18
Alder St. *Bacup* 2H 31
Alder St. *B'brn* 5K 13
Alder St. *Burn* 4H 9
Alder St. *Ross* 2H 29
Aldwych Pl. *B'brn* 2J 13
Alexander Clo. *Acc* 7F 23
Alexander Gro. *Burn* 4G 9
Alexander St. *Nels* 6D 4
Alexandra Clo. *Clay M* 4K 15
Alexandra Ho. *B'brn* 5A 20
Alexandra Pl. *Gt Har* 1J 15
Alexandra Rd. *B'brn* 6F 13
Alexandra Rd. *Dar* 3D 26
Alexandra St. *Clay M* 3K 15
Alexandra Vw. *Dar* 3D 26
Alexandria St. *Ross* 1F 29
Alfred St. *Dar* 7F 27
Algar St. *Nels* 6C 4
Alice St. *Acc* 1E 22
Alice St. *Dar* 5E 26
Alice St. *Osw* 5K 21
Alkincoats Rd. *Col* 3F 5
Alkincoats Vs. *Col* 2F 5
Allan Critchlow Way. *Rish* 5G 15
Allandale Gro. *Burn* 6G 11
Allan St. *Bacup* 4H 31
Allen Ct. *Burn* 2B 10
  (off Allen St.)
Allendale St. *Burn* 4G 9
Allendale St. *Col* 2J 5
Allen St. *Burn* 2B 10
  (in two parts)
Allerton Clo. *Dar* 3E 26
Allerton Dri. *Burn* 4J 9
Alleys Grn. *Clith* 4E 2
Alleytroyds. *Chu* 3K 21
Alliance St. *Acc* 7G 23
Allison Gro. *Col* 2J 5
All Saints Clo. *B'brn* 3E 8
All Saints Clo. *Osw* 4G 21
All Saints Clo. *Ross* 3G 25
Allsprings Clo. *Gt Har* 1J 15
Allsprings Dri. *Gt Har* 1J 15
Alma Pl. *Clith* 6D 2
Alma St. *Bacup* 3H 31
Alma St. *B'brn* 7G 13
Alma St. *Clay M* 4A 16
Alma St. *Pad* 1A 8
Almond Cres. *Ross* 5F 29
Almond St. *Dar* 5E 26
Alnwick Clo. *Burn* 3K 9
Alpha St. *Dar* 5F 27
Alpha St. *Nels* 6C 4
Alpine Clo. *Hodd* 4J 27
Alpine Gro. *B'brn* 5E 18
Altham Bus. Pk. *Alt* 1F 17
Altham Cvn. Site. *Acc* 6D 16
Altham Ind. Est. *Alt* 1E 16
Altham La. *Alt & Acc* 1F 17
Altham St. *Burn* 2B 10
Altham St. *Pad* 2C 8
Altom St. *B'brn* 6H 13
Alwin St. *Burn* 2K 9
Amber Av. *B'brn* 2J 13
Amberley St. *B'brn* 3F 19
Amberwood Dri. *B'brn* 4D 18

Ambleside Av. *Ross* 3E 28
Ambleside Clo. *Acc* 7F 17
Ambleside Clo. *B'brn* 6K 13
Ambleside Dri. *Dar* 2G 27
Amelia St. *B'brn* 2A 20
Amersham Gro. *Burn* 5E 6
Amethyst St. *B'brn* 2H 13
Anchor Av. *Dar* 1C 26
Anchor Gro. *Dar* 1C 26
Anchor Retail Pk. *Burn* 4A 10
Anchor St. *Dar* 1C 26
Andelen Clo. *Hap* 7B 8
Anderson Clo. *Bacup* 4H 31
Anderton Rd. *Wilp* 1C 14
Anderton Clo. *Ross* 6B 30
Andrew Av. *Ross* 4F 29
Andrew Clo. *B'brn* 5E 18
Andrew Rd. *Nels* 7E 4
Andrew's Ct. *Burn* 6B 10
Anemone Dri. *Has* 5A 28
Angela St. *B'brn* 4E 18
Angel Way. *Col* 3H 5
  (off King St.)
Anglesey Av. *Burn* 3F 9
Anglesey St. *B'brn* 5E 18
Angle St. *Burn* 2B 10
Anglian Clo. *Osw* 3H 21
Angus St. *Bacup* 5E 30
Annarly Fold. *Wors* 5H 11
Anne Clo. *Burn* 5C 10
Anne St. *Burn* 5C 10
Annie St. *Acc* 1D 22
Annie St. *Ross* 3G 29
Ann St. *Barfd* 5A 4
Ann St. *Brier* 3C 6
Ann St. *Clay M* 4A 16
Ansdell Ter. *B'brn* 4H 19
Antigua Dri. *Lwr D* 7J 19
Anvil St. *Bacup* 5G 31
Anyon St. *Dar* 3F 27
Appleby Clo. *Acc* 3E 22
Appleby Dri. *Barfd* 4A 4
Appleby St. *B'brn* 7K 13
Appleby St. *Nels* 1E 6
Apple Clo. *B'brn* 1F 19
Apple Ct. *B'brn* 1F 19
Applecross Dri. *Burn* 6F 11
Apple St. *B'brn* 1F 19
Apple Tree Way. *Osw* 3K 21
Approach Way. *Burn* 7K 9
Aqueduct Rd. *B'brn* 3F 19
Arago St. *Acc* 1D 22
Arbories Av. *Pad* 2A 8
Arbory Dri. *Pad* 1A 8
Arbour Dri. *B'brn* 7G 19
Arbour St. *Bacup* 2J 31
Arboury St. *Pad* 2A 8
Arcade. *Acc* 3D 22
  (off Church St.)
Arcadia. *Col* 3H 5
  (off Market Pl.)
Arch St. *Burn* 4A 10
Arch St. *Dar* 4E 26
Ardwick St. *Burn* 1B 10
Argyle St. *Acc* 2C 22
Argyle St. *Col* 3G 5
Argyle St. *Dar* 2D 26
Arkwright Fold. *B'brn* 5F 19
Arkwright St. *Burn* 3H 9
Arley Gdns. *Burn* 3A 10
Arley Ri. *Mel* 2B 12
Arlington Rd. *Dar* 5D 26
Arncliffe Av. *Acc* 4A 22
Arncliffe Gro. *Barfd* 5A 4
Arncliffe Rd. *Burn* 5F 11
Arndale Shop. Cen. *Nels* 1F 7
Arnold St. *Acc* 2D 22
Arnside Clo. *Clay M* 5K 15
Arnside Cres. *B'brn* 6B 18
Arran Av. *B'brn* 6C 20
Arran St. *Burn* 5J 9
Arthur St. *Bacup* 2K 31
Arthur St. *B'brn* 1F 19
Arthur St. *Brier* 4C 6
Arthur St. *Burn* 4K 9
Arthur St. *Clay M* 4A 16
Arthur St. *Gt Har* 1J 15
Arthur St. *Nels* 7B 4
Arthur Way. *B'brn* 1F 19
Arundel St. *Rish* 5F 15

Ascot Way. *Acc* 3E 22
Ash Av. *Has* 2C 28
Ashburnham Rd. *Col* 6D 4
Ash Clo. *Rish* 7G 15
Ash Ct. *B'brn* 5K 13
  (off Plane St.)
Ashendean Vw. *Pad* 1C 8
Ashfield Rd. *Burn* 4A 10
Ashford St. *Nels* 2F 7
Ash Gro. *Dar* 3F 27
Ash Gro. *Raw* 2G 29
  (off Prospect Rd.)
Ash La. *Gt Har* 1G 15
Ashleigh St. *Dar* 7F 27
Ashley St. *Burn* 3A 10
Ashmere Clo. *Has* 6C 28
Ash St. *Bacup* 2H 31
Ash St. *B'brn* 5K 13
Ash St. *Burn* 5C 10
Ash St. *Gt Har* 1H 15
Ash St. *Nels* 1G 7
Ash St. *Osw* 4J 21
Ash St. *Traw* 6K 5
Ashton Dri. *Nels* 3F 7
Ashton Ho. *Dar* 5F 27
Ashton La. *Dar* 5E 26
Ashton Rd. *Dar* 5F 27
Ashtree Wlk. *Barfd* 6A 4
Ashville Ter. *B'brn* 5G 19
Ashworth Clo. *B'brn* 7F 13
Ashworth La. *Ross* 2B 30
Ashworth Rd. *Ross* 3B 30
Ashworth St. *Acc* 6F 23
Ashworth St. *Bacup* 2J 31
Ashworth St. *Rish* 6G 15
Ashworth St. *Ross* 3J 29
Ashworth St. *Stac* 5F 31
Ashworth St. *Waterf* 5B 30
  (in two parts)
Ashworth Ter. *Bacup* 5D 30
Ashworth Ter. *Dar* 5D 26
Ashworth Ter. *Ross* 3B 30
  (off Burnley Rd.)
Askrigg Clo. *Acc* 2E 22
Aspen Dri. *Burn* 3D 10
Aspen Fold. *Osw* 3G 21
Aspen La. *Osw* 4G 21
Aspinall Fold. *B'brn* 4H 13
Aspley Gro. *Traw* 5K 5
  (off Skipton Rd.)
Assheton Rd. *B'brn* 7D 12
Asten Bldgs. *Ross* 6B 30
Aster Chase. *Lwr D* 6K 19
Astley Ga. *B'brn* 7H 13
Astley St. *Dar* 6E 26
Astley Ter. *Dar* 6E 26
Aston Wlk. *B'brn* 5K 19
Athens Vw. *Burn* 5D 10
  (off Athletic St.)
Atherton St. *Bacup* 5D 30
Atherton Way. *Bacup* 5D 30
Athletic St. *Burn* 5D 10
Athol St. *Nels* 1G 7
Athol St. N. *Burn* 5J 9
Athol St. S. *Burn* 5J 9
Atkinson St. *Brclf* 6G 7
Atkinson St. *Col* 5F 5
  (in two parts)
Atlas Rd. *Dar* 4E 26
Atlas St. *Clay M* 6A 16
Atrium St. *Burn* 6C 10
Auckland St. *Dar* 6F 27
Audley Clo. *Nels* 1F 7
  (off Audley Ct.)
Audley Ct. *Nels* 1F 7
Audley La. *B'brn* 7K 13
Audley Range. *B'brn* 1J 19
Audley St. *B'brn* 7K 13
Augusta St. *Acc* 4D 22
Austin St. *Bacup* 4H 31
  (off Union St.)
Austin St. *Burn* 5K 9
Austwick Way. *Acc* 3F 23
Avallon Way. *Dar* 4G 27
Avalon Clo. *Burn* 3E 8
Avebury Clo. *B'brn* 5K 19
Avenue Pde. *Acc* 2D 22
Avenue, The. *Burn* 7E 10
Aviemore Clo. *B'brn* 1K 19
Avon Clo. *B'brn* 2G 19

Avon Ct. *Burn* 3J 9
Avondale Av. *B'brn* 3D 20
Avondale Av. *Burn* 3H 9
Avondale Clo. *Dar* 3C 26
Avondale M. *Dar* 2C 26
Avondale Rd. *Dar* 3C 26
Avondale St. *Nels* 2E 6
Avondale St. *Col* 3K 5
Avonwood Clo. *Dar* 6D 6
Aylesbury Wlk. *Burn* 6D 6
Ayr Gro. *Burn* 7J 9
Ayr Rd. *B'brn* 5C 20
Ayrton St. *Col* 3H 5
Aysgarth Dri. *Acc* 2E 22
Aysgarth Dri. *Dar* 3C 26
Azalea Rd. *B'brn* 6E 12

B

Bk. Albert Rd. *Col* 4G 5
  (off Albert Rd.)
Bk. Albert St. *Pad* 2B 8
  (off Albert St.)
Bk. Altham St. *Pad* 2C 8
Bk. Arthur St. *Clay M* 4A 16
Bk. Atkinson St. *Col* 4F 5
Bk. Beehive Ter. *Ross* 7B 24
  (off Blackburn Rd.)
Bk. Bolton Rd. *Dar* 6F 27
Bk. Bond St. *Col* 3G 5
  (off Bond St.)
Bk. Boundry St. *Col* 4G 5
Bk. Brown St. *Col* 4F 5
Bk. Burnley Rd. *Acc* 2D 22
Bk. Cambridge St. *Col* 4G 5
  (off Cambridge St.)
Bk. Carr Mill St. *Ross* 7B 24
Bk. Cemetery Ter. *Bacup* 5G 31
Bk. Chapel St. *Col* 4G 5
  (off Chapel St.)
Bk. Church St. *Barfd* 5A 4
Bk. Church St. *Hap* 6B 8
  (off Church St.)
Bk. Church St. *Newc* 3A 30
Bk. Clayton St. *Nels* 7A 4
  (off Clayton St.)
Bk. Colne Rd. *Traw* 6K 5
  (off Colne Rd.)
Bk. Commons. *Clith* 4D 2
Bk. Constablelee. *Ross* 1G 29
Bk. Dover St. *Lwr D* 6J 19
Bk. Duckworth St. *Dar* 4E 26
Bk. Duke St. *Col* 4G 5
  (off Duke St.)
Bk. Earl St. *Col* 4G 5
  (off Earl St.)
Bk. East Bank. *Barfd* 4A 4
Bk. Gisburn St. *Black* 1B 4
Bk. Halifax Rd. *Brclf* 6H 7
Bk. Hall St. *Col* 4G 5
  (off Hall St.)
Bk. Harry St. *Barfd* 5A 4
Bk. Hesketh St. *Gt Har* 2H 15
  (off Blackburn Rd.)
Bk. Heys. *Osw* 5K 21
Bk. Hill St. *Brier* 3A 6
  (off Hill St.)
Bk. Hill St. *Ross* 5G 25
  (off Hill St.)
Bk. Hope St. *Bacup* 1H 31
Backhouse St. *Osw* 4K 21
Bk. King St. *Acc* 2C 22
Back La. *Acc* 6F 23
Back La. *Brclf & S'fld* 7G 5
Back La. *Ross* 2G 29
Back La. *Traw* .....
Back La. Side. *Has* 3B 28
Bk. Leach St. *Col* 4F 5
  (off Leach St.)
Bk. Lee St. *Has* 3B 28
Bk. Lord St. *Ross* 6D 25
  (off Burnley Rd.)
Bk. Lune St. *Col* 4H 5
  (off Lune St.)
Bk. Newchurch Rd. *Ross* 3J 29
Bk. Oddfellows Ter. *Ross* 2B 30
Bk. Ormerod St. *Ross* 3G 29
  (off Ormerod St.)
Bk. Parkinson St. *B'brn* 3E 18

Bk. Peter St. *Barfd* 4A **4**
Bk. Queen St. *Gt Har* 2H **15**
Bk. Regent St. *Has* 2A **28**
(off Regent St.)
Bk. Rhoden Rd. *Osw* 6J **21**
Bk. Richard St. *Brier* 4C **6**
(off Richard St.)
Bk. Rings Row. *Ross* 3G **25**
(off Burnley Rd.)
Bk. Rushton St. *Bacup* 5G **31**
Bk. St John St. *Bacup* 2H **31**
Bk. Scotland Rd. *Nels* 1E **6**
(off Scotland Rd.)
Bk. Shuttleworth St. *Pad* 2B **8**
(off Shuttleworth St.)
Bk. Spencer St. *Ross* 4G **25**
Bk. Water St. *Acc* 2D **22**
Bk. Wellington St. *Acc* 3D **22**
Bk. Willow St. *Burn* 3K **9**
Bk. York St. *Clith* 5E **2**
Bk. York St. *Ross* 5G **25**
(off York St.)
Bk. Zion St. *Col* 4G **5**
(off Zion St.)
Bacon St. *Nels* 1F **7**
Bacup Golf Course 3F **31**
Bacup Natural History Society Mus.
. . . . .2H **31**
(off Yorkshire St.)
Bacup Rd. *Ross* 3G **29**
(in two parts)
Baden Ter. *B'brn* 4G **19**
Badgebrow. *Osw* 3K **21**
Badger Clo. *Pad* 1C **8**
Badgers Clo. *Acc* 7F **17**
Bailey St. *Burn* 5K **9**
Baker St. *Bacup* 2H **31**
Baker St. *B'brn* 4A **20**
Baker St. *Burn* 5K **9**
Baker St. *Nels* 6B **4**
Balaclava St. *B'brn* 6H **13**
Bala Clo. *B'brn* 6H **13**
Balderstone Clo. *Burn* 7E **6**
Balderstone La. *Burn* 1E **10**
Baldwin Hill. *Clith* 5D **2**
Baldwin Rd. *Clith* 5D **2**
Baldwins Bldgs. *Ross* 2G **29**
(off Bank St.)
Baldwins Hill. *Burn* 7E **6**
(off Marsden Rd.)
Baldwin St. *Bacup* 5D **30**
Baldwin St. *Barfd* 4A **4**
Baldwin St. *B'brn* 2F **19**
Balfour Clo. *Brier* 4E **6**
Balfour St. *B'brn* 1F **19**
Balfour St. *Gt Har* 2J **15**
Ballam St. *Burn* 6B **10**
Ballantrae Rd. *B'brn* 5C **20**
Ballater St. *Burn* 7J **9**
Balle St. *Dar* 5E **26**
Ball Gro. Dri. *Col* 3K **5**
Balliol Clo. *Pad* 4C **8**
Ball St. *Nels* 7A **4**
Balmoral Av. *B'brn* 4C **14**
Balmoral Av. *Clith* 7C **2**
Balmoral Cres. *B'brn* 4E **20**
Balmoral Rd. *Acc* 1E **22**
Balmoral Rd. *Dar* 7F **27**
Balmoral Rd. *Has* 4A **28**
Baltic Rd. *Ross* 5A **30**
Bamburgh Dri. *Burn* 3K **9**
Bamford Cres. *Acc* 4E **22**
Bamford St. *Burn* 4B **10**
Bamford St. *Nels* 1H **7**
Banastre St. *Acc* 6B **16**
Banbury Av. *Osw* 4H **21**
Banbury Clo. *Acc* 1B **22**
Banbury Gro. *B'brn* 5C **18**
Bancroft Rd. *Burn* 2D **10**
Bancroft St. *B'brn* 7J **13**
Bangor St. *B'brn* 5J **13**
Bank Bottom. *Dar* 4E **26**
Bankcroft Clo. *Pad* 2D **8**
Bankfield. *Burn* 4B **10**
Bankfield St. *Bacup* 5F **31**
Bankfield St. *Col* 4E **4**
Bankfield Ter. *Bacup* 5F **31**
Bank Fold. *Barfd* 3B **4**
Bank Hall Ter. *Burn* 3B **10**
(off Stafford St.)

Bank Hey Clo. *B'brn* 3K **13**
Bank Hey La. N. *B'brn* 1J **13**
Bank Hey La. S. *B'brn* 3K **13**
Bank Ho. La. *Bacup* 3H **31**
Bankhouse M. *Barfd* 4B **4**
Bankhouse Rd. *Nels* 7B **4**
Bankhouse St. *Barfd* 4B **4**
Bankhouse St. *Burn* 4A **10**
(in two parts)
Bank La. *B'brn* 4C **20**
Bank Mill St. *Has* 3B **28**
Bank Pde. *Burn* 4B **10**
Bank Row. *Ross* 2F **25**
Bankside. *B'brn* 3H **19**
Bankside Clo. *Bacup* 4G **31**
Bankside La. *Bacup* 4G **31**
Banks St. *Brclf* 6J **7**
Bank St. *Acc* 2D **22**
Bank St. *Bacup* 3H **31**
Bank St. *Brier* 3C **6**
Bank St. *Chu* 2K **21**
Bank St. *Dar* 4E **26**
Bank St. *Has* 2B **28**
Bank St. *Nels* 7B **4**
Bank St. *Pad* 1B **8**
Bank St. *Ross* 3G **29**
Bank St. *Traw* 7K **5**
Bank Top. *B'brn* 2F **19**
Bank Top. *Burn* 4B **10**
Bannister Clo. *Traw* 5J **5**
Bannister Ct. *Nels* 2F **7**
(off York St.)
Bannister Way. *Col* 3H **5**
(off King La.)
Barbara Castle Way. *B'brn* 7G **13**
Barbon St. *Burn* 7D **6**
Barbon St. *Pad* 1B **8**
Barclay Av. *Burn* 6H **9**
Barcroft St. *Col* 3F **5**
(in two parts)
Barden Cft. *Clay M* 3A **16**
Barden La. *Burn* 6A **6**
Barden Rd. *Acc* 4A **22**
Barden St. *Burn* 1C **10**
Barden Vw. *Burn* 7B **6**
Bargee Clo. *B'brn* 2J **19**
Barilla St. *Chu* 2K **21**
Barkerhouse Rd. *Nels* 7B **4**
Barker La. *Mel* 2E **12**
Barker Ter. *Clith* 4E **2**
Barley Bank St. *Dar* 3D **26**
Barley Clo. *B'brn* 7G **13**
Barleydale Rd. *Barfd* 3B **4**
Barley Gro. *Burn* 4D **10**
Barley Holme Rd. *Ross* 5G **25**
Barley Holme St. *Ross* 4G **25**
Barley La. *B'brn* 7G **13**
Barley St. *Pad* 3B **8**
Barley Way. *B'brn* 1G **19**
Barlow Fold. *Ross* 5E **28**
Barlows Bldgs. *Ross* 4F **29**
Barlow St. *Acc* 2B **22**
Barlow St. *Bacup* 5E **30**
Barlow St. *Ross* 2G **29**
Barmouth Cres. *B'brn* 3H **13**
Barnard Clo. *Osw* 4H **21**
Barn Cft. *Clith* 6D **2**
Barnes Av. *Ross* 3F **29**
Barnes Ct. *Burn* 6E **10**
Barnes Sq. *Clay M* 4A **16**
Barnes St. *Acc* 2D **22**
(in two parts)
Barnes St. *Burn* 8B **10**
Barnes St. *Chu* 2K **21**
Barnes St. *Clay M* 4K **15**
Barnes St. *Has* 1B **28**
Barnfield Av. *Burn* 4G **11**
Barnfield Bus. Cen. *Nels* 3G **7**
Barnfield Clo. *Col* 3K **5**
Barnfield St. *Acc* 3E **22**
Barnfield Way. *Alt* 2F **17**
Barn Mdw. Cres. *Rish* 6H **15**
Barnmeadow La. *Gt Har* 2H **15**
Barnoldswick Rd. *Black* 1C **4**
Baron Fold. *Ross* 5A **30**
Barons Clo. *Lwr D* 6K **19**
Baron St. *Dar* 3C **26**
Baron St. *Ross* 4J **29**
Barons Way. *Lwr D* 7K **19**

Barracks Rd. *Burn* 4J **9**
Barrett St. *Burn* 2B **10**
Barritt Rd. *Ross* 3F **29**
Barrowdale Av. *Nels* 2G **7**
Barrowford Rd. *Col* 3D **4**
(in two parts)
Barrowford Rd. *Pad & Fence* . . .1A **6**
(in two parts)
Barry St. *Burn* 4H **9**
Bar St. *Burn* 2C **10**
Bartle St. *Burn* 5J **9**
Barton St. *B'brn* 7H **13**
Basil St. *Col* 4G **5**
Basnett St. *Burn* 1D **10**
Bastwell Rd. *B'brn* 5J **13**
Bates St. *Clay M* 4K **15**
Bath St. *Acc* 4C **22**
Bath St. *Bacup* 3J **31**
Bath St. *B'brn* 1F **19**
Bath St. *Col* 3H **5**
Bath St. *Dar* 4E **26**
Bath St. *Nels* 1G **7**
Bathurst St. *B'brn* 7G **13**
Bawdlands. *Clith* 5D **2**
Baxenden Golf Course. 5H **23**
Bayard St. *Burn* 4F **9**
Bayley Fold. *Clith* 5E **2**
Bayley St. *Clay M* 4K **15**
Baynes St. *Hodd* 4K **27**
Bay St. *B'brn* 5K **13**
Baywood St. *B'brn* 5J **13**
Beachley Sq. *Burn* 3J **9**
Beacon Clo. *Col* 5F **5**
Beaconsfield St. *Acc* 3E **22**
Beaconsfield St. *Gt Har* 1H **15**
Beaconsfield St. *Has* 2B **28**
Beale Rd. *Nels* 1C **6**
Beardsworth St. *B'brn* 4K **13**
Beardwood. *B'brn* 5D **12**
Beardwood Brow. *B'brn* 5D **12**
Beardwood Dri. *B'brn* 5D **12**
Beardwood Fold. *B'brn* 5D **12**
Beardwood Mdw. *B'brn* 5D **12**
Beardwood Pk. *B'brn* 5E **12**
Bear St. *Burn* 4D **8**
Beatie St. *Brier* 3C **6**
Beatrice Av. *Burn* 3H **9**
Beatrice Pl. *B'brn* 5K **19**
Beatrice Ter. *Dar* 5F **27**
Beaufort St. *Nels* 2E **6**
Beaumaris Av. *B'brn* 4D **18**
Beaumaris Clo. *Has* 4B **28**
Beaver Clo. *Wilp* 3B **14**
Beaver Ter. *Bacup* 2J **31**
Beckenham Ct. *Burn* 6E **6**
Beckett St. *Dar* 5E **26**
Beckside Clo. *Traw* 5K **5**
Beck Way. *Col* 5E **4**
Beddington St. *Nels* 7A **4**
Bedford Clo. *Osw* 4H **21**
Bedford M. *Dar* 1D **26**
Bedford Pl. *Pad* 3C **8**
Bedfordshire Av. *Burn* 3G **9**
Bedford St. *Barfd* 1D **6**
Bedford St. *B'brn* 3F **19**
Bedford St. *Dar* 1D **26**
Bedford Ter. *Has* 5A **28**
Beech Av. *Dar* 3F **27**
Beech Bank. *Wadd* 1B **2**
Beech Clo. *Bacup* 2J **31**
Beech Clo. *Clay D* 2A **14**
Beech Clo. *Clith* 5D **2**
Beech Clo. *Osw* 6H **21**
Beech Clo. *Rish* 7G **15**
Beech Cres. *Alt W* 6B **16**
Beech Dri. *Has* 3C **28**
Beech Gro. *Acc* 4B **22**
Beech Gro. *Burn* 5D **6**
Beech Gro. *Chat* 1K **3**
Beech Gro. *Dar* 7G **19**
Beech Ind. Est. *Bacup* 2J **31**
(off Vale Rd.)
Beech Mt. *Rams* 1J **13**
Beech Mt. *Wadd* 1B **2**
Beech St. *Acc* 3D **22**
Beech St. *Bacup* 2J **31**
Beech St. *B'brn* 5K **13**
Beech St. *Clay M* 6A **16**
Beech St. *Clith* 5D **2**
Beech St. *Gt Har* 1H **15**

Beech St. *Nels* 7B **4**
Beech St. *Pad* 3C **8**
Beech St. *Ross* 2G **29**
Beechthorpe Av. *Wadd* 1B **2**
Beech Tree Clo. *Nels* 2F **7**
Beechwood Av. *Acc* 5E **22**
Beechwood Av. *Burn* 7K **9**
Beechwood Av. *Clith* 7E **2**
Beechwood Ct. *B'brn* 5J **13**
Beechwood Dri. *B'brn* 5B **18**
Beechwood M. *B'brn* 5K **19**
Beechwood Rd. *B'brn* 5K **13**
Beetham Ct. *Clay M* 5K **15**
Begonia St. *Dar* 4F **27**
Belfield Rd. *Acc* 3C **22**
Belford St. *Burn* 3A **10**
Belgarth Rd. *Acc* 1D **22**
Belgrave Clo. *B'brn* 2E **18**
Belgrave Ct. *Burn* 3A **10**
(off Belgrave St.)
Belgrave Rd. *Col* 2G **5**
Belgrave Rd. *Dar* 5D **26**
Belgrave Sq. *Dar* 4E **26**
Belgrave St. *Acc* 4A **24**
Belgrave St. *Brier* 4B **6**
Belgrave St. *Burn* 3A **10**
Belgrave St. *Nels* 1G **7**
Belle Vue La. *Wadd* 1B **2**
Belle Vue Pl. *Burn* 4K **9**
Belle Vue St. *B'brn* 7F **13**
Belle Vue St. *Burn* 4K **9**
Bell La. *Clay M* 3C **16**
Bells Arc. *Burn* 2B **10**
(off Ardwick St.)
Bell St. *Has* 2B **28**
Belmont Clo. *B'brn* 5D **12**
Belmont Gro. *Burn* 5E **10**
Belmont Rd. *Gt Har* 2G **15**
Belmont Ter. *Barfd* 5A **4**
(off Nora St.)
Belper St. *B'brn* 6K **13**
Belshaw Ct. *Burn* 7F **9**
Belvedere Av. *Ross* 4C **30**
Belvedere Rd. *B'brn* 1K **13**
Belvedere Rd. *Burn* 4C **10**
Bence St. *Col* 4H **5**
Bennett St. *Nels* 6C **4**
Bennington St. *B'brn* 2J **19**
Benson Ho. *B'brn* 1A **20**
Benson St. *B'brn* 1A **20**
Bentcliffe Gdns. *Acc* 4E **22**
Bent Gap La. *B'brn* 1F **19**
Bentgate Clo. *Has* 5D **28**
Bentham Av. *Burn* 6C **6**
Bentham Clo. *B'brn* 4E **18**
Bentham Rd. *B'brn* 4E **18**
Bent La. *Col* 2K **5**
Bentley St. *Bacup* 2H **31**
Bentley St. *B'brn* 3B **20**
Bentley St. *Dar* 6G **27**
Bentley St. *Nels* 2E **6**
Bents. *Col* 2K **5**
Bent St. *B'brn* 1G **19**
Bent St. *Has* 5D **28**
Bent St. *Osw* 5J **21**
Bentwood Rd. *Has* 2A **28**
Beresford Rd. *B'brn* 5G **13**
Beresford St. *Nels* 3G **7**
Bergen St. *Burn* 5G **9**
Berkeley Clo. *Nels* 2F **7**
Berkeley Cres. *Pad* 1B **8**
Berkeley St. *Brier* 4B **6**
Berkeley St. *Nels* 3F **7**
Berkshire Av. *Burn* 3G **9**
Berkshire Clo. *Wilp* 1B **14**
Berridge Av. *Burn* 4F **9**
Berriedale Rd. *Nels* 7D **4**
Berry St. *Brier* 4C **6**
Berry St. *Burn* 6A **10**
Bertha St. *Acc* 2E **22**
Berwick Dri. *Burn* 3K **9**
Beryl Av. *Burn* 2J **13**
Bethel Rd. *B'brn* 5K **13**
Bethel St. *Col* 4E **4**
Bethesda Clo. *B'brn* 2G **19**
Bethesda St. *Burn* 4A **10**
Bevan Pl. *Nels* 6C **4**
Beverley Clo. *Clith* 7D **2**
Beverley Dri. *Clith* 7D **2**

Beverley Rd.—Brookhouse Bus. Cen.

Beverley Rd. *Black* 1A 4
Beverley St. *B'brn* 4E 18
Beverley St. *Burn* 5K 9
Beverley Ter. B'brn 4E 18
(off Broadway St.)
Bevington Clo. *Burn* 5K 9
Bicknell St. *B'brn* 6H 13
Billinge Av. *B'brn* 7D 12
Billinge Clo. *B'brn* 7E 12
Billinge End. *B'brn* 6D 12
Billinge End Rd. *B'brn* 7B 12
Billinge Side. *B'brn* 7C 12
Billinge St. *B'brn* 1K 19
Billinge Vw. *B'brn* 3C 18
Billington Av. *Ross* 7G 25
Billington Rd. *Burn* 7F 9
Binns St. *Craw* 5G 25
Birch Av. *Has* 2C 28
Birchbank Gdns. *B'brn* 6J 13
Birch Clo. *Acc* 5F 17
Birch Cotts. *Ross* 5E 28
Birch Cres. *Osw* 5A 22
Birchenlee La. *Col* 5G 5
Birch Hall Av. *Dar* 1C 26
Birch St. *Acc* 2C 22
Birch St. *Bacup* 2H 31
Birch Ter. *Acc* 5E 22
Birch Wlk. *B'brn* 4A 20
Bird St. *Brier* 4C 6
Birkbeck Way. *Burn* 1B 10
Birkett Rd. *Acc* 1D 22
Birley Pl. *Burn* 2B 10
Birley St. *B'brn* 6J 13
Birtwistle Av. *Col* 2F 5
Birtwistle Clo. *Brier* 4C 6
Birtwistle Fold. *Col* 3H 5
Birtwistle Hyde Pk. *Col* 3G 5
Birtwistle Standroyd Bungalows.
Col 3K 5
Birtwistle St. *Acc* 3D 22
Birtwistle St. *Gt Har* 2G 15
Bisham Clo. *Dar* 5G 27
Bishopdale Clo. *B'brn* 6A 18
Bishopstone Clo. *B'brn* 5K 19
Bishop St. *Acc* 3D 22
Bishop St. *Burn* 1C 10
Bishop St. *Nels* 1E 6
Bispham Rd. *Nels* 3F 7
Bivel St. *Burn* 4J 9
Black Abbey St. *Acc* 3D 22
Blackamoor Rd. *Guide* 6K 19
Blackburn Cathedral 1H 19
Blackburn Golf Course 5E 12
Blackburn Mus. & Art Gallery
7H 13
Blackburn Old Rd. *Gt Har* 2D 14
Blackburn Old Rd. *Rish* 5B 14
(in two parts)
Blackburn Rd. *Acc* 7G 23
Blackburn Rd. *Alt & Pad* 1F 17
Blackburn Rd. *B'brn & Osw* 3D 20
Blackburn Rd. *Chu* 2K 21
Blackburn Rd. *Clay M* 6J 15
Blackburn Rd. *Dar* 7H 19
(in two parts)
Blackburn Rd. *Gt Har* 3H 15
Blackburn Rd. *Has* 2A 28
Blackburn Rd.
Has & Ram 7D 28
Blackburn Rd. *Rish* 1C 20
Blackburn Rovers F.C. 5G 19
(Ewood Pk.)
Blackburn Shop. Cen. B'brn 7H 13
(off Church St.)
Blackburn St. *B'brn* 6H 13
Blackburn St. *Burn* 4A 10
Blacker St. *Burn* 7B 6
Black Ho. La. *Brclf* 7K 7
Blacklane Cft. Clith 4E 2
(off Railway Vw.)
Black La. Cft. *Clith* 4E 2
Blackpool St. *Chu* 3K 21
Blackpool St. *Dar* 7F 27
Blacksnape Rd. *Hodd* 4H 27
Blackthorn Cres. *Bacup* 2H 31
Blackthorn La. *Bacup* 1H 31
Blackwood Rd. *Bacup* 6D 30
Blake Gdns. *Gt Har* 3G 15
Blake St. *Acc* 2C 22
Blakewater Rd. *B'brn* 1A 20
Blakey Moor. *B'brn* 7G 13
Blakey St. *Burn* 4B 10
Blannell St. *Burn* 4K 9
Blascomay Sq. Col 4G 5
(off Raglan St.)
Blea Clo. *Burn* 2H 9
Bleasdale Av. *Clith* 6C 2
Blenheim Clo. *B'brn* 3H 13
Blenheim St. *Col* 3K 5
Blucher St. *Col* 4H 5
Bluebell Av. *Has* 5A 28
Board St. *Burn* 1B 10
Boarsgreave La. *Ross* 7B 30
Boathorse La. *Burn* 4J 9
Bobbin Clo. *Acc* 3B 22
Bocholt Way. *Ross* 3G 29
Bog Height Rd. *Dar* 7E 18
Boland St. *B'brn* 5K 13
Bold St. *Acc* 2D 22
Bold St. *Bacup* 4H 31
Bold St. *B'brn* 6H 13
Bold St. *Col* 4H 5
Bolland Clo. *Clith* 5F 3
Bolland Prospect. *Clith* 5F 3
Bolton Av. *Acc* 6E 16
Bolton Gro. *Barfd* 5A 4
Bolton Rd. *B'brn* 4G 19
Bolton Rd. *Dar* 4E 26
Bolton's Ct. B'brn 7H 13
(off Exchange Ter.)
Bolton St. *Col* 4E 4
Bolton St. *Newc* 4A 30
Bombay St. *B'brn* 2F 19
Bonchurch St. *B'brn* 4B 20
Bond St. *Acc* 3B 22
Bond St. *Burn* 2B 10
Bond St. *Col* 3G 5
Bond St. *Dar* 2E 26
Bond St. *Nels* 2E 6
Bonfire Hill Clo. *Ross* 5H 25
Bonfire Hill Rd. *Ross* 5G 25
Bonsall St. *B'brn* 3D 18
Booth Ct. Burn 2B 10
(off Old Hall St.)
Booth Cres. *Ross* 4C 30
Boothman Pl. *Nels* 6B 4
Boothman St. *B'brn* 3G 19
Booth Pl. *Ross* 4B 30
Booth Rd. *Ross & Bacup* 4B 30
Booth St. *Acc* 3D 22
Booth St. *Bacup* 3H 31
Booth St. *Has* 1A 28
Booth St. *Nels* 1E 6
Booth St. *Ross* 5A 30
Boot Way. *Burn* 5B 10
Borough Rd. *Dar* 5D 26
Borrowdale Av. *B'brn* 5B 20
Borrowdale Clo. *Acc* 6E 16
Borrowdale Clo. *Burn* 6D 6
Borrowdale Dri. *Burn* 5D 6
Bosley Clo. *Dar* 5H 27
Boston Rd. *Bacup* 2H 31
Bostons. *Gt Har* 2G 15
Boston St. *Nels* 3G 7
Bott Ho. La. *Col* 6D 4
(in two parts)
Bottomgate. *B'brn* 3A 20
Bottomley Bank La. *Ross* 5G 25
Bottomley St. *Nels* 1F 7
Bottom's Row. *Ross* 7B 30
Boulder St. *Ross* 5G 25
Bouldsworth Rd. *Burn* 5F 11
Boulevard, The. *B'brn* 1H 19
Boulsworth Cres. *Nels* 7E 4
Boulsworth Dri. *Traw* 7K 5
Boulsworth Gro. *Col* 3K 5
Boulsworth Rd. *Traw* 7K 5
Boulview Ter. *Col* 3K 5
Boundary Rd. *Acc* 1D 22
Boundary St. *Burn* 7D 6
Boundary St. *Col* 4G 5
Bowden Av. *Pleas* 4A 18
Bowen St. *B'brn* 3E 18
Bower Clo. *B'brn* 3E 18
Bower St. *B'brn* 3E 18
Bowland Av. *Burn* 5F 11
Bowland Ct. *Clith* 5E 2
Bowland Ho. B'brn 6J 13
(off Primrose Bank)
Bowland Vw. *Brier* 5E 6
Bowling Grn. Clo. *Dar* 7E 26
Bowman Ct. B'brn 7J 13
(off Cleaver St.)
Bowness Av. *Nels* 3F 7
Bowness Clo. *B'brn* 6K 13
Bowness Rd. *Pad* 1B 8
Boxwood Dri. *B'brn* 5C 18
Boxwood St. *B'brn* 4J 13
Boyle St. *B'brn* 6J 13
Bracewell Clo. *Nels* 1F 7
Bracewell St. *Burn* 1C 10
Bracewell St. *Nels* 1F 7
Bracken Clo. *B'brn* 5C 18
Bracken Gro. *Has* 5A 28
Bracken Hey. *Clith* 5G 3
Bradda Rd. *B'brn* 4H 19
Bradford St. *Acc* 2E 22
Bradley Fold. *Nels* 7B 4
Bradley Gdns. *Burn* 5G 9
Bradley Hall Rd. *Nels* 7C 4
Bradley Rd. *Nels* 7B 4
Bradley Rd. E. *Nels* 7B 4
Bradley St. *Col* 3J 5
Bradley Vw. *Nels* 7B 4
Bradshaw Clo. *B'brn* 4H 13
Bradshaw Clo. *Nels* 2F 7
Bradshaw Row. *Chu* 2A 22
Bradshaw St. *Chu* 2A 22
Bradshaw St. *Nels* 2E 6
Bradshaw St. E. *Acc* 2D 22
Bradshaw St. W. *Acc* 2A 22
Braeside. *B'brn* 6F 13
Brambles, The. *B'brn* 4D 12
Bramble St. *Burn* 1B 10
Bramley Av. *Burn* 2H 9
Bramley Clo. *Osw* 3K 21
Branch Rd. *B'brn & Lwr D* 6H 19
Branch Rd. *Burn* 5B 10
Branch Rd. *Clay M* 4A 16
Branch Rd. *Wadd* 1B 2
Branch St. *Bacup* 5F 31
Branch St. *Nels* 1G 7
Brandwood. Ross 4A 30
(off Staghills Rd.)
Brandwood Gro. *Burn* 4D 10
Brandwood Pk. *Bacup* 5C 30
Brandwood Rd. *Bacup* 5D 30
Brandwood St. *Dar* 4F 27
Brandy Ho. Brow. *B'brn* 3J 19
Brantfell Dri. *Burn* 2G 9
Brantfell Rd. *B'brn* 5G 13
Brantfell Rd. *Gt Har* 1H 15
Brantwood. *Clay M* 5K 15
Brantwood Av. *B'brn* 3D 20
Brassey St. *Burn* 3H 9
Bread St. Burn 4J 9
(off Redruth St.)
Brearley St. *Bacup* 5F 31
Brecon Av. *Osw* 4H 21
Brecon Rd. *B'brn* 3B 20
Brendon Ho. Has 2B 28
(off Pleasant St.)
Brennand St. *Burn* 1C 10
Brennand St. *Clith* 4E 2
Brent St. *Burn* 6D 6
Brentwood Av. *Burn* 7K 9
Brentwood Rd. *Nels* 7D 4
Brett Clo. *Clith* 6G 3
Brewery St. *B'brn* 7G 13
Briarcroft. *Lwr D* 7K 19
Briar Hill Clo. *B'brn* 1K 19
Briar Rd. *B'brn* 4J 13
Briar St. *Bacup* 4J 31
Briar Ter. *Bacup* 4J 31
Brick St. *Burn* 4A 10
Bridge Clo. *Ross* 4B 30
Bridge Ct. *Clith* 3F 3
Bridge Cft. *Clay M* 3K 15
Bri. End Clo. *Helm* 6A 28
Bridgefield Clo. *Rish* 5G 15
Bridgefield St. *Hap* 6B 8
Bridgemill Rd. *B'brn* 1J 19
Bri. Mill Rd. *Nels* 1D 6
Bridge Rd. *Chat* 1K 3
Bridge St. *Acc* 2D 22
Bridge St. *B'brn* 1H 19
Bridge St. *Brier* 3C 6
Bridge St. *Burn* 4B 10
Bridge St. *Chu* 2K 21
Bridge St. *Col* 4F 5
Bridge St. *Dar* 4E 26
Bridge St. *Gt Har* 2H 15
(in two parts)
Bridge St. *Newc* 4B 30
Bridge St. *Pad* 2A 8
Bridge St. *Rish* 5G 15
Bridge St. *Ross* 6A 30
Bridgewater Ho. B'brn 1F 19
(off Bath St.)
Bridleway. *Ross* 3B 30
Brief St. *Burn* 2B 10
Briercliffe Av. *Col* 5E 4
Briercliffe Rd. *Burn* 1C 10
Briercliffe St. *Col* 5E 4
Brier Cres. *Nels* 3E 6
Brierh Gdns. Clo. *Brier* 4E 6
Brigg Fld. *Clay M* 3A 16
Brighton Rd. *Burn* 6D 6
Brighton Ter. *B'brn* 6E 12
Brighton Ter. *Dar* 3C 26
Bright St. *Bacup* 3H 31
Bright St. *Burn* 1B 10
Bright St. *Clith* 5F 3
Bright St. *Col* 3G 5
Bright St. *Dar* 3D 26
Bright St. *Osw* 5J 21
Bright St. *Pad* 2C 8
Bright St. *Ross* 2G 29
Bright Ter. *Traw* 6J 5
Brigsteer Clo. *Clay M* 5K 15
Brindle St. *B'brn* 4F 19
Brisbane St. *Clay M* 6B 16
Bristol Clo. *B'brn* 1J 19
Bristol St. *Burn* 7J 9
Bristol St. *Col* 2H 5
Britannia Av. *Bacup* 3J 31
Britannia St. *Gt Har* 2H 15
Britannia Wlk. Burn 6C 10
(off Tarleton St.)
Britannia Way. *Ross* 5A 28
British in India Mus. 3H 5
Britten Clo. *B'brn* 3K 19
Britten St. *Dar* 3D 26
Britwell Clo. *B'brn* 5K 19
Broadfield. *Osw* 6A 22
Broadfield Rd. *Acc* 5B 22
Broadfield St. *Osw* 5A 22
Broadfield Ter. Osw 5A 22
(off Broadfield St.)
Broadfold Av. *B'brn* 5K 13
Broad Ga. *Dar* 3F 27
Broadhurst Way. *Brier* 5D 6
Broading Ter. *Ross* 1G 25
Broadley St. *Ross* 2G 29
Broadness Dri. *Nels* 3F 7
Broad Oak Rd. *Acc* 3D 22
Broad St. *Nels* 1E 6
Broadtree Clo. *Mel* 1A 12
Broadway. *Acc* 2D 22
Broadway. *B'brn* 2H 13
Broadway. *Has* 5A 28
Broadway. *Nels* 1E 6
Broadway Cres. *Has* 5A 28
Broadway Pl. *Barfd* 5A 4
Broadway Pl. *Nels* 7D 4
Broadway St. *B'brn* 4E 18
Brock Bank. *Ross* 1B 30
Brock Clough Rd. *Ross* 1B 30
Brockenhurst St. *Burn* 5D 10
Brocklehurst Av. *Acc* 5C 22
Broderick St. *Dar* 2D 26
Brodick Rd. *B'brn* 5C 20
Broken Banks. *Col* 4H 5
Broken Stone Rd. *Dar* 6C 18
Bromley Ho. B'brn 7F 13
(off Bromley St.)
Bromley St. *B'brn* 7F 13
Bromsgrove Rd. *Burn* 2C 10
Bronte Av. *Burn* 4E 10
Brooden Dri. *Brier* 5D 6
Brookbank. Barfd 4B 4
(off Bankhouse St.)
Brook Ct. *Ross* 5G 25
Brooke Clo. *Acc* 6F 23
Brookes St. *Bacup* 5F 31
Brookfield. *Mel* 2B 12
Brookfield St. *B'brn* 6H 13
Brookford Clo. *Burn* 2J 9
Brookhouse Bus. Cen.
B'brn 6J 13

A-Z Blackburn 35

Brookhouse Clo.—Cecil St.

Brookhouse Clo. B'brn 6J 13
Brookhouse Gdns. B'brn 6J 13
Brookhouse La. B'brn 6J 13
Brookland Clo. Clay M 3A 16
Brooklands. Ross 4B 30
(Burnley Rd. E.)
Brooklands. Ross 4F 29
(Bury Rd.)
Brooklands Av. Burn 7C 10
Brooklands Av. Ross 6B 28
Brooklands Rd. Burn 7C 10
Brooklands Ter. B'brn 5K 13
Brookland St. Ross 4K 29
Brookland Ter. Ross 6B 30
Brooklyn Rd. Clay D 3B 14
Brookside. Ross 5E 28
Brookside Bus. Pk. Ross 1F 29
Brookside Ind. Pk. Osw 5H 21
Brookside La. Osw 5E 20
Brookside St. Osw 5H 21
Brookside Vw. Osw 4H 21
Brook St. B'brn 3E 18
Brook St. Clith 4F 3
Brook St. Col 3G 5
Brook St. Dar 3E 26
Brook St. Has 7B 24
Brook St. Nels 1F 7
Brook St. Osw 5K 21
Brook St. Pad 3C 8
Brook St. Rish 6G 15
Brookway. B'brn 5E 18
Broomfield Pl. B'brn 2E 18
Brothers St. B'brn 4D 18
Brotherton Mdw. Clith 5F 3
Brougham St. Burn 3A 10
Broughton Clo. B'brn 4K 19
Broughton St. Burn 4J 9
Broughton St. Dar 3D 26
Brow Edge. Ross 4K 29
Browhead Ct. Burn 2C 10
Browhead Rd. Burn 2C 10
Brown Birks Rd. Acc 7F 17
Brownhill Av. Burn 4D 10
Brownhill Dri. B'brn 2J 13
Brown Hill La. Col 1J 5
Brownhill Rd. B'brn 1J 13
Browning Av. Osw 3H 21
Browning Clo. Col 2G 5
Browning St. Hodd 4K 27
Brownlow St. B'brn 4C 20
Brownlow St. Clith 6E 2
Brownside Mill. B'brn 4F 11
Brownside Rd. Burn 5F 11
Brown's Sq. Burn 4B 10
(off Forest St.)
Brown St. Acc 3B 22
Brown St. Bacup 1H 31
Brown St. B'brn 7H 13
Brown St. Burn 4A 10
Brown St. Clith 6D 2
Brown St. Col 4F 5
Brown St. E. Col 3G 5
Brown St. W. Col 4F 5
Browsholme Av. Burn 4D 10
Brow Vw. Burn 2C 10
Bruce St. B'brn 2A 20
Bruce St. Burn 5J 9
Brundhurst Fold. Mel 2A 12
Brunel Dri. B'brn 1J 19
Brunel St. Burn 3H 9
Brunel Wlk. B'brn 1J 19
Brungerley Av. Clith 4E 2
Brunshaw Av. Burn 5D 10
Brunshaw Rd. Burn 4C 10
Brun St. Burn 4A 10
Brunswick Dri. Col 5D 4
Brunswick St. B'brn 1G 19
Brunswick St. Burn 6B 10
(in two parts)
Brunswick St. Dar 5F 27
Brunswick St. Nels 1F 7
Brunswick Ter. Acc 2C 22
Brunswick Ter. Bacup 5F 31
Brun Ter. Burn 5G 11
Brush St. Burn 5H 9
Brussells Rd. Dar 4G 27
Bryan St. B'brn 3H 19
Bryer's Cft. Wilp 2B 14
Buccleuch Av. Clith 5D 2
Buccleuch Clo. Clith 5D 2
Buccleuch Rd. Nels 7A 4
Buccleuch St. Burn 5K 9
Buckden Ga. Barfd 5A 4
Buckden Rd. Acc 4A 22
Buckingham Clo. Has 4A 28
Buckingham Gro. Chu 1A 22
Buck St. Burn 5K 9
Buck St. Col 3H 5
Buff St. Dar 5E 26
Bulcock St. Burn 1D 10
Buller St. Ross 3G 29
Bullough Clo. Acc 3B 22
Bull St. Burn 4B 10
Buncer La. B'brn 7D 12
Bunkers Hill Clo. B'brn 5E 18
Burdett St. Burn 5J 9
Burford Clo. B'brn 5B 18
Burgess St. B'brn 3B 20
Burgess St. Has 2B 28
Burleigh St. Burn 2A 10
Burlington St. B'brn 7F 13
Burlington St. Nels 2D 6
Burnham Clo. Burn T 5K 9
Burnham Ga. Burn 5J 9
Burnham Trad. Pk. Burn 4K 9
(off Blannel St.)
Burnley Bus. Cen. Burn 4B 10
(off Bank Pde.)
Burnley Clo. B'brn 3A 20
Burnley F.C. 4C 10
(Turf Moor)
Burnley La. Hun & Acc 6G 17
Burnley Rd. Acc 2D 22
Burnley Rd. Bacup 1H 31
Burnley Rd. B'brn 3B 20
Burnley Rd. Brclf 6G 7
Burnley Rd. Brier 5C 6
Burnley Rd. Clay M 5B 16
Burnley Rd. Col 6D 4
Burnley Rd. Good & Dunn 3G 25
Burnley Rd. Hap 6H 17
Burnley Rd. Pad 2B 8
Burnley Rd. Ram 7D 28
Burnley Rd. Traw 7J 5
Burnley Rd. E. Ross 1A 30
Burnley Rd. E. Waterf 5A 30
Burnsall Clo. Burn 6F 7
Burnsall Rd. Acc 4A 22
Burns Av. Osw 3J 21
Burns Dri. Acc 6F 23
Burns St. Burn 3A 10
Burns St. Hap 6B 8
Burns St. Nels 7A 4
Burns St. Pad 3C 8
Burns Wlk. Dar 4F 27
Burns Way. Gt Har 3G 15
Burrans Mdw. Col 4G 5
Burrell Av. Col 2G 5
Burton Gdns. Brier 4C 6
Burton Rd. Acc 1D 22
Burton St. Burn 5C 10
Burton St. Rish 6H 15
Burwen Clo. Burn 7J 9
Bury Fold. Dar 7E 26
Bury Fold Clo. Dar 6E 26
Bury Fold La. Dar 7E 26
Bury Rd. Has 2B 28
Bury Rd. Ross 7E 28
Bury St. Dar 4E 26
Bury St. Osw 5J 21
Bush St. Burn 1B 10
Bute Rd. B'brn 5C 20
Bute St. Burn 7J 9
Butler St. Burn 2B 10
Butler St. Rish 6H 15
Butterfield St. Barfd 5A 4
Buttermere Av. Col 2J 5
Buttermere Clo. B'brn 6J 13
Buttermere Dri. Osw 3J 21
Buttermere Rd. Burn 5G 11
Butts. Gt Har 2G 15
(off Delph Rd.)
Butts Gro. Clith 3E 2
Butts Mt. Gt Har 2G 15
Buxton St. Acc 3B 22
Byrom St. B'brn 1G 19
Byron Clo. Acc 6F 23
Byron Clo. Osw 4H 21
Byron Rd. Col 3H 5
Byron Sq. Gt Har 3G 15
Byron St. Burn 3E 8
Byron Ter. B'brn 2E 18

C

Cabin End Row. B'brn 4D 20
Cadogan St. Barfd 6A 4
Cadshaw Clo. B'brn 4H 13
Caernarvon Av. Burn 3F 9
Caernarvon Rd. Has 4A 28
Cairo St. Burn 4J 9
Calcott St. Burn 7K 9
Caldbeck Clo. Nels 3F 7
Calder Av. Dar 1B 26
Calder Banks. B'brn 5J 13
(in two parts)
Calderbrook Av. Burn 7K 9
Calderbrook Pl. Burn 7K 9
Calder Clo. Nels 7A 4
Calder Ct. Alt 1F 17
Calder Pl. Gt Har 1K 15
Calder Rd. Ross 1G 29
Calder St. B'brn 5J 13
Calder St. Burn 4A 10
Calder St. Col 4F 5
Calder St. Nels 7A 4
Calder St. Pad 2B 8
Calder Ter. Nels 1C 6
Calder Va. Barfd 6A 4
Calder Vale Rd. Burn 4A 10
Calder Vw. Barfd 3B 4
Caleb St. Nels 7B 4
Calendar St. B'brn 7H 13
Calf Hey. Clay M 3A 16
Calgary Av. B'brn 4E 12
Calico Clo. Osw 4G 21
Calico St. B'brn 4G 19
Calva Clo. Burn 2G 9
Cambrian Clo. B'brn 1J 13
Cambrian Way. Has 4B 28
Cambridge Clo. B'brn 1J 19
Cambridge Clo. Pad 4C 8
Cambridge Dri. B'brn 4D 20
Cambridge Dri. Pad 3C 8
Cambridge Ho. Dar 4G 27
Cambridge St. Acc 1D 22
Cambridge St. B'brn 1J 19
Cambridge St. Brier 4C 6
Cambridge St. Burn 5J 9
Cambridge St. Col 4G 5
Cambridge St. Dar 4G 27
Cambridge St. Gt Har 2J 15
Cambridge St. Has 3B 28
Cambridge St. Nels 2E 6
Camden St. Barfd 5A 4
Camden St. Nels 2E 6
Cameron St. Burn 1B 10
Camms Vw. Has 5A 28
Campbell Pl. B'brn 2E 18
(off Spring La.)
Campbell St. B'brn 3J 13
Campbell St. Burn 3E 8
Campion Ct. Osw 4K 21
Campion Dri. Has 5A 28
Camp St. Burn 6F 7
Canal M. Nels 1E 6
(off Carr Rd.)
Canalside. B'brn 2J 19
Canalside. Nels 6A 4
Canal St. B'brn 4E 18
Canal St. Burn 4A 10
Canal St. Chu 2K 21
Canal St. Clay M 5A 16
Candlemakers Ct. Clith 5E 2
Canning St. Burn 3A 10
(in two parts)
Canning St. Pad 3C 8
Cannon St. Acc 3C 22
Cannon St. Nels 7C 4
Canterbury St. B'brn 1G 19
Cape St. Ross 3G 29
Captain's Cotts. Wors 5J 11
(off Wallstreams La.)
Cardigan Av. Burn 3F 9
Cardigan Av. Clith 5D 2
Cardigan Av. Osw 4H 21
Cardigan Clo. Clith 5D 2
Cardinal St. Burn 1C 10
Cardwell Pl. B'brn 7G 13
Cardwell St. Pad 3C 8
Carham Rd. B'brn 4H 13
Carholme Av. Burn 4D 10
Carleton Rd. Col 5D 4
Carleton St. Nels 2F 7
Carley St. Dar 3C 26
Carlinghurst Rd. B'brn 1G 19
Carlisle Rd. Acc 7E 16
Carlisle St. B'brn 1J 19
Carlton Clo. Col 3E 4
Carlton Gdns. B'brn 6H 13
Carlton Pl. Clith 6F 3
Carlton Rd. B'brn 6H 13
Carlton Rd. Burn 5K 9
Carlton St. Bacup 2J 31
Carlton St. Brier 4C 6
Carluke St. B'brn 3B 20
Carlyle St. Burn 6D 6
Carnarvon Rd. B'brn 7E 12
Carnforth Clo. B'brn 4K 19
Caroline Ct. Burn 6G 9
Carradice Clo. Nels 1E 6
Carr Hall Dri. Barfd 1C 6
Carr Hall Rd. Barfd 1C 6
Carr Hall St. Has 7B 24
Carr Head. Traw 6K 5
Carrington Av. B'brn 5F 19
Carr La. B'brn 6B 12
Carr La. New H 4F 29
Carr La. Waterf 5A 30
Carr Mill St. Has 7B 24
Carr Mt. Ross 4F 29
Carr Rd. Burn 7K 9
Carr Rd. Col 2H 5
Carr Rd. Dar 5F 27
Carr Rd. Nels 7A 4
Carr Rd. Ross 4F 29
Carrs Ind. Est. Has 2A 28
Carr St. B'brn 6H 13
Carr St. Has 7B 24
Carrs Wood. B'brn 6C 12
Carr Vw. Traw 7K 5
Carrwood Grn. Pad 2B 8
Carry La. Col 3H 5
Carside. Brier 1C 6
Carter Av. Hap 6B 8
Carter Fold. Mel 2B 12
Carter St. Acc 4C 22
Carter St. Burn 3H 9
Cartmel Av. Acc 5B 22
Cartmel Dri. Burn 2G 9
Cartmel Rd. B'brn 2D 18
Carus Av. Hodd 4J 27
Carus St. Hodd 4K 27
Casserley Rd. Col 2J 5
Castercliff Bank. Col 5F 5
Castercliffe Rd. Nels 1J 7
Casterton Av. Burn 6C 6
Castle Clo. Col 2H 5
Castle Clough Cotts. Burn 6A 8
Castlegate. Clith 5E 2
Castlerigg Dri. Burn 2G 9
Castle Rd. Col 2H 5
Castle St. B'brn 3A 20
Castle St. Brier 3C 6
Castle St. Burn 3A 10
Castle St. Clith 5E 2
Castle St. Hap 6B 8
Castle St. Nels 1G 7
Castletown Dri. Bacup 5K 31
Castle Vw. Clith 5E 2
Cathedral Clo. B'brn 7H 13
(off Church St.)
Catlow Hall St. Osw 5K 21
Catterall St. B'brn 5F 19
Cattle St. Gt Har 2H 15
Causeway. Gt Har 2G 15
Causeway Cft. Clith 4E 2
Causeway Head. Has 5A 28
Causeway St. Dar 6G 27
Causey Foot. Nels 2D 6
Cavalry Way. Burn 4J 9
Cavendish Pl. B'brn 2E 18
Cavendish St. Dar 2D 26
Cave St. B'brn 4E 18
Cavour St. Burn 3A 10
Cecilia Rd. B'brn 3C 18
Cecil St. B'brn 6K 13
Cecil St. Osw 4K 21
Cecil St. Rish 5H 15

Cedar Av.—Colbran St.

Cedar Av. Has 2C 28
Cedar Av. Raw 3E 28
Cedar Clo. Rish 7G 15
Cedar Ct. B'brn 5J 13
Cedar St. Acc 2D 22
Cedar St. B'brn 4J 13
Cedar St. Burn 5C 10
Celia St. Burn 5D 10
Cemetery La. Burn 6F 9
Cemetery Rd. Dar 7F 27
Cemetery Rd. Pad 3B 8
Centenary Way. Burn 5A 10
Central Av. Clith 6D 2
Central Av. Osw 4H 21
Central Bldgs. Pad 1B 8
(off Factory La.)
Central Sq. Has 2B 28
Central Vw. Bacup 3J 31
Chad St. Col 6D 4
Chadwick St. B'brn 2G 19
Challenge Way. B'brn 1B 20
Chancel Pl. Dar 5G 27
Chancel Way. Dar 5G 27
Chancery Wlk. Burn 4B 10
Change Clo. Bacup 1K 31
Chapel Clo. Clith 5B 2
Chapel Clo. Traw 6J 5
Chapel Ct. Brclf 6H 7
Chapel Fld. Col 4G 5
Chapel Hill La. Ross 1H 29
Chapel Ho. Rish 6H 15
(off Chapel St.)
Chapel Ho. Rd. Nels 3E 6
Chapel La. Good 3G 25
Chapels. Dar 2E 26
Chapels Brow. Dar 2E 26
(in two parts)
Chapel St. Acc 3D 22
Chapel St. Bacup 5E 30
Chapel St. B'brn 1G 19
Chapel St. Brier 3C 6
Chapel St. Burn 4B 10
Chapel St. Clay M 4K 15
Chapel St. Col 4G 5
Chapel St. Dar 5E 26
Chapel St. Good 4G 25
Chapel St. Has 2B 28
Chapel St. Nels 1F 7
Chapel St. Newc 4A 30
Chapel St. Osw 4K 21
Chapel St. Rish 6H 15
Chapel St. Wors 5H 11
Chapel Ter. Ross 1B 30
Chapel Wlk. Pad 1B 8
Chapman Rd. Hodd 4K 27
Chapter Rd. Dar 5G 27
Charles La. Has 3A 28
Charles St. B'brn 3G 19
Charles St. Clay M 4K 15
Charles St. Col 3H 5
Charles St. Dar 3E 26
Charles St. Gt Har 3H 15
Charles St. Nels 7A 4
Charles St. Osw 5K 21
Charles St. Ross 3B 30
Charlotte St. B'brn 6H 13
Charlotte St. Burn 5A 10
Charnley St. B'brn 3F 19
Charnwood Clo. B'brn 4D 12
Charter Brook. Gt Har 2J 15
Charterhouse Pl. B'brn 2E 18
Charter St. Acc 3A 22
Chase, The. Burn 2J 9
Chatburn Av. Burn 5E 10
Chatburn Av. Clith 4F 3
Chatburn Clo. Gt Har 2K 15
Chatburn Clo. Ross 1G 29
Chatburn Old Rd. Chat 1J 3
Chatburn Old Rd. Clith 2F 3
Chatburn Pk. Av. Brier 3B 6
Chatburn Pk. Dri. Brier 3B 6
Chatburn Pk. Dri. Clith 3F 3
Chatburn Rd. Clith 4F 3
Chatburn St. B'brn 7F 13
Chatham Cres. Col 2H 5
Chatham St. Col 2H 5
Chatham St. Nels 7A 4
Chatsworth Clo. B'brn 3H 13
Chatterton Dri. Acc 6F 23
Chaucer Gdns. Gt Har 3G 15
Cheetham St. B'brn 7F 13
Chelburn Gro. Burn 4D 10
Chelston Dri. Ross 6A 28
Cheltenham Av. Acc 7D 16
Cheltenham Rd. B'brn 7F 13
Chequers. Clay M 5A 16
Cherry Clo. B'brn 3A 20
Cherryclough Way. B'brn 5D 18
Cherry Cres. Osw 6J 21
Cherry Cres. Ross 5F 29
Cherry Lea. B'brn 4C 18
Cherry St. B'brn 3A 20
Cherry Tree La. B'brn 5B 18
Cherry Tree La. Ross 4F 29
Cherry Tree M. Burn 7J 9
(off Bristol St.)
Cherry Tree Ter. B'brn 4C 18
Cherry Tree Way. Ross 6A 28
Chessington Grn. Burn 6E 6
(off Hillingdon Rd. N.)
Chester Av. Clith 4E 2
Chester Clo. B'brn 2K 19
Chester Cres. Has 5B 28
Chester St. Acc 3B 22
Chester St. B'brn 1K 19
Chestnut Dri. Ross 5F 29
Chestnut Gdns. B'brn 5J 13
Chestnut Gro. Acc 4B 22
Chestnut Gro. Clay M 3B 16
Chestnut Gro. Dar 7E 26
Chestnut Ri. Burn 6A 10
Chestnut Wlk. B'brn 3A 20
(off Longton St.)
Chevassut Clo. Barfd 7A 4
Cheviot Av. Burn 5F 11
Chichester Clo. Burn 4C 10
Chicken St. B'brn 1F 19
Childrey Wlk. B'brn 5K 19
(off Ridgeway Av.)
Chiltern Av. Burn 5E 10
China St. Acc 2A 22
Chingford Bank. Burn 6D 6
Chipping Gro. Burn 6E 10
Chipping St. Pad 1C 8
Chislehurst Gro. Burn 5E 6
Chorlton Clo. Burn 7E 6
Chorlton Gdns. B'brn 6J 13
Chorlton St. B'brn 5J 13
Christchurch Sq. Acc 3D 22
Christchurch St. Acc 3D 22
Christchurch St. Bacup 2J 31
Christleton Clo. Brclf 6G 7
Church All. Clay M 5A 16
Church Av. Acc 7F 23
Church Bank. Chu 1K 21
Chu. Bank St. Dar 4E 26
Church Brow. Clith 4E 2
Chu. Brow Gdns. Clith 4E 2
Church Clo. Clith 4E 2
Church Clo. Mel 2B 12
Church Clo. Wadd 1B 2
Church Hall. Acc 1A 22
Churchill Av. Rish 7F 15
Churchill Rd. Acc 5E 22
Churchill Rd. Barfd 1C 6
Churchill Rd. B'brn 5K 13
Churchill Way. Brier 1B 6
Church La. Clay M 6B 16
Church La. Gt Har 1H 15
Church La. Mel 2B 12
Church La. Newc 4A 30
Church La. Pad 1B 8
Church Meadows. Col 3G 5
Church Pad. Ross 3G 29
Church Sq. Wors 5J 11
(off Ravenoak La.)
Church St. Acc 3D 22
Church St. Bacup 5E 30
Church St. Barfd 4A 4
Church St. B'brn 7H 13
Church St. Brclf 7G 7
Church St. Brier 4C 6
Church St. Burn 3B 10
Church St. Chu 1K 21
Church St. Clay M 5A 16
Church St. Clith 5E 2
Church St. Col 3G 5
Church St. Dar 4E 26
Church St. Good 3G 25
Church St. Gt Har 2H 15
Church St. Hap 6B 8
Church St. Has 2B 28
Church St. Newc 4A 30
Church St. Osw 5J 21
Church St. Pad 2A 8
Church St. Rish 6F 15
Church St. Ross 5A 30
Church St. Traw 6K 5
Church Ter. Dar 4E 26
Churchtown Cres. Bacup 4J 31
Church Vw. Traw 6K 5
(off Ash St.)
Church Wlk. B'brn 1J 13
Church Wlk. Clith 5E 2
Church Way. Nels 3E 6
Cicely Ct. B'brn 1J 19
Cicely La. B'brn 7J 13
Cicely St. B'brn 1J 19
Circus, The. Dar 4E 26
Clare Av. Col 6D 4
Claremont Av. Clith 6F 3
Claremont Dri. Clith 6F 3
Claremont Rd. Acc 7C 16
Claremont St. Brier 4B 6
Claremont St. Burn 4J 9
Claremont St. Col 3J 5
Claremont Ter. Nels 2E 6
Clarence Av. Has 4A 28
Clarence Pk. B'brn 5E 12
Clarence Rd. Acc 4B 22
Clarence St. B'brn 6G 13
Clarence St. Burn 6C 10
Clarence St. Col 3K 5
Clarence St. Dar 2D 26
Clarence St. Osw 5H 21
Clarence St. Ross 5G 25
Clarence St. Traw 6K 5
Clarendon Rd. B'brn 4J 13
Clarendon Rd. E. B'brn 4K 13
Clarendon St. Acc 2E 22
Clarendon St. Col 3K 5
Clare St. Burn 4K 9
Claret St. Acc 3B 22
Clarke Holme St. Ross 3B 30
Clarke St. Rish 6G 15
Claughton St. Burn 1C 10
Claybank. Pad 1B 8
Clay St. Burn 5H 9
Clayton Av. Ross 5E 28
Clayton Bus. Pk. Clay M 5J 15
Clayton Clo. Nels 7A 4
Clayton Gro. Clay D 2A 14
Clayton Hall Dri. Clay M 3A 16
Clayton St. B'brn 1H 19
Clayton St. Clay M 6B 16
Clayton St. Col 4H 5
Clayton St. Gt Har 2H 15
Clayton St. Nels 1E 6
(in two parts)
Clayton St. Osw 3K 21
Clayton St. Ind. Est. Nels 7A 4
Clayton Way. Clay M 4B 16
Cleaver St. B'brn 7J 13
Cleaver St. Burn 2C 10
Clegg St. Bacup 5E 30
Clegg St. Brier 4C 6
Clegg St. Burn 2B 10
Clegg St. Has 2B 28
Clegg St. Nels 3F 7
Clegg St. Wors 5H 11
Clegg St. E. Burn 2B 10
(off Grey St.)
Clematis St. B'brn 7E 12
Clements Dri. Brier 5D 6
Clement St. Acc 4D 22
Clement St. Dar 5E 26
Clement Vw. Nels 1E 6
Clerkhill St. B'brn 3A 20
Clery St. Burn 5F 9
Cleveland Ho. Has 2B 28
(off Pleasant St.)
Clevelands Gro. Burn 6K 9
Clevelands Mt. Burn 6A 10
(off Clevelands Gro.)
Clevelands Rd. Burn 6K 9
Cleveland St. Col 2J 5
Cleveland Ter. Dar 5F 27
Cleveleys Rd. Acc 7B 16
Cleveleys Rd. B'brn 4J 19
Cliffe La. Gt Har 1H 15
Cliffe St. Nels 7B 4
Clifford St. Col 3H 5
Cliff St. Col 5E 4
Cliff St. Pad 1C 8
Cliff St. Rish 5G 15
Clifton Av. Acc 7D 16
Clifton Dri. Gt Har 1H 15
Clifton Gro. Wilp 4B 14
Clifton Rd. Brier 5D 6
Clifton Rd. Burn 3H 9
Clifton St. Acc 4B 22
Clifton St. B'brn 1H 19
Clifton St. Burn 4K 9
Clifton St. Col 3G 5
Clifton St. Dar 1D 26
Clifton St. Rish 6G 15
Clifton St. Traw 6J 5
Clifton Ter. Hodd 3J 27
Clinkham Rd. Gt Har 2E 14
Clinton St. B'brn 6K 13
Clipper Quay. B'brn 2J 19
Clitheroe By-Pass. Clith 7G 3
Clitheroe Castle Mus. 5E 2
Clitheroe Rd. Brier 4A 6
Clitheroe Rd. Chat 2J 3
Clitheroe Rd. Wadd 1B 2
Clitheroe Rd. W Brad 1E 2
Clitheroe St. Pad 1B 8
Clive St. Burn 2A 10
Clockhouse Av. Burn 6E 6
Clockhouse Ct. Burn 6E 6
Clockhouse Gro. Burn 6E 6
Clod La. Has 6C 28
Clogg Head. Traw 6K 5
Cloister Dri. Dar 4F 27
Close, The. Acc 4A 24
Close, The. Clay M 3A 16
Cloth Hall St. Col 3G 5
Clough Bank. Chat 1K 3
Clough End Rd. Has 7B 24
Clough Rd. Bacup 2J 31
Clough Rd. Nels 1H 7
Clough St. Bacup 5F 31
Clough St. Burn 5J 9
(in two parts)
Clough St. Dar 7G 27
Clough St. Ross 4B 30
Clough, The. Dar 7G 27
Clover Cres. Burn 2J 9
Cloverfields. B'brn 6K 13
Clover Hill Rd. Nels 2G 7
Clover St. Bacup 2J 31
Clover Ter. Dar 2E 26
Clyde St. B'brn 2E 18
Clynders Cotts. Burn 1H 9
Coach Rd. Chu 3K 21
Coal Clough La. Burn 5K 9
Coal Hey St. Has 2B 28
(off Peel St.)
Coal Pit La. Acc 4A 22
Coal Pit La. Bacup 2K 31
Coal Pit La. Col 4J 5
Coal Pit La. Ross 2C 30
Coal St. Burn 4A 10
Cobbs La. Osw 7K 21
Cob Castle Rd. Has 2A 28
Cobden Ct. B'brn 7H 13
(off Blackburn Shop. Cen.)
Cobden Ho. Ross 4K 29
Cobden St. Bacup 5K 31
Cobden St. Brclf 6G 7
Cobden St. Burn 2C 10
Cobden St. Dar 5E 26
Cobden St. Hap 6B 8
Cobden St. Nels 2E 6
Cobden St. Pad 1C 8
Cobham Ct. Ross 4A 30
Cobham Rd. Acc 3E 22
Cobourg Clo. B'brn 3J 19
Cob Wall. B'brn 6K 13
Cochran St. Dar 5E 26
Cockerill St. Has 1B 28
Cockermouth Clo. B'brn 6J 19
Cocker St. Dar 6G 27
Cockridge Clo. B'brn 5E 18
Coddington St. B'brn 3A 20
Cog La. Burn 5H 9
Cog St. Burn 5J 9
Colbran St. Burn 1C 10
Colbran St. Nels 6C 4

A-Z Blackburn 37

Coldstream Pl. *B'brn* 3H 19
Coldweather Av. *Nels* 4G 7
Coleman St. *Nels* 1G 7
Colenso Rd. *B'brn* 5G 13
Coleridge Clo. *Col* 2G 5
Coleridge Dri. *Acc* 6F 23
Coleridge Pl. *Gt Har* 3G 15
Coleridge St. *B'brn* 2F 19
Coleshill Av. *Burn* 5D 10
Colin St. *Burn* 5J 9
Colldale Ter. *Has* 3B 28
College Clo. *Pad* 4C 8
College St. *Acc* 2B 22
Collier's Row. *Guide* 7E 20
Colliers Sq. *Acc* 3K 21
(off Colliers St.)
Colliers St. *Osw* 3K 21
Collier St. *Osw* 6F 23
Collinge Fold La. *Ross* 1F 29
Collinge St. *Pad* 3B 8
Collinge St. *Ross* 1F 29
Collingwood. *Clay M* 5K 15
Collingwood St. *Col* 4E 4
Collins Dri. *Acc* 6F 23
Colne La. *Col* 4H 5
Colne Rd. *Barfd & Col* 4B 4
Colne Rd. *Brier* 3C 6
(in two parts)
Colne Rd. *Burn* 5C 6
Colne Rd. *Traw* 6J 5
Colthirst Dri. *Clith* 3F 3
Columbia Way. *B'brn* 4D 12
Colville Rd. *Dar* 1C 26
Colville St. *Burn* 2B 10
Commerce St. *Bacup* 3H 31
Commerce St. *Has* 2A 28
(in two parts)
Commercial Rd. *Gt Har* 2H 15
Commercial Rd. *Nels* 1F 7
Commercial St. *Bacup* 5F 31
Commercial St. *Brier* 3C 6
Commercial St. *Chu* 2K 21
Commercial St. *Gt Har* 2H 15
Commercial St. *Osw* 5J 21
Commercial St. *Rish* 5G 15
Commercial St. *Ross* 1G 25
Como Av. *Burn* 6H 9
Company St. *Rish* 6G 15
Compston Av. *Ross* 3G 25
Comrie Cres. *Burn* 7J 9
Conduit St. *Nels* 7A 4
Coniston Av. *Acc* 4A 22
Coniston Av. *Bacup* 1J 31
Coniston Av. *Pad* 1B 8
Coniston Dri. *Dar* 3G 27
Coniston Gro. *Col* 2K 5
Coniston Rd. *B'brn* 5K 13
Coniston St. *Burn* 4H 9
Coniston Way. *Rish* 6E 14
Constable Av. *B'brn* 7A 10
Constable Lee Ct. *Ross* 1G 29
(off Burnley Rd.)
Constable Lee Cres. *Ross* 1G 29
Conway Av. *B'brn* 5H 13
Conway Av. *Clith* 6C 2
Conway Clo. *Has* 4B 28
Conway Dri. *Osw* 4G 21
Conway Gro. *Burn* 6D 6
Conway Rd. *Ross* 2J 29
Cook Ct. *B'brn* 6D 12
Cook Gdns. *B'brn* 4A 20
Cook Ho. Rd. *Col* 2H 5
Cooperage, The. *Osw* 5J 21
Co-operation St. *Bacup* 3J 31
Co-operation St. *Craw* 5G 25
Co-operation St. *Ross* 3H 29
(Bacup Rd.)
Co-operation St. *Ross* 3B 30
(Burnley Rd. E.)
Coopers Clo. *Osw* 5J 21
(off Peel St.)
Cooper St. *Bacup* 2H 31
Cooper St. *Burn* 5B 10
Cooper St. *Nels* 7B 4
Copperfield Clo. *Burn* 4G 11
Copperfield St. *B'brn* 2J 19
Coppice Av. *Acc* 1E 22
Coppice Clo. *Nels* 6D 4
Coppice, The. *B'brn* 5D 12
Coppice, The. *Clay M* 3A 16

Copse, The. *Acc* 3A 22
Copster Hill Clo. *Guide* 7C 20
Copthurst St. *Pad* 1B 8
Copy Nook. *B'brn* 7K 13
Copy St. *B'brn* 7K 13
Corbridge Ct. *Clith* 4E 2
Corlass St. *Barfd* 5A 4
Cornel Gro. *Burn* 6H 9
Cornelian St. *B'brn* 2J 13
Cornfield Gro. *Burn* 2F 9
Cornfield St. *Dar* 3F 27
Cornhill. *Acc* 2D 22
Cornhill Arc. *Acc* 2D 22
(off Cornhill)
Cornholme. *Burn* 7F 7
Corn Mill La. *Ross* 2G 29
(off Greenfield St.)
Corn Mill Yd. *Clay M* 5A 16
Cornwall Av. *B'brn* 4D 20
Cornwall Pl. *Chu* 1A 22
Cornwall Rd. *Rish* 6F 15
Coronation Av. *Burn* 6A 18
Coronation Av. *Pad* 4B 8
Coronation Gro. *Ross* 4A 30
Coronation Pl. *Barfd* 5A 4
Coronation Rd. *Brier* 4D 6
Coronation St. *Gt Har* 1J 15
Corporation St. *Acc* 3B 22
Corporation St. *B'brn* 7H 13
Corporation St. *Clith* 5D 2
Corporation St. *Col* 5D 4
Corporation Way. *B'brn* 6H 13
Cotswold Ho. *Has* 2B 28
(off Warwick St.)
Cotswold M. *B'brn* 5K 19
Cottam Cft. *Clay M* 3A 16
Cotton Ct. *Col* 5F 5
Cotton Hall St. *Dar* 3E 26
Cotton St. *Acc* 3C 22
Cotton St. *Burn* 4J 9
Cotton St. *Pad* 3B 8
Cotton Tree La. *Col* 3K 5
Coultate St. *Burn* 4H 9
Coulton Rd. *Brier* 2C 6
Countess Rd. *Lwr D* 6J 19
Countess St. *Acc* 2A 22
Court Gro. *Clay D* 2A 14
Courtyard, The. *Bacup* 2J 31
Coverdale Dri. *B'brn* 6A 18
Coverdale Way. *Burn* 3J 9
Cowan Brae. *B'brn* 6G 13
Cowell Way. *B'brn* 7G 13
Cowes Av. *Has* 3C 28
Cowgill St. *Bacup* 2J 31
Cowhill La. *Rish* 1E 20
Cow La. *Burn* 4A 10
Cowley Cres. *Pad* 3D 8
Cowper Av. *Clith* 4E 2
Cowpe Rd. *Ross & Waterf* 5A 30
Cowper St. *B'brn* 5J 13
Cowtoot La. *Bacup* 2H 31
Crabtree Av. *Bacup* 4J 31
Crabtree Av. *Ross* 3B 30
Crabtree Av. *B'brn* 3A 20
Crabtree St. *Brier* 4C 6
Crabtree St. *Col* 4F 5
Crabtree St. *Ross* 1B 30
Cracoe Gill. *Barfd* 5A 4
Craddock Rd. *Col* 3H 5
Cragg St. *Col* 3F 5
Cranberry Chase. *Dar* 6G 27
Cranberry Clo. *Dar* 7H 27
Cranberry La. *Dar* 6G 27
Cranberry Ri. *Love* 2G 25
Cranborne Ter. *B'brn* 6F 13
Cranbourne Dri. *Chu* 7B 16
Cranbourne St. *Col* 2H 5
Cranbrook Av. *Osw* 4H 21
Cranbrook St. *B'brn* 3G 19
Cranfield Vw. *Dar* 7G 27
Crangle Way. *Clith* 3G 3
Crankshaw St. *Ross* 2G 29
Cranmer St. *Burn* 4K 9
Cranshaw Dri. *B'brn* 4H 13
Cranshaw St. *Acc* 2C 22
Cravendale Av. *Nels* 5B 4
Craven's Av. *B'brn* 6H 19
Craven's Brow. *B'brn* 6H 19

Cravens Heath. *B'brn* 7H 19
Cravens Hollow. *B'brn* 7G 19
Craven St. *Acc* 3B 22
Craven St. *Brier* 4C 6
Craven St. *Burn* 5B 10
Craven St. *Clith* 6E 2
Craven St. *Col* 3K 5
Craven St. *Nels* 1D 6
Craven St. *Ross* 3F 29
Crawford St. *Nels* 7B 4
Crawshaw Dri. *Ross* 6G 25
Crawshaw Grange. *Craw* 6G 25
Crawshaw La. *S'fld* 3K 7
Crediton Clo. *B'brn* 5F 19
Crescent, The. *B'brn* 4B 18
Crescent, The. *Burn* 5C 6
Crescent, The. *Clith* 5D 2
Crescent, The. *Col* 2G 5
Crescent, The. *Has* 4B 28
Crescent, The. *Wors* 5H 11
Creswick Av. *Burn* 7A 10
Creswick Clo. *Burn* 7A 10
Crewdson St. *Dar* 3D 26
Cribden End La. *Has* 1B 28
Cribden La. *Raw* 1E 28
Cribden St. *Ross* 1F 29
Criccieth Clo. *Has* 4B 28
Crimea St. *Bacup* 3J 31
Cringle Fold. *Clith* 3G 3
Croasdale Av. *Burn* 7E 6
Croasdale Dri. *Clith* 6F 3
Croasdale Sq. *B'brn* 2K 19
Crocus Clo. *Ross* 5A 28
Croft Clo. *Ross* 7G 25
Cft. Head Rd. *Whi I* 6A 14
Croft St. *Bacup* 2H 31
Croft St. *Burn* 5B 10
Croft St. *Clith* 6E 2
Croft St. *Dar* 4E 26
Croft St. *Gt Har* 3H 15
Croft, The. *B'brn* 5G 13
Croft, The. *Col* 1H 5
Croft Wood Ter. *B'brn* 4D 18
Cromer Av. *Burn* 1D 10
Cromer Gro. *Burn* 1D 10
Cromer Pl. *B'brn* 5H 13
Crompton Pl. *B'brn* 7E 12
Cromwell Av. *Acc* 7C 16
Cromwell St. *B'brn* 1K 19
Cromwell St. *Burn* 3A 10
Cromwell Ter. *Barfd* 5A 4
Cronkshaw St. *Burn* 3B 10
Crooked Shore. *Bacup* 2H 31
Crookhalgh Av. *Burn* 4G 11
Crosby Clo. *Dar* 7F 27
Crosby Rd. *B'brn* 4H 19
Crosley Clo. *Acc* 5C 22
Cross Bank. *Pad* 2C 8
(off Hambledon St.)
Cross Barn Gro. *Dar* 5F 27
Cross Barn Wlk. *Dar* 5F 27
Cross Ct. *Bacup* 2J 31
Cross Edge. *Osw* 7B 22
Crossfield St. *B'brn* 2J 19
Cross Gates. *Gt Har* 2H 15
Cross Hagg St. *Col* 4G 5
Cross Helliwell St. *Col* 4G 5
Crosshill Rd. *B'brn* 7E 12
Crosshills. *Pad* 1B 8
(off East St.)
Crossland St. *Acc* 3B 22
Crossley Fold. *Burn* 6J 9
Cross School St. *Col* 4G 5
Cross Skelton St. *Col* 3H 5
Cross St. *Acc* 3D 22
Cross St. *Brclf* 7G 7
Cross St. *Brier* 4C 6
Cross St. *Clay M* 4K 15
Cross St. *Clith* 5D 2
Cross St. *Dar* 6F 27
Cross St. *Lwr D* 6J 19
Cross St. *Nels* 1E 6
Cross St. *Osw* 4J 21
Cross St. *Ross* 5G 25
Cross St. *Wors* 4J 11
Cross St. N. *Has* 1B 28
Cross St. S. *Has* 1B 28
Cross St. W. *Col* 4E 4
Croston Clo. *B'brn* 3A 20
Croston St. *B'brn* 3B 20

Crown Ho. *Dar* 1D 26
Crown St. *Acc* 3B 22
Crown St. *Dar* 5E 26
Crown Way. *Col* 3F 5
Crowther Ct. *Wors* 4J 11
(off Showfield)
Crowther St. *Burn* 6C 10
Crowther St. *Clay M* 4K 15
Crow Tree Av. *Bacup* 5D 30
Crow Tree Gdns. *Chat* 1K 3
Crow Trees Brow. *Chat* 1K 3
Crow Wood Av. *Ross* 3J 9
Crow Wood Ct. *Burn* 3K 9
Crow Wood Rd. *Ross* 7D 28
Crow Woods. *Ram* 7D 28
Croydon St. *B'brn* 7F 13
Cuba St. *Nels* 1E 6
Cuckoo Brow. *B'brn* 4G 13
Cuckstool La. *Fence* 3A 6
Cuerdale St. *Burn* 6F 7
Cuerden St. *Col* 5E 4
Culshaw St. *B'brn* 7K 13
(off Higher Audley St.)
Culshaw St. *Burn* 5D 10
Cumberland Av. *Burn* 3F 9
Cumberland Av. *Clay M* 4B 16
Cumberland St. *B'brn* 1K 19
Cumberland St. *Col* 3H 5
Cumberland St. *Nels* 7B 4
Cumbrian Way. *Burn* 2G 9
Cumpstey St. *B'brn* 2H 19
Cuncliffe St. *Clay M* 5A 16
Cunliffe Clo. *B'brn* 6A 14
Cunliffe Ho. *Ross* 4K 29
(off Bacup Rd.)
Cunliffe Rd. *B'brn* 6A 14
Cunningham Gro. *Burn* 4G 9
Curate St. *Gt Har* 2H 15
Curlew Clo. *B'brn* 4H 13
Curlew Clo. *Osw* 5J 21
Curlew Gdns. *Burn* 5G 9
Curtis St. *Ross* 2G 29
Curven Edge. *Ross* 6A 28
Curve St. *Bacup* 4H 31
Curzon Pl. *B'brn* 2F 19
Curzon St. *Burn* 4A 10
(in two parts)
Curzon St. *Clith* 5D 2
Curzon St. *Col* 4H 5
Cut La. *Rish* 6E 14
(in two parts)
Cutler Clo. *B'brn* 7G 13
Cutler Cres. *Bacup* 6F 31
Cutler La. *Bacup* 6F 31
Cypress Ridge. *B'brn* 5C 18
Cypress St. *Bacup* 5E 30
Cyprus St. *Dar* 7F 27

D

Daffodil Clo. *Has* 5A 28
Dahlia Clo. *Lwr D* 6K 19
Daisy Bank. *Bacup* 2H 31
Daisy Bank Cres. *Burn* 5G 11
Daisyfield St. *Dar* 1C 26
Daisy Hill. *Ross* 2G 29
Daisy La. *B'brn* 6J 13
Daisy St. *B'brn* 6J 13
Daisy St. *Col* 4G 5
Dalby Cres. *B'brn* 4D 18
Dalby Lea. *B'brn* 4D 18
Dale Clo. *Burn* 4J 9
(off Tunnel St.)
Dale Cres. *B'brn* 5B 18
Dalesford. *Has* 4B 28
Dale St. *Acc* 2B 22
Dale St. *Bacup* 2H 31
Dale St. *B'brn* 1G 19
Dale St. *Brier* 4B 6
Dale St. *Burn* 4J 9
Dale St. *Col* 3F 5
Dale St. *Has* 2B 28
Dale St. *Nels* 1D 6
Dale St. *Osw* 4K 21
Dale St. *Stac* 5E 30
Dalesway. *Barfd* 5A 4
Dale Ter. *Chat* 1K 3
Dale Vw. *B'brn* 7H 19
Dale Vw. *Ross* 4G 29

Dalkeith Rd.—Edinburgh Rd.

Dalkeith Rd. Nels 1D 6
Dall St. Burn 6B 10
Dalton Clo. B'brn 7K 13
Dalton St. Burn 7J 9
Dalton St. Nels 7B 4
Dame Fold. Pad 2B 8
Dam Side. Col 4G 5
Dandy Row. Dar 2G 27
Dandy Wlk. B'brn 1H 19
Danes Ho. Rd. Burn 2B 10
Dane St. Burn 3B 10
Daniell St. Rish 5F 15
Daniel St. Clay M 4K 15
Danvers St. Rish 5G 15
Dark La. Ross 5K 29
(in two parts)
Darnley St. Burn 5D 10
Dartford Clo. B'brn 1J 19
Darwen Enterprise Cen. Dar 3E 26
Darwen Golf Course. 2A 26
Darwen St. B'brn 1H 19
Darwen St. Pad 2B 8
Darwin St. Burn 7B 6
Davenham Rd. Dar 2C 26
David St. Bacup 5F 31
David St. Barfd 4A 4
David St. Burn 6A 10
Davies Rd. B'brn 2C 20
Davitt Clo. Has 2B 28
Davy Fld. Rd. B'brn 7K 19
Dawlish Clo. B'brn 5F 19
Dawson Sq. Burn 3B 10
Day St. Nels 2F 7
Deal St. B'brn 5J 13
Dean La. Gt Har & Whal 1G 15
(in three parts)
Dean Mdw. Clith 6D 2
Dean Rd. Has 4A 28
Dean Rd. Helm 5B 28
Deansgrave. Has 3A 28
Deansgreave Rd. Bacup 5K 31
Dean St. B'brn 1H 19
Dean St. Burn 4K 9
Dean St. Dar 2D 26
Dean St. Pad 1C 8
Dean St. Traw 6J 5
Dearden Cft. Has 2B 28
(off Ratcliffe St.)
Dearden Ga. Has 2B 28
Deardengate Cft. Has 2B 28
Dearden Nook. Ross 4G 29
Deepdale Ct. Barfd 5A 4
Deepdale Dri. Burn 6D 6
Deepdale Grn. Barfd 5A 4
Deer Pk. Acc 7F 17
Deer Pk. Rd. Burn 5F 11
(in two parts)
Deerplay Clo. Burn 7F 7
Deerstone Av. Burn 4D 10
Deerstone Rd. Nels 1J 7
Deganwy Av. B'brn 5H 13
De Lacy St. Clith 5D 2
Delamere Clo. B'brn 3E 18
Delamere Rd. Brclf 6G 7
Delius Clo. B'brn 4K 19
Dell La. Hap 6B 8
Dell, The. B'brn 7G 19
Delma Rd. Burn 5F 11
Delph App. B'brn 4B 20
Delph Clo. B'brn 4B 20
Delph Ct. Gt Har 2H 15
Delph La. B'brn 4B 20
Delph Mt. Gt Har 1G 15
Delph Mt. Nels 2E 6
Delph Rd. Gt Har 2G 15
Delph Sq. Burn 7E 6
(off Marsden Rd.)
Delph St. B'brn 3J 19
Delph St. Dar 2F 27
Delph St. Has 1B 28
Delves La. S'fld 2K 7
Denbigh Dri. Clith 3F 3
Denbigh Gro. Burn 3F 9
Dene Bank Rd. Osw 5K 21
Dene, The. B'brn 4D 12
Dentdale Clo. B'brn 6A 18
Dent Row. Burn 5A 10
Dent St. Col 5E 4
Denville Rd. B'brn 7G 13
Denville St. B'brn 7G 13
Derby Clo. Dar 7F 27
Derby St. Acc 1D 22
Derby St. B'brn 6K 13
Derby St. Burn 5A 10
Derby St. Clith 5F 3
Derby St. Col 3G 5
Derby St. Nels 7B 4
Derby St. Rish 6H 15
Derham St. B'brn 2H 19
Derwent Av. Burn 7B 6
Derwent Av. Pad 1B 8
Derwent Clo. Col 2K 5
Derwent Clo. Rish 6E 14
Derwent Cres. Clith 6C 2
Derwent St. Dar 3D 26
Devon Av. Osw 3G 21
Devon Cres. Has 5B 28
Devon Gro. Burn 3F 9
Devon Pl. Chu 3K 21
Devonport Ct. B'brn 7F 13
(off Johnston St.)
Devonport Rd. B'brn 7F 13
Devon Rd. B'brn 3B 20
Devonshire Dri. Clay M 4A 16
Devonshire Rd. Burn 3B 10
Devonshire Rd. Rish 6F 15
Devonshire St. Acc 1C 22
Devonshire Ter. Burn 3B 10
(off Devonshire Rd.)
Devon St. Col 2H 5
Devon St. Dar 7F 27
Dewan Ind. Est. Has 5B 28
Dewhurst Clo. Dar 7F 27
Dewhurst St. B'brn 1K 19
(in two parts)
Dewhurst St. Col 5G 5
Dewhurst St. Dar 7F 27
Dickens St. B'brn 2J 19
Dickinson Clo. B'brn 2F 19
Dickinson St. B'brn 2G 19
Dickson St. Burn 4H 9
Dickson St. Col 2H 5
Didsbury St. B'brn 3B 20
Dill Hall La. Chu 1A 22
Dimmock St. B'brn 3F 19
Dinckley Sq. B'brn 6E 12
Dineley St. Chu 2A 22
Disraeli St. Burn 7B 6
Dixon St. Barfd 5A 4
Dixon St. B'brn 1F 19
Dobbin Clo. Ross 3J 29
Dobbin Ct. Ross 3J 29
(off Dobbin La.)
Dobbin Fold. Ross 3J 29
Dobbin La. Ross 3J 29
Dobson St. Dar 3D 26
Dockray St. Col 3H 5
Dock St. B'brn 7K 13
Dombey St. B'brn 1K 19
(in two parts)
Dominica Av. Lwr D 7J 19
Dominion Ct. Burn 6G 9
Dominion Rd. B'brn 4F 13
Dorchester Av. Osw 3H 21
Dorchester Clo. B'brn 5A 20
Doris St. Burn 4C 10
Dorothy St. B'brn 5F 19
Dorritt St. B'brn 2K 19
Dorset Av. Dar 2D 26
Dorset Av. Pad 3C 8
Dorset Dri. B'brn 4D 20
Dorset Dri. Clith 3F 3
Dorset Dri. Has 5A 28
Dorset Pl. Chu 1A 22
Dorset Rd. Rish 6F 15
Dorset St. Burn 4F 9
Double Row. Pad 2A 8
Doughty St. Col 4G 5
Douglas Gro. Dar 1B 26
Douglas Pl. B'brn 3J 13
Douglas Rd. Bacup 4J 31
Douglas Rd. Brclf 6H 7
Douglas St. Col 2H 5
Douglas Way. Brclf 6H 7
Dove Ct. Burn 7C 6
(off Shuttleworth St.)
Dovedale Clo. Burn 5D 6
Dovedale Dri. Burn 2H 9
Dove La. Dar 3D 26
Dover Clo. B'brn 4B 20
Dover St. Acc 4B 22
Dover St. Lwr D 6J 19
Dover St. Nels 7B 4
Downham Av. Gt Har 1K 15
Downham Av. Ross 1G 29
Downham Dri. Acc 5B 22
Downham Gro. Burn 5E 10
Downham Rd. Chat 1K 3
Downham St. B'brn 1F 19
Dowry St. Acc 2D 22
Dragon St. Pad 2B 8
Drammen Av. Burn 5G 9
Drew St. Burn 5G 9
(in two parts)
Driver St. Ross 5G 25
Drive, The. Bacup 3H 31
(off Market St.)
Driving Ga. Ross 3G 25
Dryden Gro. Gt Har 3G 15
Dryden St. Clay M 4A 16
Dryden St. Pad 3C 8
(in two parts)
Duchess St. Lwr D 6J 19
Duckett St. Burn 4K 9
Duckshaw Rd. Dar 7D 26
Duck St. Clith 5F 3
Duckworth Hall Brow. Acc 7F 21
Duckworth Hill La. Osw 7F 21
Duckworth La. Ross 5E 28
Duckworth St. Barfd 6A 4
Duckworth St. B'brn 2G 19
Duckworth St. Chu 2K 21
Duckworth St. Dar 3D 26
Duddon Av. Dar 2C 26
Dudley Av. Osw 4H 21
Dudley St. Brier 4D 6
Dudley St. Col 3J 5
Duerden St. Nels 1E 6
Dugdale Rd. Burn 3G 9
Dugdale St. Burn 5B 10
(off Red Lion St.)
Duke of Sussex St. B'brn 5E 18
Dukes Brow. B'brn 6E 12
Dukes Ct. B'brn 6E 12
Dukes Dri. Hodd 4J 27
Duke St. B'brn 7G 13
Duke St. Brclf 6G 7
Duke St. Burn 6C 10
Duke St. Clay M 5A 16
Duke St. Col 4G 5
Duke St. Gt Har 2G 15
Duke St. Osw 5J 21
Duke St. Ross 5A 30
Duncan Clo. Burn 5G 11
Duncan St. Burn 5F 9
Dun Cft. Clo. Clith 3E 2
Dundas St. Col 4F 5
(off John St.)
Dundee Dri. B'brn 1K 19
Dunderdale Av. Nels 2D 6
Dundonnell Rd. Nels 7D 4
Dunkenhalgh Way. Acc 6K 15
Dunny Shop Av. Acc 4B 22
Dunoon Dri. B'brn 5C 20
Dunoon St. Burn 5J 9
Dunsop St. B'brn 6J 13
Dunster Av. Osw 3H 21
Dunster Gro. Clith 7C 2
Durban Gro. Burn 6K 9
Durham Av. Burn 3G 9
Durham Clo. B'brn 1J 19
Durham Dri. B'brn 2B 14
Durham Dri. Osw 5A 22
Durham Rd. Dar 3C 26
Durham Rd. Wilp 2B 14
Durham St. Acc 1E 22
Dutton St. Acc 2D 22
Duxbury St. Dar 7F 27
Dyke Nook. Clith 6F 3
Dyneley Av. Burn 6G 11
Dyneley Rd. B'brn 1B 20
Dyson St. B'brn 3G 19

E

Eachill Gdns. Rish 7G 15
Eachill Rd. Rish 6G 15
Eagle St. Acc 3C 22
Eagle St. B'brn 4B 20
Eagle St. Nels 7C 4
Eagle St. Osw 6H 21
Eagley Rd. Brier 5D 6
Eanam. B'brn 7J 13
Eanam Old Rd. B'brn 7J 13
Eanam Wharf. B'brn 7J 13
Eanam Wharf Vis. Cen. 7J 13
(off Eanam Wharf)
Earls Dri. Hodd 4J 27
Earl St. B'brn 5H 13
Earl St. Burn 2C 10
Earl St. Clay M 5A 16
Earl St. Col 4G 5
Earl St. Gt Har 2G 15
Earl St. Nels 7C 4
Earnsdale Av. Dar 3B 26
Earnsdale Clo. Dar 3C 26
Earnsdale Rd. Dar 2C 26
Earnshaw Rd. Bacup 2H 31
Easedale Clo. Burn 2G 9
Easington Wlk. B'brn 2J 19
East Bank. Barfd 4A 4
E. Bank Av. Has 3B 28
Eastcott Clo. B'brn 5K 19
East Cres. Acc 7C 16
East Cft. Nels 7E 4
Eastern Av. Burn 2D 10
Eastgate. Acc 2C 22
East Ga. Has 2B 28
Eastham Pl. Burn 4C 10
Eastham St. Burn 5C 10
Eastham St. Clith 4E 2
East Lancashire Railway. 4F 29
E. Lancashire Rd. B'brn 1J 13
Eastmoor Dri. Clith 6F 3
East Pde. Ross 2G 29
East Pk. Av. B'brn 5G 13
East Pk. Av. Dar 5D 26
East Pk. Rd. B'brn 6G 13
East St. B'brn 2F 19
East St. Brier 4D 6
East St. Fen 5A 18
East St. Hap 6B 8
East St. Helm 6A 28
East St. Nels 7A 4
East St. Pad 1B 8
East St. Raw 7F 25
East Vw. Acc 4A 24
(off Hoyle St.)
East Vw. Bacup 3H 31
East Vw. Ross 4B 30
East Vw. Traw 6K 5
Eastwood Cres. Ross 3J 29
Eastwood St. B'brn 5K 13
Eastwood St. Ross 3J 29
Eaves Clo. Hun 6G 17
Ebony St. B'brn 5K 13
Ebor St. Burn 7C 6
Eccleshill Cotts. E'hill 1G 27
Eccleshill Gdns. E'hill 1H 27
Eccleshill St. Pad 2B 8
Eccles St. Acc 1C 22
Eccles St. B'brn 2H 19
Eclipse Rd. B'brn 5A 18
Ecroyd St. Nels 1D 6
Edale Av. Has 3C 28
Eden Clo. Barfd 4A 4
Edensor Ter. Dar 3D 26
Eden St. Acc 3B 22
Eden St. B'brn 7K 13
Edgar St. Acc 2C 22
Edgar St. Hun 5F 17
Edgar St. Nels 6C 4
Edge End. Gt Har 2G 15
Edge End Av. Brier 3E 6
Edge End La. Gt Har 2G 15
(in two parts)
Edge End La. Nels 3D 6
Edge End La. Ross 6G 25
Edge End Rd. Gt Har 2G 15
Edge La. Ross 3J 29
Edgeley Ct. Burn 3J 9
Edge Nook Rd. B'brn 7C 20
Edgeside. Gt Har 2G 15
Edgeside La. Ross 2B 30
Edgeware Rd. B'brn 6F 13
Edge Yate La. Ross 7H 25
Edgworth Gro. Burn 4D 10
Edinburgh Dri. Osw 5A 22
Edinburgh Rd. Has 5A 28

Edisford Rd. Clith 6B 2
Edisford Rd. Wadd 1B 2
Edison St. Dar 4D 26
Edith St. B'brn 1K 19
Edith St. Nels 1G 7
Edleston St. Acc 3A 22
Edmonton Dri. B'brn 4D 12
Edmund Gennings Ct. Chat 1K 3
Edmundson St. B'brn 7F 13
Edmundson St. Chu 2K 21
Edmund St. Acc 3D 22
Edmund St. B'brn 6G 19
Edmund St. Burn 1C 10
Edmund St. Dar 4F 27
Edward Ct. Chu 2K 21
Edward St. Bacup 2J 31
Edward St. Bax 7F 23
Edward St. Burn 4B 10
Edward St. Chu 2K 21
Edward St. Craw 4G 25
Edward St. Dar 3E 26
Edward St. Gt Har 2H 15
Edward St. Has 6B 24
Edward St. Nels 5C 4
(in two parts)
Edward St. Rish 6G 15
Egypt Mt. Ross 3E 28
Egypt Ter. Ross 4E 28
Elder Ct. Acc 7F 17
Elder St. Nels 6C 4
Eldon Rd. B'brn 5G 13
Eldwick St. Burn 1D 10
Eleanor St. B'brn 7J 13
Eleanor St. Nels 7B 4
Electricity St. Acc 1C 22
Elgar Clo. B'brn 3K 19
Elgin Cres. Burn 6J 9
Elim Gdns. B'brn 4F 19
Elim Pl. B'brn 4F 19
Elim Vw. B'brn 7E 6
Elizabeth Dri. Has 5A 28
Elizabeth Ho. B'brn 5A 20
Elizabeth Ho. Dar 4F 27
Elizabeth St. Acc 3A 22
Elizabeth St. B'brn 7J 13
Elizabeth St. Burn 5B 10
Elizabeth St. Nels 7B 4
Elizabeth St. Pad 3B 8
Elizabeth St. Ross 1B 30
Eliza St. Burn 5C 10
Elland Rd. Brier 3D 6
Ellenshaw Clo. Dar 4F 27
Ellen St. Dar 6E 26
Ellen St. Nels 1E 6
Ellerbeck Clo. Burn 6F 7
Ellerbeck Rd. Acc 1C 22
Ellerbeck Rd. Dar 4F 27
Ellesmere Av. Col 3J 5
Ellesmere Rd. Dar 2C 26
Elliott Av. Dar 7F 27
Elliott St. Dar 5D 10
Ellison Fold. Clay M 4K 15
Ellison Fold La. Dar 4G 27
Ellison Fold Ter. Dar 4F 27
Ellison St. Acc 2C 22
Ellison St. Dar 3E 26
Ellis St. Burn 5K 9
Elm Clo. Has 2B 28
Elm Clo. Rish 7G 15
Elmfield St. Chu 1A 22
Elm Gro. Dar 2F 27
Elm Mill. B'brn 2B 10
Elm St. Bacup 2J 31
Elm St. B'brn 5K 13
Elm St. Burn 1B 10
Elm St. Col 2H 5
Elm St. Gt Har 3H 15
Elm St. Has 2B 28
Elm St. Nels 7B 4
Elm St. Raw 2G 29
Elmwood Clo. Acc 2E 22
Elmwood St. Burn 5J 9
Elswick Gdns. Mel 1A 12
Elswick Lodge. Mel 1B 12
Elswick St. Dar 4F 27
Ely Clo. Dar 4G 27
Ely Clo. Wilp 2B 14
Emerald Av. B'brn 2J 13
Emerald St. B'brn 2J 13
Emily St. B'brn 6K 13

Emily St. Burn 6B 10
Emma St. Acc 2A 22
Empire St. Gt Har 1J 15
Empress St. Acc 2A 22
Empress St. Col 3H 5
Empress St. Lwr D 6J 19
End St. Col 4E 4
Enfield Rd. Acc 5E 16
Ennerdale Av. B'brn 5B 20
Ennerdale Clo. Clith 6C 2
Ennerdale Clo. Osw 3J 21
Ennerdale Rd. Burn 5F 11
Ennerdale Rd. Clith 6C 2
Ennismore St. Burn 1D 10
Enterprise Ct. Hun I 6E 16
Enterprise Way. Col 5C 4
Entwistle Rd. Acc 7C 16
Entwistle St. Dar 4E 26
Epsom Way. Acc 3E 22
Epworth St. Dar 7F 27
Equity St. Dar 5E 26
Ermine Clo. B'brn 5K 19
Ernest St. Bacup 5K 31
Ernest St. Chu 2K 21
Ernest St. Clay M 6A 16
Ernest St. B'brn 5D 18
Escar St. Burn 5A 10
Escott Gdns. Burn 2B 10
Eshton Ter. Clith 6D 2
Eskdale Clo. Burn 5C 6
Eskdale Cres. B'brn 5B 18
Eskdale Gdns. Pad 1B 8
(off Windermere Rd.)
Esplanade, The. Rish 7E 14
Essex Av. Burn 3G 9
Essex Clo. B'brn 2G 19
Essex Rd. Rish 6F 15
Essex St. Acc 2E 22
Essex St. Col 4H 5
Essex St. Dar 4F 27
Essex St. Nels 7B 4
Etherate St. B'brn 3B 20
Ethersall Rd. Nels 3F 7
Eton Av. Acc 1D 22
Eton Clo. Pad 4D 8
Euro Trad. Est. B'brn 5J 13
Evans St. Burn 6A 10
Evelyn Rd. Dar 1C 26
Evelyn St. Burn 1B 10
Evergreens, The. B'brn 5C 18
Everton. B'brn 4K 19
Everton St. Dar 4D 26
Every St. Brier 3C 6
Every St. Burn 5K 9
Every St. Nels 2D 6
Evesham Clo. Acc 1B 22
Ewood. B'brn 4G 19
Ewood Ct. B'brn 3F 19
Ewood La. Has 6C 28
Exchange St. Acc 3A 22
Exchange St. B'brn 7H 13
Exchange St. Col 4G 5
Exchange St. Dar 3E 26
Exeter St. B'brn 3F 19
Exmouth St. Burn 5B 10
Exton St. Brier 4B 6
Extwistle Rd. Wors 5J 11
Extwistle Sq. Burn 5K 9
Extwistle St. Burn 2B 10
Extwistle St. Nels 2E 6

F

Factory La. Barfd 4A 4
Factory La. Pad 1B 8
Fairbairn Av. Burn 2H 9
Fairbank Wlk. Love 2G 25
Fairclough Rd. Acc 5B 22
Fairfield Av. Ross 3B 30
Fairfield Clo. Clith 6C 2
Fairfield Dri. Burn 6C 6
Fairfield Dri. Clith 6C 2
Fairfield Rd. Nels 1J 7
Fairfields Dri. Lwr D 7J 19
Fairfield St. Acc 4A 22
Fairfield St. B'brn 4J 19
Fair Hill. Ross 6A 28
Fairhill Ter. Ross 6A 28
Fairholme Rd. Burn 7C 10

Fairhope Ct. B'brn 6F 13
Fairview. Ross 7F 25
Fair Vw. Cres. Bacup 3K 31
Fair Vw. Rd. Burn 5C 10
Fairways Ct. Wilp 3B 14
Fairweather Ct. Pad 1C 8
Falcon Av. Dar 2C 26
Falcon Clo. B'brn 4G 13
Falcon Ct. Clay M 5A 16
Fallbarn Cres. Ross 4F 29
Fallbarn Rd. Ross 3H 29
(in two parts)
Fallowfield Dri. Burn 2J 9
Falmouth Av. Has 3C 28
Faraday Av. Clith 5D 2
Faraday St. Burn 3H 9
Farholme La. Bacup 5F 31
Farm Av. Bacup 1H 31
Farm Ho. Clo. B'brn 4B 20
Farndean Way. Col 4H 5
Faroes Clo. B'brn 4J 19
Farrer St. Nels 1D 6
Farrington Clo. Burn 7H 9
Farrington Ct. Burn 7H 9
Farrington Pl. Burn 7H 9
Farrington Rd. Burn 7G 9
Favordale Rd. Col 2K 5
Fawcett Clo. B'brn 2G 19
Fearns Moss. Bacup 4C 30
Fecitt Brow. B'brn 4B 20
Fecitt Rd. B'brn 6E 12
Feilden Pl. B'brn 5A 18
Feilden St. B'brn 1G 19
Felix St. Burn 3C 10
Fell Rd. Wadd 1B 2
Fell Vw. Burn 6E 6
Feniscliffe Dri. B'brn 3C 18
Fennyfold Ter. Pad 4B 8
Fenwick St. Burn 7J 9
Fern Av. Osw 5A 22
Fernbank Ct. Nels 2F 7
Ferndale. B'brn 6K 13
Ferndale St. Burn 2D 10
Fern Gore Av. Acc 5B 22
Fernhill Av. Bacup 5G 31
Fernhill Clo. Bacup 5G 31
Fernhill Cres. Bacup 5G 31
Fernhill Dri. Bacup 5F 31
Fernhill Gro. Bacup 4G 31
Fernhill Pk. Bacup 5G 31
Fernhill Way. Bacup 5G 31
Fernhurst St. B'brn 5G 19
Fernlea Av. Osw 5A 22
Fernlea Clo. B'brn 5E 18
Fernlea Dri. Clay M 3K 15
Fern Lea St. Ross 5K 29
Fern Rd. Burn 6K 9
Ferns, The. Bacup 4J 31
Fern St. Bacup 2H 31
Fern St. Col 2J 5
Fern St. Ross 4B 30
Fern Ter. Has 2A 28
Fernville Ter. Bacup 5F 31
Ferrier Clo. B'brn 3B 20
Ferrier Ct. B'brn 3B 20
Fielden St. Burn 5H 9
Fielding Cres. B'brn 4D 18
Fielding La. Gt Har 2G 15
Fielding La. Osw 5K 21
Fielding St. Rish 6H 15
Fields Rd. Has 4C 28
Field St. B'brn 3E 18
Field St. Pad 3B 8
Fife St. Acc 3B 22
Fifth Av. Burn 7C 6
Finch Clo. B'brn 6J 13
Finch St. Dar 3D 26
Finsbury Pl. B'brn 6G 19
Finsley Ga. Burn 5A 10
Finsley St. Brclf 6F 7
Finsley Vw. Brclf 6G 7
Fir Ct. Acc 7F 17
Fir Gro. Rd. Burn 6C 10
Fir Mt. Bacup 4J 31
First Av. Chu 6B 16
Fir St. Burn 5C 10
Fir St. Has 3C 28

Fir St. Nels 1G 7
Firtrees Dri. B'brn 5C 18
Fishmoor Dri. B'brn 5J 19
Fish Rake La. Ross 7D 28
Flag St. Bacup 5G 31
Flax Clo. Has 5A 28
Flaxmoss Clo. Helm 5A 28
Fleet St. Nels 7B 4
Fleet Wlk. Burn 4B 10
Fleetwood Clo. B'brn 4J 19
Fleetwood Rd. B'brn 7D 6
Fleetwood Rd. Pad 2C 8
Fleming Sq. B'brn 1H 19
Fletcher Rd. Rish 7F 15
Fletcher St. B'brn 2G 19
Fletcher St. Nels 2G 7
Flimby Clo. B'brn 5J 19
Flip Rd. Has 2A 28
Florence Av. Burn 5H 9
Florence Pl. B'brn 6K 13
Florence St. B'brn 6K 13
Florence St. Burn 5H 9
Florence St. Chu 2K 21
Folds St. Burn 2A 10
Fold, The. Barfd 3B 4
Folly Bank. Ross 4G 25
Folly Ter. Ross 4G 25
Forbes Ct. Burn 7F 9
Fordside Av. Clay M 3K 15
Ford St. Barfd 4B 4
Ford St. Burn 1C 10
Foreside. Barfd 3B 4
Forest Bank. Ross 5G 25
Forest Bank Rd. Ross 5G 25
Fore St. Lwr D 6J 19
Forestside. B'brn 6G 19
Forest St. Bacup 3H 31
Forest St. Burn 4B 10
Forest St. Nels 7A 4
(in two parts)
Forest Vw. Barfd 5A 4
Forest Vw. Brier 4B 6
Forfar Gro. Burn 7J 9
Forfar St. Burn 7J 9
Forge St. Bacup 3H 31
Formby Clo. B'brn 5J 19
Forrest St. B'brn 7K 13
Fort St. Acc 2C 22
Fort St. B'brn 7K 13
Fort St. Clay M 4A 16
Fort St. Clith 6D 2
Fort St. Ind. Est. B'brn 6K 13
Fosse Clo. B'brn 5K 19
Foster St. Acc 1D 22
Fothergill St. Col 3F 5
Fould Clo. Col 5F 5
Foulds Rd. Traw 5J 5
Foulds Ter. Traw 6K 5
Foundry St. Bacup 3H 31
Foundry St. B'brn 1F 9
Foundry St. Burn 4A 10
Foundry St. Dar 4E 26
Foundry St. Has 3B 28
Foundry St. Ross 4F 29
Fountain Pl. Acc 3C 22
Fountain Retail Pk. Acc 2B 22
Fountains Av. B'brn 7A 14
Fountain Sq. Barfd 4A 4
Fountain St. Acc 4B 22
Fountain St. Col 4G 5
Fountain St. Dar 5E 26
Fountain St. Nels 7B 4
Fountains Way. Osw 3G 21
Fouracre. Mel 2B 12
Four La. Ends Rd. Burn 5D 30
Fowler Height Clo. B'brn 6E 18
Foxcroft. Burn 2J 9
Foxdale Clo. Bacup 4J 31
Foxhill Bank. Chu 3J 21
Foxhill Bank Brow. Chu 3K 21
Foxhill Dri. Ross 1B 30
Foxhill Ter. Acc 4K 21
Foxhill W. Osw 4K 21
Fox Ho. St. B'brn 7F 13
Foxstones Cres. B'brn 5D 18
Foxstones La. Cliv 7H 11
Fox St. Acc 2C 22
Fox St. Burn 4E 8
Fox St. Clith 4E 2
Foxwell Clo. Has 3C 28

Foxwood Chase. Acc 7F 17
Frances St. Dar 3D 26
France St. B'brn 1G 19
France St. Chu 2K 21
Francis Av. Barfd 3B 4
Francis St. B'brn 4E 18
Francis St. Burn 1B 10
Francis St. Clay M 4A 16
Francis St. Col 5E 4
Franklin Rd. B'brn 2D 18
Franklin St. Burn 4H 9
Franklin St. Clith 6D 2
Franklin St. Dar 4E 26
Frank St. Clay M 6B 16
Fraser St. Acc 4B 22
Fraser St. Burn 1C 10
Freckleton St. B'brn 1G 19
(in two parts)
Frederick Row. B'brn 3A 20
Frederick St. Acc 2B 22
Frederick St. B'brn 2H 19
Frederick St. Dar 3E 26
Frederick St. Osw 4K 21
Free La. Ross 7A 28
Free Trade St. Burn 4A 10
French Clo. B'brn 1E 18
French Rd. B'brn 1E 18
Freshfield Av. Clay M 4K 15
Friar Ct. Acc 2D 22
Fry St. Nels 1G 7
Fulham St. Nels 6C 4
Fullers Ter. Bacup 4H 31
(off Park Rd.)
Full Vw. B'brn 5E 18
Furness Av. B'brn 7A 14
Furness St. Burn 1C 10
Further Ga. B'brn 3A 20
Furthergate Ind. Est. B'brn .3A 20
Further La. Sam & Mel 3A 12
Further Wilworth. B'brn ...2H 13

G

Gables, The. Dar 1C 26
Gadfield St. Dar 5F 27
Gaghills Rd. Ross 4B 30
Gaghills Ter. Ross 4B 30
(off Gaghills Rd.)
Gainsborough Av. B'brn ...6F 13
Gainsborough Av. Burn 7K 9
Galligreaves St. B'brn 2G 19
Galligreaves Way. B'brn ...2F 19
Gambleside Clo. Ross 3G 25
Game St. Gt Har 2H 15
Gannow La. Burn 4G 9
Garbett St. Acc 4B 22
Garden Sq. Traw 6J 5
Garden St. Acc 1C 22
Garden St. B'brn 1F 19
Garden St. Brier 4C 6
Garden St. Col 4G 5
Garden St. Gt Har 3H 15
Garden St. Nels 1F 7
Garden St. Osw 4J 21
Garden St. Pad 1B 8
Garden Va. Bus. Pk. Col ...4E 4
Garfield St. Acc 3E 22
Garnett Rd. Clith 6C 2
Garnett St. Barfd 6A 4
Garnett St. Dar 4F 27
Garrick St. Nels 6C 4
Garsdale Av. Burn 5C 6
Garsden Av. B'brn 6D 20
Garstang St. Dar 3E 26
Garswood Clo. Burn 7A 6
Gas St. Bacup 3H 31
Gas St. Burn 4A 10
Gas St. Has 4A 28
Gatefield St. B'brn 6B 10
(off Hollingreave Rd.)
Gate St. B'brn 7K 13
Gawthorpe Edge Pk. Pad ...3E 8
Gawthorpe Hall. 1E 8
Gawthorpe Rd. Burn 3J 9
Gawthorpe St. Pad 1B 8
Gayle Way. Acc 3C 22
(off Lynton Rd.)
Geddes St. B'brn 3C 18
Genoa St. Burn 6H 9

George Av. Gt Har 3G 15
George's Row. Ross 5B 30
George St. Acc 4A 22
George St. Bacup 3J 31
George St. B'brn 1H 19
George St. Burn 5A 10
George St. Clay M 4A 16
George St. Clith 7D 2
George St. Dar 3E 26
George St. Gt Har 2H 15
George St. Has 2B 28
George St. Nels 7A 4
George St. Osw 3K 21
George St. Rish 6G 15
George St. Stac 5E 30
George St. W. B'brn 1F 19
(off Kirkgate)
Gertrude St. Nels 6C 4
Gib Fld. Rd. Col 5D 4
Gib Hill La. Ross 3H 25
Gib Hill Rd. Nels 7E 4
Gib La. B'brn 5D 18
Gibraltar St. B'brn 6E 12
Gibson St. Nels 6C 4
Gilbert St. Burn 7F 7
Gilbert St. Ross 4K 29
Giles St. Clith 6E 2
Giles St. Nels 7B 4
Gillibrand St. Dar 2D 26
Gillies St. Acc 2D 22
Gillies St. B'brn 2J 19
Gills Cft. Clith 7F 3
Gill St. Burn 4K 9
Gill St. Col 5E 4
Gill St. Nels 7A 4
Girvan Gro. Burn 5J 9
Gisburn Gro. Burn 5E 10
Gisburn Rd. Barfd 6A 4
Gisburn Rd. Black 1A 4
Glade, The. B'brn 7H 19
Gladstone Cres. Bacup 3J 31
Gladstone St. Bacup 3J 31
Gladstone St. B'brn 2A 20
Gladstone St. Gt Har 2H 15
Gladstone Ter. Barfd 5A 4
Gladstone Ter. B'brn 4C 18
Glamorgan Gro. Burn 3F 9
Glasson Clo. Acc 4J 19
Glebe Clo. Acc 3C 22
Glebe St. Burn 6B 10
Glebe St. Gt Har 2H 15
Glenborough Av. Bacup 5E 30
Glenbrook Clo. B'brn 5E 18
Glencarron Clo. Hodd 5K 27
Glencoe Av. Hodd 4J 27
Glen Cres. Bacup 5C 30
Glendale Clo. Burn 7B 10
Glendale Dri. Mel 2B 12
Glendene Pk. Clay D 3A 14
Glendor Rd. Burn 5F 11
Gleneagles Av. Hodd 4J 27
Gleneagles Ct. B'brn 5B 20
Glenfield Clo. B'brn 1A 20
Glenfield Pk. Bus. Cen. B'brn .1A 20
Glenfield Pk. Ind. Est. B'brn .7A 14
Glenfield Pk. Ind. Est. Nels .7D 4
Glenfield Rd. Nels 7C 4
Glengreave Av. Rams 1H 13
Glenluce Cres. B'brn 5C 20
Glenmore Clo. Acc 6F 23
Glen Rd. Ross 5B 30
Glenroy Av. Col 2G 5
Glenshiels Av. Hodd 4J 27
Glen Sq. Burn 7A 10
Glen St. Bacup 5G 31
Glen St. Burn 4K 9
Glen St. Col 2G 5
Glen Ter. Ross 5B 30
Glen Vw. Rd. Burn 7K 9
Glen, The. B'brn 7G 19
Glen Way. Brier 4B 6
Global Way. Dar 1E 26
Gloucester Av. Acc 1B 22
Gloucester Av. Clay M 4A 16
Gloucester Rd. B'brn 3B 20
Gloucester Rd. Rish 6E 14
Glynn St. Chu 1A 22
Godiva St. Burn 1B 10

Godley St. Burn 4C 10
Goitside. Nels 7B 4
Goit St. B'brn 3F 19
Goldacre La. Gt Har 1G 15
Goldfield Av. Burn 4G 11
Goldfinch Grn. Burn 5H 9
Goldhey St. B'brn 5K 13
Goodshaw Av. B'brn 4H 13
Goodshaw Av. Ross 3G 25
Goodshaw Av. N. Ross 2G 25
Goodshaw Clo. B'brn 4H 13
Goodshaw Fold Clo. Raw ..2G 25
Goodshaw Fold Rd. Ross ...2F 25
Goodshaw La. Ross 4G 25
Goodshaw La. Stone 7J 23
Goosebutts La. Clith 6F 3
Goose Ho. La. Dar 1E 26
Goose La. Traw 6J 5
Gordon Av. Acc 4B 22
Gordon Rd. Nels 7A 4
Gordonstoun Pl. B'brn 2F 19
Gordon St. Bacup 1H 31
Gordon St. Burn 3A 10
Gordon St. Chu 3K 21
Gordon St. Clay M 5B 16
Gordon St. Col 3H 5
Gordon St. Dar 2E 26
Gordon St. Ross 3F 29
Gordon St. Wors 4J 11
Gorple Grn. Wors 5J 11
Gorple Rd. Wors 5J 11
Gorse St. Burn 6F 7
Gorse Gro. Helm 5A 28
Gorse Rd. B'brn 7E 12
Gorse St. B'brn 2A 20
Grafton Av. Acc 6F 23
Grafton Av. Burn 4C 6
Grafton Ct. Dar 3D 26
Grafton St. Bacup 4J 31
(off Rockcliffe La.)
Grafton St. B'brn 3G 19
Grafton St. Clith 5F 3
Grafton St. Nels 7C 4
Grafton Ter. Dar 3D 26
(off Grafton Ct.)
Grafton Vs. Bacup 4H 31
Graham St. Hodd 4K 27
Graham St. Pad 3C 8
Granby St. Burn 4J 9
Grane Pk. Has 3A 28
Grane Rd. Has 3A 28
Grane St. Has 2B 28
Grange Av. Barfd 3C 4
Grange Av. Gt Har 1H 15
Grange Av. Ross 2H 29
Grange Clo. Gt Har 1H 15
Grange Clo. Osw 5B 22
Grange Clo. Raw 3H 29
Grange Cres. Ross 3G 29
Grange La. Acc 3D 22
Grange Rd. B'brn 3E 18
Grange Rd. Ross 3G 29
Grange St. Acc 3D 22
Grange St. Burn 5K 9
Grange St. Clay M 4K 15
Grange St. Ross 3G 29
Grange Ter. Ross 2G 29
Grange, The. Wilp 3B 14
Grant Rd. B'brn 3E 18
Grant St. Acc 2B 22
Grant St. Burn 5K 9
Granville Gdns. Acc 4E 22
Granville Rd. Acc 4E 22
(in two parts)
Granville Rd. B'brn 7E 12
Granville Rd. Brier 3D 6
Granville Rd. Dar 5D 26
Granville Rd. Gt Har 1J 15
Granville St. Brclf 6G 7
Granville St. Burn 2B 10
Granville St. Col 3H 5
Granville St. Ross 6A 28
Grasmere Av. B'brn 3F 13
Grasmere Av. Pad 1B 8
Grasmere Clo. Acc 7E 16
Grasmere Clo. Col 3K 5
Grasmere Clo. Rish 6F 15
Grasmere Rd. Has 5C 28

Grasmere St. Burn 7B 6
Grassington Dri. Burn 6E 6
Grassmere Ter. Bacup 1H 31
Gt. Bolton St. B'brn 2H 19
Great Harwood Golf Course.
.........1A 16
Greave Clo. Bacup 2K 31
Greave Clo. Ross 1G 29
Greave Clough Clo. Bacup ..2J 31
Greave Clough Dri. Bacup ..2J 31
Greave Cres. Bacup 2J 31
(off Greave Clough Clo.)
Greave Rd. Bacup 2K 31
Greaves St. Gt Har 3H 15
Greaves St. Has 3A 28
Greave Ter. Bacup 2K 31
Greenacre. Lwr D 7J 19
Greenacre St. Clith 6E 2
Green Bank. Bacup 5F 31
Grn. Bank Bus. Pk. B'brn ..1A 20
(in two parts)
Greenbank Pk. Ross 3H 29
Greenbank Rd. B'brn 2A 20
Greenbank St. Ross 3H 29
Green Bank Ter. Lwr D 7J 19
Grn. Bridge N. Ross 6A 30
Grn. Bridge S. Ross 6A 30
Greenbrook Clo. Burn 4E 8
Greenbrook Rd. Burn 4E 8
Greendale Av. Ross 4A 30
Green Dri. Clith 3G 3
Grn. End Clo. Bacup 2J 31
Greenfield Av. Clith 5C 2
Greenfield Gdns. Has 2B 28
Greenfield Rd. Burn 6E 10
Greenfield Rd. Col 4D 4
(in three parts)
Greenfields. B'brn 6G 19
Greenfield St. Dar 7G 27
Greenfield St. Has 2B 28
Greenfield St. Raw 2G 29
Greenfield Ter. Osw 7F 21
Greenfield Vw. Lwr D 6K 19
Greenfold Dri. Ross 2G 25
Greengate Clo. Burn 3J 9
Green Gown. B'brn 4H 13
Green Haworth Golf Course.
.........7C 22
Grn. Haworth Vw. Osw 6B 22
Greenhead Av. B'brn 1A 20
Greenhead La. Fence & Burn ..5A 6
Green Hill. Bacup 4J 31
Grn. Hill Rd. Bacup 4J 31
Greenhurst Clo. B'brn 1G 19
Green La. B'brn 4C 18
Green La. Pad 2B 8
Green Mdw. Traw 6J 5
Greenock Clo. Burn 6J 9
Greenock St. Burn 3F 19
Grn. Pk. Clo. B'brn 3F 19
Greenridge Clo. Brier 4E 6
Green Rd. Col 4F 5
Green Row. Live 7E 18
Greenside Av. B'brn 5D 18
Greens La. Bacup 6E 31
Greens La. Bacup 6B 28
(Cutler La.)
Greens La. Bacup 6B 28
(Todmorden Old Rd.)
Greens La. Ross 6B 28
Greensnook La. Bacup 2H 31
Greensnook M. Bacup 2J 31
Greensnook Ter. Bacup 2J 31
Green St. Burn 1C 10
Green St. Dar 4E 26
Green St. Gt Har 2G 15
Green St. Osw 6H 21
Green St. Pad 3B 8
Green St. Ross 2H 29
Green St. E. Dar 4E 26
Green Ter. Wors 5J 11
(off Wallstreams La.)
Green, The. Col 2J 5
Green, The. Dar 4E 26
Green, The. Nels 6E 4
Greenthorne Ter. Nels 5E 26
(off Ashworth Ter.)
Greenthorne Ter. Dar 3C 26
(off Avondale Rd.)
Greenway St. Dar 2D 26

Gregory Fold. *Ross* 6A **28**
Gregson St. *B'brn* 7G **13**
Gregson St. *Dar* 5E **26**
Grenada Clo. *Lwr D* 7J **19**
Gresham St. *Ross* 4B **30**
Gretna Rd. *B'brn* 3J **13**
Gretna Wlk. *B'brn* 3J **13**
Greystoke Av. *B'brn* 5B **18**
Grey St. *Barfd* 5A **4**
Grey St. *Burn* 1B **10**
Griffin Clo. *Acc* 6G **17**
Griffin Clo. *Burn* 6G **9**
Griffin Ct. *B'brn* 3F **19**
Griffin St. *B'brn* 2E **18**
Grime St. *Dar* 3D **26**
Grimshaw Pk. *B'brn* 2J **19**
Grimshaw Retail Pk. *B'brn* 2H **19**
Grimshaw St. *Acc* 2B **22**
Grimshaw St. *Barfd* 4A **4**
Grimshaw St. *Burn* 5B **10**
Grimshaw St. *Chu* 2K **21**
Grimshaw St. *Clay M* 5A **16**
Grimshaw St. *Dar* 6F **27**
Grimshaw St. *Gt Har* 2H **15**
Grindlestone Hurst. *Col* 5F **5**
Grindleton Gro. *Burn* 6E **10**
Grindleton Rd. *B'brn* 1F **19**
Grisedale Av. *B'brn* 6B **20**
Grisedale Dri. *Burn* 2G **9**
Grizedale Clo. *Clay M* 5K **15**
Grosvenor St. *Burn* 3A **10**
Grosvenor St. *Col* 3J **5**
Grosvenor Way. *B'brn* 7H **13**
Groundwork Countryside Cen.
.........4E **28**
Grove Ct. *Osw* 5H **21**
Grove La. *Pad* 1C **8**
Grove St. *Acc* 2B **22**
Grove St. *Bacup* 2J **31**
Grove St. *Barfd* 5A **4**
Grove St. *B'brn* 3H **19**
Grove St. *Burn* 5J **9**
Grove St. *Nels* 1F **7**
Grove St. *Osw* 5H **21**
Grove, The. *Burn* 4G **9**
Grove, The. *Clith* 4F **3**
Guernsey Av. *B'brn* 4J **19**
Guilford St. *Brier* 4C **6**
Gunsmith Pl. *Burn* 4B **10**
Gurney St. *B'brn* 2E **18**
Guy St. *Pad* 1B **8**
Guysyke. *Col* 4F **5**

H

Habergham Dri. *Burn* 2E **8**
Habergham St. *Pad* 1B **8**
Hacking St. *Dar* 4E **26**
Hacking St. *Nels* 6C **4**
Hagg St. *Col* 4F **5**
Haldane Rd. *Dar* 1C **26**
Haldane St. *Burn* 7C **6**
Hale St. *Burn* 6B **10**
Halifax Rd. *Brclf* 6H **7**
Halifax Rd. *Brier* 4C **6**
Halifax Rd. *Nels* 3E **6**
Hallam Cres. *Nels* 1H **7**
Hallam Rd. *Nels* 7C **4**
Hallam St. *Acc* 6B **16**
Hall Carr Rd. *Ross* 4G **29**
Hall Clo. *Ross* 6G **25**
Halley Rd. *Dar* 2C **26**
Hallfield Rd. *Gt Har* 1J **15**
Hall Hill St. *Pad* 1B **8**
(off St Giles St.)
Halliwell St. *Acc* 6E **22**
Hall Meadows. *Traw* 5J **5**
Hallows St. *Burn* 7B **6**
Hall Pk. Av. *Burn* 6G **11**
Hall Rd. *Traw* 5J **5**
Hall St. *Bacup* 2H **31**
Hall St. *B'brn* 3H **19**
Hall St. *Burn* 4B **10**
Hall St. *Clith* 6E **2**
Hall St. *Col* 4G **5**
Hall St. *Has* 3B **28**
Hall St. *Raw* 2G **29**
Hall St. *Wors* 5H **11**
Hallwell St. *Burn* 2B **10**

Hallwood Clo. *Burn* 5C **6**
Halstead Clo. *Barfd* 4A **4**
Halstead La. *Barfd* 4A **4**
Halstead St. *Burn* 5A **10**
Halstead St. *Wors* 4H **11**
Hambledon St. *Pad* 2C **8**
Hambledon Ter. *Burn* 3E **8**
Hambledon Vw. *Burn* 3E **8**
Hameldon App. *Burn* 5J **9**
Hameldon Av. *Acc* 6F **23**
Hameldon Clo. *Hap* 7B **8**
Hameldon Rd. *Hap* 5K **17**
Hameldon Rd. *Ross* 2G **25**
Hameldon Vw. *Gt Har* 2J **15**
Hamer Av. *B'brn* 3C **20**
Hamer Av. *Ross* 3G **25**
Hamer St. *Ross* 3G **29**
Hamilton Rd. *Barfd* 1D **6**
Hamilton Rd. *Col* 6D **4**
Hamilton St. *Burn* 3G **19**
Hamlet Clo. *B'brn* 2F **19**
Hammerton Grn. *Bacup* 2H **31**
Hammerton St. *Bacup* 1H **31**
Hammerton St. *Burn* 5A **10**
Hammond Av. *Bacup* 5F **31**
Hammond St. *Nels* 2G **7**
Hampden Av. *Dar* 6F **27**
Hampden St. *Burn* 6C **10**
Hampden St. *Hap* 6B **8**
Hampshire Clo. *Wilp* 1C **14**
Hampshire Rd. *Rish* 6F **15**
Hancock St. *B'brn* 3B **8**
(in two parts)
Hannah St. *Acc* 3C **22**
Hannah St. *Bacup* 2J **31**
Hannah St. *Dar* 4F **27**
Hanover Ct. *Burn* 7J **9**
Hanover St. *Col* 2G **5**
Hanson St. *Gt Har* 3H **15**
Hanson St. *Rish* 6H **15**
Hapton Rd. *Pad* 3B **8**
Hapton St. *Pad* 2C **8**
Hapton Way. *Ross* 2G **25**
Harcourt Rd. *Acc* 5E **22**
Harcourt Rd. *B'brn* 6F **19**
Harcourt St. *Bacup* 2H **31**
Harcourt St. *Burn* 5J **9**
Hardacre. *Nels* 2F **7**
Hardman Av. *Ross* 4G **29**
Hardman Clo. *B'brn* 4E **20**
Hardman Clo. *Ross* 6B **30**
Hardman Dri. *Ross* 6B **30**
Hardman St. *B'brn* 2F **19**
Hardman Ter. *Bacup* 5F **31**
Hardman Way. *Dar* 4E **26**
Hardy Av. *Brier* 3C **6**
Hardy Ct. *Nels* 1F **7**
Hardy St. *B'brn* 3J **13**
Hardy St. *Brier* 3C **6**
Harebell Clo. *B'brn* 5A **18**
Hare Clough Clo. *B'brn* 2J **19**
Hareden Brook Clo. *B'brn* 2J **19**
Harefield Ri. *Burn* 2J **9**
(in two parts)
Hareholme La. *Ross* 4K **29**
Hargher St. *Burn* 5J **9**
Hargreaves Ct. *Clith* 6C **2**
Hargreaves Dri. *Ross* 3F **29**
Hargreaves La. *B'brn* 2H **19**
Hargreaves Rd. *Osw* 4G **21**
Hargreaves St. *Acc* 3D **22**
Hargreaves St. *Brclf* 6G **7**
Hargreaves St. *Burn* 4A **10**
Hargreaves St. *Col* 4E **4**
Hargreaves St. *Has* 2B **28**
Hargreaves St. *Hodd* 4K **27**
Hargreaves St. *Nels* 1D **6**
Hargreaves St. *Ross* 1A **30**
Hargrove Av. *Burn* 3J **9**
Hargrove Av. *Pad* 1B **8**
Harlech Clo. *Has* 4B **28**
Harlech Dri. *Osw* 4H **21**
Harling St. *Burn* 4H **9**
Harold Av. *Burn* 6H **9**
Harold St. *Burn* 6J **9**
Harold St. *Col* 4F **5**
Harrier Dri. *B'brn* 4G **13**
Harriet St. *Burn* 6K **9**
Harrington St. *Clay M* 6B **16**

Harris Ct. *Clith* 5E **2**
Harrison Dri. *Col* 2F **5**
Harrison St. *Bacup* 5K **31**
Harrison St. *B'brn* 1G **19**
Harrison St. *Brclf* 7G **7**
Harrogate Cres. *Burn* 7D **6**
Harrow Av. *Acc* 1D **22**
Harrow Clo. *Pad* 4D **8**
Harrow Dri. *B'brn* 5A **20**
Harrow St. *Osw* 4K **21**
Harry St. *Barfd* 5A **4**
Hartington Rd. *Dar* 1C **26**
Hartington St. *Brier* 4C **6**
Hartington St. *Rish* 6F **15**
Hartlands Clo. *Burn* 6E **6**
Hartley Av. *Acc* 5B **22**
Hartleys Ter. *Col* 4H **5**
Hartley St. *B'brn* 6H **13**
Hartley St. *Burn* 5H **9**
Hartley St. *Col* 3G **5**
Hartley St. *Gt Har* 1J **15**
Hartley St. *Has* 2B **28**
Hartley St. *Nels* 2F **7**
Hartley St. *Osw* 4K **21**
Hartmann St. *Acc* 2B **22**
Hart St. *B'brn* 1J **19**
Hart St. *Burn* 4B **10**
Harvey Longworth Ct. *Ross* 3G **25**
Harvey St. *Nels* 7B **4**
Harvey St. *Osw* 4H **21**
Harwood Ga. *B'brn* 6K **13**
Harwood La. *Gt Har* 1J **15**
Harwood New Rd. *Gt Har* 1K **15**
Harwood Rd. *Rish* 5F **15**
Harwood's La. *Hodd* 4H **27**
Harwood St. *B'brn* 5K **13**
(in two parts)
Harwood St. *Dar* 3C **26**
Haslingden Old Rd. *Ross* 3D **28**
Haslingden Rd. *B'brn & Acc* 4C **20**
Haslingden.
B'brn & Guide 2J **19**
(in two parts)
Haslingden Rd. *Ross* 4C **28**
Hastings Clo. *B'brn* 4B **20**
Haston Lee Av. *B'brn* 1J **13**
Hatfield Rd. *Acc* 7E **16**
Hathaway Fold. *Pad* 3C **8**
Hattersley St. *Burn* 4K **9**
Haulgh St. *Burn* 7C **6**
Havelock Clo. *B'brn* 2G **19**
Havelock St. *B'brn* 3F **19**
Havelock St. *Burn* 4G **9**
Havelock St. *Osw* 5J **21**
Havelock St. *Pad* 1B **8**
Haven St. *Burn* 5D **10**
Haverholt Clo. *Col* 3F **5**
Haverholt Rd. *Col* 3F **5**
Hawarden St. *Nels* 2F **7**
Hawer St. *Dar* 5F **27**
Hawes Dri. *Col* 2J **5**
Hawes Ter. *Burn* 7D **6**
Haweswater Rd. *Acc* 6E **16**
Hawkins St. *B'brn* 3E **18**
Hawks Gro. *Ross* 4G **29**
Hawkshaw Av. *Dar* 2C **26**
Hawkshaw Bank Rd. *B'brn* 4G **13**
Hawkshead Clo. *B'brn* 1E **18**
Hawkshead St. *B'brn* 1E **18**
Hawkstone Clo. *Acc* 6G **17**
Hawk St. *Burn* 4B **10**
Hawkswood Gdns. *Brier* 5B **6**
Hawksworth Rd. *Acc* 7C **16**
Hawley St. *Col* 4F **5**
Haworth Art Gallery. 5E **22**
(Tiffany Glass)
Haworth Av. *Acc* 5E **22**
Haworth Av. *Ross* 3F **29**
Haworth Dri. *Bacup* 4E **30**
Haworth St. *Acc* 6C **16**
Haworth St. *Osw* 4K **21**
Haworth St. *Rish* 6G **15**
Hawthorn Av. *Dar* 3G **27**
Hawthorn Av. *Osw* 4K **21**
Hawthorn Bank. *Alt* 5B **16**
Hawthorn Clo. *Nels* 1J **7**
Hawthorn Dri. *Rish* 7G **15**
Hawthorne Av. *Burn* 4C **6**
Hawthorne Gro. *Barfd* 5A **4**
Hawthorne Ind. Est. *Clith* 4G **3**

Hawthorne Meadows. *Craw* 4G **25**
Hawthorne Pl. *Clith* 4E **2**
Hawthorne Rd. *Burn* 6K **9**
Hawthorne St. *B'brn* 4J **13**
Hawthorn Gdns. *Clay M* 4B **16**
Hawthorn Rd. *Bacup* 3J **31**
Hawthorns, The. *B'brn* 2B **14**
Hawthorns, The. *Ross* 4B **30**
(off Booth Rd.)
Haydock Sq. *Gt Har* 2H **15**
Haydock St. *B'brn* 3H **13**
Haydock St. *Burn* 1D **10**
Hayfield. *B'brn* 5D **12**
Hayhurst Farm Ter. *Clith* 6F **3**
Hayhurst St. *Clith* 6F **3**
Haywood Clo. *Acc* 7C **16**
Haywood Rd. *Acc* 7C **16**
Hazel Av. *Clay M* 2A **16**
Hazel Av. *Dar* 2F **27**
Hazel Bank. *B'brn* 6F **13**
Hazel Clo. *B'brn* 1F **19**
Hazeldene Av. *Has* 3B **28**
Hazel Gro. *Bacup* 2K **31**
Hazel Gro. *Burn* 3D **20**
Hazel Gro. *Burn* 7E **6**
Hazel Gro. *Clay M* 5A **16**
Hazel Gro. *Clith* 6C **2**
Hazel Gro. *Ross* 1F **29**
Hazels, The. *B'brn* 2A **14**
Hazel St. *Acc* 4A **24**
Hazelwood Clo. *B'brn* 3K **13**
Hazelwood Rd. *Nels* 1H **7**
Headingley Clo. *Acc* 6G **17**
Heald Rd. *Burn* 7B **6**
Healdwood Clo. *Burn* 6A **6**
Healdwood Dri. *Burn* 6A **6**
Healey Ct. *Burn* 5A **10**
Healey Mt. *Burn* 5A **10**
Healey Row. *Burn* 6A **10**
Healey Wood Rd. *Burn* 5A **10**
(in two parts)
Healey Wood Rd. Ind. Est.
Burn 6A **10**
Heaning Av. *Acc* 7E **16**
Heaning Av. *B'brn* 4C **20**
Heap St. *Brier* 4B **6**
Heap St. *Burn* 1C **10**
Heap St. *Ross* 4G **25**
Heap St. *Wors* 4J **11**
Heartwood Clo. *B'brn* 4D **12**
Heasandford Ind. Est. *Burn* 2E **10**
(Bancroft Rd.)
Heasandford Ind. Est. *Burn* 1E **10**
(Widow Hill Rd., in two parts)
Heathbourne Rd. *Bacup* 5D **30**
Heather Bank. *Burn* 6H **9**
Heather Bank. *Ross* 4F **29**
Heather Clo. *Brier* 5E **6**
Heather Clo. *Has* 5A **28**
Heatherleigh Gdns. *B'brn* 7G **13**
Heathfield Av. *Bacup* 5E **30**
Heathfield Pk. *B'brn* 6C **12**
Heathfield Rd. *Bacup* 5E **30**
Heath Hill Dri. *Bacup* 5E **30**
Heath St. *Burn* 2C **10**
Heatley Clo. *B'brn* 4A **20**
Heaton St. *B'brn* 1H **19**
Heber St. *Dunn* 1H **25**
Hebrew Rd. *Burn* 2B **10**
(in two parts)
Hebrew Sq. *Burn* 2B **10**
Heckenhurst Av. *Burn* 4G **11**
Hector Rd. *Dar* 1C **26**
Hedgerow, The. *B'brn* 4D **12**
Height Barn La. *Bacup* 5H **31**
Height Cft. *Brier* 4F **7**
Heights Cotts. *Acc* 4G **23**
Heightside Av. *Ross* 3A **30**
Height Side La. *Ross* 5H **25**
Heightside M. *Ross* 3A **30**
Heights Rd. *Nels* 3E **6**
Heirshouse La. *Col* 2E **4**
Helena St. *Burn* 5C **10**
Helm Clo. *Burn* 7J **9**
Helmcroft. *Has* 4A **28**
Helmcroft Ct. *Has* 4B **28**
Helmn Way. *Nels* 6C **4**
Helmsdale Rd. *Nels* 7D **4**
Helmshore Rd. *Holc & Helm* 7A **28**
Helmshore Textile Mus. 5A **28**

Helston Clo. Burn 6G 9
Helton Clo. Barfd 4A 4
Helvellyn Dri. Burn 2G 9
Hemingway Pl. Nels 1G 7
Hempshaw Av. Ross 2G 25
Hemp St. Bacup 4H 31
Hendon Rd. Nels 1G 7
Henfield Clo. Clay M 4B 16
Henrietta St. Bacup 3H 31
Henrietta St. B'brn 7F 13
(off Johnston St.)
Henrietta St. Ind. Est. Bacup ...3H 31
(off Henrietta St.)
Henry Gdns. Brier 4C 6
Henry St. Acc 4E 22
Henry St. Chu 2K 21
Henry St. Clay M 5B 16
Henry St. Col 4F 5
Henry St. Nels 7A 4
Henry St. Rish 6G 15
Henry St. Ross 3F 29
Henry Whalley St. B'brn 3D 18
Henthorn Clo. Clith 6D 2
Henthorn Rd. Clith 7B 2
Herbert St. Bacup 5F 31
Herbert St. B'brn 3G 19
Herbert St. Burn 5K 9
Herbert Av. Pad 3C 8
Hereford Av. Burn 3G 9
Hereford Clo. Acc 1C 22
Hereford Dri. Clith 6F 3
Hereford Rd. B'brn 3B 20
Hereford Rd. Col 6D 4
Hereford St. Nels 1D 6
Herkomer Av. Burn 7K 9
Hermitage St. Rish 6H 15
Heron Clo. B'brn 4G 13
Heron Ct. Burn 5H 9
Heron Way. Osw 5K 21
Herschel Av. Burn 2H 9
Herschell St. B'brn 4E 18
Hertford St. B'brn 3F 19
Hesketh Clo. Dar 7G 27
Hesketh St. Gt Har 2H 15
Hesse St. Dar 5E 26
Hetton Lea. Barfd 5A 4
Hexham Clo. Acc 5F 23
Heyfold Gdns. Dar 2D 26
Hey Head Av. Ross 5C 30
Heyhead St. Brier 4D 6
Heyhurst Rd. B'brn 7G 13
Heymoor Av. Gt Har 1J 15
Heys Av. Has 2A 28
Heys Clo. B'brn 6F 19
Heys Clo. Ross 3J 29
Heys Ct. B'brn 5F 19
Heys Ct. Osw 5K 21
Heysham Cres. B'brn 4J 19
Heys La. Dar 3D 26
Heys La. Gt Har 2J 15
(in two parts)
Heys La. Hodd 5J 27
Heys La. Live & B'brn 7E 18
Heys La. Osw 5K 21
Heys St. Bacup 3H 31
Heys St. Has 2A 28
Heys St. Raw 4J 29
Hey St. Nels 7B 4
Heywood St. Gt Har 3H 15
Heyworth Av. B'brn 6F 19
Hibson Rd. Nels 3E 6
(in two parts)
Hick's Ter. Rish 6G 15
Higgin St. Burn 5C 10
Higgin St. Col 3G 5
Higgin St. Wors 5J 11
Higham St. Pad 1C 8
Highbank. B'brn 3J 13
Highbrake Ter. Acc 5F 17
Highbury Pl. B'brn 6G 13
High Clo. Burn 4D 8
Higher Antley St. Acc 3B 22
Higher Audley St. B'brn 1J 19
Higher Avondale Rd. Dar 3C 26
Higher Bank St. B'brn 6E 12
Higher Barn St. B'brn 7K 13
Higher Blackthorn. Bacup 1H 31
Higher Booths La. Craw 3G 25
Higher Causeway. Barfd 5A 4
Higher Change Vs. Bacup 1K 31

Higher Chu. St. Dar 4F 27
Higher Cockcroft. B'brn 7H 13
Higher Cft. Rd. Lwr D 5J 19
Higher Cross Row. Bacup 2H 31
Higher Dri. Clay M 4B 16
Higher Eanam. B'brn 7K 13
Higher Ga. Acc 6G 17
Highergate Clo. Hun 5G 17
Higher Ga. Rd. Acc 6G 17
Higher Heys. Osw 5K 21
Higherhouse Clo. B'brn 6D 18
Higher La. Has 1B 28
Higher Lawrence St. Dar 3D 26
Higher Mill St. Ross 2G 29
Higher Peel St. Osw 5J 21
Higher Perry St. Dar 3F 27
Higher Ramsgreave Rd.
  Rams 1E 12
Higher Reedley Rd. Brier 5D 6
Higher Saxifield. Burn 6F 7
Higher S. St. Dar 4F 27
Higher Tentre. Burn 5C 10
Higher Watermill. 5A 28
Higher Witton Rd. B'brn 1E 18
Highfield. Bacup 3H 31
Highfield. Gt Har 2G 15
Highfield. Ross 5G 25
Highfield Av. Burn 6C 6
Highfield Clo. Osw 5A 22
Highfield Cres. Barfd 5A 4
Highfield Cres. Nels 5B 4
Highfield Gdns. B'brn 3H 19
Highfield M. Dar 5F 27
Highfield Pk. Has 3A 28
Highfield Rd. B'brn 2H 19
Highfield Rd. Clith 6E 2
Highfield Rd. Dar 4F 27
Highfield Rd. Rish 6F 15
Highfield Rd. Ross 4K 29
Highfield St. Dar 5F 27
Highfield St. Has 3A 28
Highgate. Nels 3E 6
Highmoor. Nels 3G 7
Highmoor Pk. Clith 5F 3
High St. Acc 5A 22
High St. B'brn 7H 13
High St. Brier 4C 6
High St. Clith 5B 2
High St. Col 3H 5
High St. Dar 4E 26
High St. Has 1B 28
High St. Nels 2E 6
High St. Osw 4C 22
High St. Pad 1C 8
High St. Rish 6G 15
Hightown. Ross 1A 30
Hightown Rd. Ross 1A 30
Higson St. B'brn 7G 13
Hilary St. Burn 1B 10
Hill Crest. Bacup 4F 31
Hill Crest Av. Burn 6G 11
Hillcrest Rd. B'brn 3C 18
Hill End. Traw 6K 5
Hill End La. Ross 4J 29
Hillhouses. Dar 6E 26
Hillingdon Rd. Burn 6E 6
Hillingdon Rd. N. Burn 5D 6
Hill Pl. Nels 3E 6
Hill Ri. Has 4C 28
Hillsborough Av. Brier 4E 6
Hillside. Burn 7J 9
Hillside Av. B'brn 4B 20
Hillside Av. Burn 5D 6
Hillside Av. Dar 5E 26
Hillside Clo. Brier 4D 6
Hillside Clo. Burn 7J 9
Hillside Clo. Clith 7E 2
Hillside Clo. Gt Har 1H 15
Hillside Gdns. Dar 6E 26
Hillside Rd. Has 3B 28
Hillside Wlk. B'brn 4B 20
Hill St. Acc 3D 22
(Hollins La.)
Hill St. Acc 6E 22
(Wellington St.)
Hill St. B'brn 2A 20

Hill St. Brier 3A 6
(Burnley Rd.)
Hill St. Brier 4C 6
(Montford Rd.)
Hill St. Clay M 6B 16
Hill St. Col 4G 5
Hill St. Osw 3J 21
Hill St. Pad 2B 8
Hill St. Ross 5G 25
Hill Top. Barfd 4A 4
Hilltop Dri. Has 6C 28
Hilltop Rd. Nels 7C 4
Hill Vw. B'brn 3H 13
Hill Vw. Ross 4F 29
Hilton Rd. Dar 5F 27
Hilton St. Dar 5E 26
Hindle Ct. Dar 3E 26
Hindle Fold La. Gt Har 1H 15
Hindle St. Acc 2C 22
Hindle St. Bacup 5F 31
Hindle St. Dar 3C 26
Hindle St. Has 2B 28
Hind St. Burn 7C 6
Hinton St. Burn 5C 10
Hippings La. Ross 4B 30
Hippings Va. Osw 4J 21
(off Holly St.)
Hirst St. Burn 6C 10
(in two parts)
Hirst St. Pad 1B 8
Hobart St. Burn 4C 10
Hobson St. Osw 4K 21
Hodder Gro. Clith 6C 2
Hodder Gro. Dar 1C 26
Hodder Pl. B'brn 6J 13
(in two parts)
Hodder St. Acc 2E 22
Hodder St. B'brn 6J 13
Hodder St. Burn 6D 6
Hoddlesden Fold. Hodd 4K 27
Hoddlesden Rd. Hodd 4J 27
Hodge Bank Pk. Nels 6A 4
Hodgson St. Dar 4F 27
Hodgson St. Osw 4K 21
Hogarth Av. Burn 7K 9
Hoghton Av. Bacup 4J 31
Holbeck St. Burn 1B 10
Holcombe Dri. Burn 4C 10
Holcombe Rd. Ross 6A 28
Holden Fold. Dar 2F 27
Holden Rd. Brier 4B 6
Holden Rd. Burn 6C 6
Holden St. Acc 3C 22
Holden St. B'brn 1F 19
Holden St. Burn 4A 10
Holden St. Clith 5F 3
Holden Wood Dri. Has 4A 28
Hole Ho. St. B'brn 3B 20
Holgate St. Brclf 6G 7
Holgate St. Gt Har 2H 15
Holker Bus. Cen. Col 4E 4
Holker St. Col 4E 4
Holker St. Dar 5F 27
Holland Av. Ross 1F 29
Holland St. Acc 3A 22
Holland St. B'brn 6G 13
Holland St. Pad 2A 8
Hollies Clo. B'brn 5C 18
Hollies Rd. Wilp 1C 14
Hollin Bank St. Brier 3C 6
Hollin Bri. St. B'brn 1B 30
(in two parts)
Hollin Clo. Ross 1B 30
(off Foxhill Dri.)
Hollingreave Rd. Burn 6B 10
Hollin Gro. Ross 1G 29
(off Hollin La.)
Hollington St. Col 3K 5
Hollin Hill. Burn 7C 10
Hollin La. Ross 1G 29
Hollin Mill St. Brier 3C 6
Hollins Av. Burn 6G 11
Hollins Clo. Acc 4D 22
Hollins Gro. St. Dar 2D 26
Hollins La. Acc 4D 22
Hollins Rd. Dar 1C 26
Hollins Rd. Nels 6D 4
Hollin St. B'brn 3F 19

Hollin Way. Raw 1G 29
Hollin Way. Ross 6G 25
Hollinwood Dri. Raw 7G 25
Hollowhead Av. Wilp 3B 14
Hollowhead Clo. Wilp 3C 14
Hollowhead La.
  B'brn & Wilp 3B 14
Holly Av. Has 4C 28
Holly Bank. Acc 4D 22
Holly Mt. Ross 6A 28
Holly St. Burn 5C 10
Holly St. Nels 1G 7
Holly St. Osw 4J 21
Holly Ter. B'brn 4J 13
Holly Tree Clo. Dar 7E 26
Holly Tree Clo. Ross 7F 25
Holly Tree Way. B'brn 5C 18
Holmbrook Clo. B'brn 5J 19
Holmby St. Burn 7C 6
Holme Bank. Ross 4F 29
Holme Cres. Traw 5J 5
Holme End. Burn 5A 6
Holmefield Ct. Barfd 5A 4
Holme Hill. Clith 3E 2
Holme La. Has & Ross 5D 28
(in two parts)
Holme Lea. Clay M 3A 16
Holme Rd. Burn 3K 9
Holme Rd. Clay M 3K 15
Holmes Dri. Bacup 1H 31
Holmes La. Bacup 2H 31
Holmes Sq. Burn 5C 10
Holmes St. Burn 5C 10
Holmes St. Pad 2C 8
Holmes St. Ross 2H 29
Holmes Ter. Reed 7F 25
Holmes, The. Reed 7F 25
Holmestrand Av. Burn 6F 9
Holme St. Acc 2C 22
Holme St. Bacup 5F 31
Holme St. Barfd 6A 4
Holme St. Dar 5E 26
Holme St. Nels 1F 7
Holmeswood Pk. Ross 5E 28
Holme Ter. Nels 1D 6
Holme Ter. Tow F 5E 28
Holmsley St. Burn 5C 10
Holt Mill Rd. Ross 5K 29
Holt Sq. Barfd 3B 4
Holt St. Rish 5H 15
Holt St. Ross 5A 30
Holyoake St. Burn 4E 8
Homer St. Burn 5H 9
Honey Hole. B'brn 3H 19
Honister Rd. Burn 6C 6
Honiton Av. B'brn 5F 19
Hood Ho. St. B'brn 6K 9
Hood St. Acc 1D 22
Hope St. Acc 3C 22
Hope St. Bacup 1H 31
Hope St. B'brn 7G 13
Hope St. Brier 4C 6
Hope St. Dar 4D 26
Hope St. Gt Har 3H 15
Hope St. Has 3B 28
Hope St. Nels 2E 6
Hope St. Pad 2C 8
Hope St. Raw & Ross 4J 29
Hope St. Wors 4J 11
Hope Ter. B'brn 6F 13
Hopkinson St. Traw 5J 5
Hopkinson Ter. Traw 5J 5
(off Skipton Rd.)
Hopwood St. Acc 4C 22
Hopwood St. B'brn 2H 19
Hopwood St. Burn 4K 9
Horace St. Burn 4J 9
Horden Rake. B'brn 6A 18
Horden Vw. B'brn 6B 18
Hordley St. Burn 4F 9
Horeb Clo. Pad 3C 8
(off Victoria Rd.)
Hornby Ct. B'brn 1F 19
(off Garden St.)
Hornby St. Burn 5B 10
Hornby St. Osw 5K 21
Horncliffe Clo. Ross 5E 28
Horncliffe Heights. Brier 4F 7
Horncliffe Vw. Has 5B 28

Horne St. *Acc* ...1D **22**
Horning Cres. *Burn* ...7E **6**
Horsfall Clo. *Acc* ...1C **22**
Horsfield Clo. *Col* ...3J **5**
Horton Av. *Burn* ...6C **6**
Howard Clo. *Acc* ...3A **22**
Howard St. *Burn* ...5J **9**
Howard St. *Nels* ...1D **6**
Howard St. *Rish* ...6F **15**
Howarth Av. *Chu* ...1A **22**
Howe Cft. *Clith* ...5F **3**
Howe Wlk. *Burn* ...4B **10**
Howgill Clo. *Nels* ...3G **7**
Howorth Clo. *Burn* ...7B **10**
Howorth Rd. *Burn* ...7B **10**
Howsin St. *Burn* ...1B **10**
Hoyle St. *Acc* ...4A **24**
Hoyle St. *Bacup* ...5G **31**
Hozier St. *B'brn* ...3B **20**
Hubie St. *Burn* ...3A **10**
Hud Hey Ind. Est. *Ross* ...6B **24**
Hud Hey Rd. *Has* ...6A **24**
Hud Rake. *Has* ...7B **24**
Hudson Clo. *B'brn* ...4F **13**
Hudson Pl. *B'brn* ...4E **12**
Hudson St. *Acc* ...4D **22**
Hudson St. *Brier* ...4C **6**
Hudson St. *Burn* ...5J **9**
Hufling Ct. *Burn* ...6C **10**
(off Hufling La.)
Hufling La. *Burn* ...7C **10**
Hugh Bus. Pk. *Ross* ...5B **30**
Hughes St. *Burn* ...5B **10**
Hugh Rake. *Ross* ...6F **25**
Hull St. *Burn* ...5C **10**
(in two parts)
Hulton Dri. *Nels* ...3F **7**
Humber Sq. *Burn* ...6D **6**
Humphrey St. *Brier* ...3C **6**
Huncoat Ind. Est. *Acc* ...6D **16**
Hunslet St. *Acc* ...4C **10**
Hunslet St. *Nels* ...2G **7**
Hunters Dri. *Burn* ...2J **9**
Hunters Lodge. *B'brn* ...4C **18**
Hunter St. *Brier* ...5C **6**
Huntington Dri. *Dar* ...6E **26**
Huntroyde Av. *Pad* ...2A **8**
Huntroyde Clo. *Burn* ...3J **9**
Hurst Cres. *Ross* ...2H **29**
Hurstead St. *Acc* ...7F **23**
Hurst La. *Raw & Ross* ...2G **29**
Hurst Wood Av. *B'brn* ...4D **18**
Hurstwood Av. *Burn* ...5E **10**
Hurstwood Enterprise Pk.
   Has ...3A **28**
Hurstwood Gdns. *Brier* ...5E **6**
Hurstwood La. *Wors* ...6J **11**
Hurtley St. *Burn* ...2B **10**
Hutch Bank Rd. *Ross* ...3A **28**
Hutchinson Ct. *Dar* ...4D **26**
Hutchinson St. *B'brn* ...2H **19**
Huttock End La. *Bacup* ...5F **31**
Hutton Dri. *Burn* ...3K **9**
Hutton St. *B'brn* ...7K **13**
Hyacinth Clo. *Has* ...5A **28**
Hygiene. *Clay M* ...5K **15**
Hynd Brook Ho. *Acc* ...3B **22**
(off Dale St.)
Hyndburn Bri. *Clay M* ...2A **16**
Hyndburn Dri. *Dar* ...1B **26**
Hyndburn Rd. *Acc & Chu* ...1A **22**
Hyndburn Rd. *Gt Har* ...2K **15**
Hyndburn St. *Acc* ...2A **22**
Hyndburn Ter. *Clay M* ...3K **15**
Hynings, The. *Gt Har* ...1G **15**
Hythe Clo. *B'brn* ...4B **20**

I

Icconhurst Clo. *Acc* ...6F **23**
Ice St. *B'brn* ...5H **13**
Idstone Clo. *B'brn* ...5K **19**
Ightenhill Pk. La. *Burn* ...1G **9**
Ightenhill Pk. M. *Burn* ...3H **9**
Ightenhill St. *Pad* ...1B **8**
Ighten Rd. *Burn* ...2H **9**
Imperial Gdns. *Nels* ...1E **6**
(off Carr Rd.)
Inchfield. *Wors* ...4J **11**

India St. *Acc* ...2A **22**
India St. *Dar* ...5F **27**
Industrial Cotts. *Ross* ...5B **30**
(off Wood Lea Rd.)
Industrial Pl. *Bacup* ...3H **31**
(off St James St.)
Industrial St. *Bacup* ...3J **31**
Industry St. *Dar* ...3E **26**
Infant St. *Acc* ...2D **22**
Infirmary Clo. *B'brn* ...3G **19**
Infirmary Rd. *B'brn* ...3G **19**
Infirmary St. *B'brn* ...3G **19**
Ingdene Clo. *Col* ...4E **4**
Ingham St. *Barfd* ...4A **4**
Ingham St. *Pad* ...1C **8**
Ingleby Clo. *B'brn* ...3C **20**
Inglehurst Rd. *Burn* ...5G **9**
Ingle Nook. *Burn* ...6G **11**
Ingleton Clo. *Acc* ...3E **22**
Inkerman St. *Bacup* ...3J **31**
Inkerman St. *B'brn* ...6H **13**
Inkerman St. *Pad* ...2B **8**
Inskip St. *Pad* ...2B **8**
Institute St. *Pad* ...2C **8**
Intake Cres. *Col* ...2J **5**
Inverness Rd. *Dar* ...5D **26**
Irene Pl. *B'brn* ...7E **12**
Irene St. *B'brn* ...5D **10**
Iron St. *B'brn* ...2G **19**
Irvine St. *Nels* ...6C **4**
Irving Pl. *B'brn* ...7E **12**
Irwell Ho. *Ross* ...5A **30**
(off Cowpe Rd.)
Irwell St. *Bacup* ...3H **31**
Irwell St. *Burn* ...4F **9**
Irwell Ter. *Bacup* ...2H **31**
Irwell Va. Rd. *Ross* ...7C **28**
Isherwood St. *B'brn* ...4G **19**
Isle of Man. *Rams* ...4A **14**
Islington. *B'brn* ...2H **19**
Islington Clo. *Burn* ...6E **6**
Ivan St. *Burn* ...7C **6**
Ivegate. *Col* ...3G **5**
Ivinson Rd. *Dar* ...2F **27**
Ivory St. *Burn* ...4H **9**
Ivy Av. *Has* ...2G **29**
Ivy Gro. *Ross* ...3G **19**
Ivy St. *Burn* ...1C **10**
Ivy St. *Col* ...6D **4**
Ivy St. *Ross* ...5B **30**
Ivy Ter. *Dar* ...7F **27**

J

Jacks Key Dri. *Dar* ...7G **27**
Jackson St. *Burn* ...2B **10**
Jackson St. *Chu* ...3K **21**
Jackson St. *Clay M* ...4A **16**
Jacob St. *Acc* ...3D **22**
James Av. *Gt Har* ...2G **15**
James St. *Acc* ...5F **17**
James St. *Bacup* ...6C **30**
James St. *Barfd* ...4A **4**
James St. *B'brn* ...7H **13**
James St. *Burn* ...1B **10**
James St. *Clay M* ...4A **16**
James St. *Col* ...4H **5**
(off West St.)
James St. *Dar* ...4D **26**
James St. *Gt Har* ...2G **15**
James St. *Has* ...3A **28**
James St. *Osw* ...4J **21**
James St. *Rish* ...6H **15**
James St. *Ross* ...3G **29**
James St. W. *Dar* ...4E **26**
Jannat Clo. *Acc* ...3C **22**
Jasper St. *B'brn* ...3J **13**
Jenny La. *Nels* ...3E **6**
Jepson St. *Dar* ...5E **26**
Jersey St. *B'brn* ...4E **18**
Jessel St. *B'brn* ...3E **18**
Jewel Holme. *Brier* ...4B **6**
Jib Hill Cotts. *Burn* ...6E **6**
Jobing St. *Col* ...5E **4**
Jockey St. *Burn* ...5H **9**
Joe Connolly Way. *Waterf* ...5A **30**
Johnny Barn Clo. *Ross* ...3K **29**
Johnny Barn Cotts. *Ross* ...3K **29**

John o'Gaunt St. *Pad* ...1B **8**
(off Guy St.)
Johnson New Rd. *Hodd* ...3J **27**
Johnson Rd. *E'hill & Waters* ...1G **27**
Johnston Clo. *B'brn* ...7F **13**
Johnston St. *B'brn* ...7F **13**
John St. *Barfd* ...4B **4**
John St. *Brier* ...3C **6**
John St. *Chu* ...1K **21**
John St. *Clay M* ...4A **16**
John St. *Col* ...4F **5**
John St. *Dar* ...4D **26**
John St. *Has* ...2B **28**
John St. *Osw* ...5J **21**
John St. *Waterf* ...4B **30**
John Wall Ct. *Clith* ...5D **2**
(Bawdlands)
John Wall Ct. *Clith* ...6E **2**
(Eshton Ter.)
Joiners All. *Gt Har* ...2H **15**
Joiners Row. *B'brn* ...2J **19**
Jonathan Clo. *Has* ...5A **28**
Joseph St. *Barfd* ...6A **4**
Joseph St. *Dar* ...4F **27**
Jubilee Clo. *Has* ...4A **28**
Jubilee Ct. *Has* ...4A **28**
Jubilee M. *Has* ...3A **28**
Jubilee Rd. *Chu* ...1A **22**
Jubilee Rd. *Has* ...3A **28**
Jubilee St. *B'brn* ...1H **19**
Jubilee St. *Brclf* ...6G **7**
Jubilee St. *Clay M* ...6B **16**
Jubilee St. *Dar* ...4E **26**
Jubilee St. *Osw* ...4K **21**
Jubilee Tower. ...5B **26**
Jude St. *Nels* ...1E **6**
Judge Fields. *Col* ...2G **5**
July St. *B'brn* ...1K **19**
Junction St. *Brier* ...3C **6**
Junction St. *Burn* ...3J **9**
(in two parts)
Junction St. *Col* ...5C **4**
Junction St. *Dar* ...6F **27**
June St. *B'brn* ...1K **19**
Juniper Ct. *Hun* ...7F **17**
Juniper St. *B'brn* ...5K **13**
Juno St. *Nels* ...6C **4**

K

Kay Fold Lodge. *B'brn* ...2G **13**
Kay Gdns. *Acc* ...5C **10**
Kay St. *B'brn* ...2H **19**
Kay St. *Brier* ...4C **6**
Kay St. *Clith* ...6D **2**
Kay St. *Dar* ...4F **27**
Kay St. *Osw* ...5J **21**
Kay St. *Pad* ...1C **8**
Kay St. *Ross* ...3G **29**
Keats Clo. *Acc* ...6F **23**
Keats Clo. *Col* ...2G **5**
Keats Fold. *Burn* ...3D **8**
Keele Wlk. *B'brn* ...1J **19**
Keighley Av. *Col* ...2G **5**
Keighley Rd. *Col* ...3H **5**
Keighley Rd. *Traw* ...6K **5**
Keirby Wlk. *Burn* ...4B **10**
Keith St. *Burn* ...4H **9**
Kelbrook Rd. *Burn* ...7K **9**
Kelsall Av. *B'brn* ...7A **14**
Kelswick Dri. *Nels* ...3F **7**
Kelvin St. *Dar* ...4D **26**
Kemp Ct. *B'brn* ...1J **13**
Kemple St. *Clith* ...7C **2**
Kempton Ri. *B'brn* ...2J **19**
Kendal Av. *Barfd* ...4A **4**
Kendal St. *B'brn* ...6H **13**
Kendal St. *Clith* ...4F **3**
Kendal St. *Nels* ...7A **4**
Kenilworth Clo. *Pad* ...2C **8**
Kenilworth Dri. *Clith* ...7C **2**
Kensington Pl. *Burn* ...6J **9**
Kensington St. *Nels* ...2D **6**
Kent Ct. *Barfd* ...4A **4**
Kentmere Clo. *B'brn* ...2G **9**
Kentmere Dri. *B'brn* ...5B **18**
Kent St. *B'brn* ...1J **19**
Kent St. *Burn* ...3A **10**

Kent Wlk. *Has* ...5A **28**
Kenworthy St. *B'brn* ...6J **13**
Kenyon Rd. *Brier* ...2B **6**
Kenyon St. *Acc* ...2D **22**
Kenyon St. *Bacup* ...5K **31**
Kenyon St. *B'brn* ...3B **20**
Kenyon St. *Ross* ...2G **29**
Keppel Pl. *Burn* ...5K **9**
Kershaw Clo. *Ross* ...5G **25**
(off Burnley Rd.)
Kershaw St. *Bacup* ...3H **31**
(off Union St.)
Kershaw St. *Chu* ...1K **21**
Kestrel Clo. *B'brn* ...4G **13**
Kestrel Dri. *Dar* ...2B **26**
Keswick Clo. *Acc* ...6E **16**
Keswick Dri. *B'brn* ...5B **18**
Keswick Rd. *Burn* ...7B **6**
Kew Rd. *Nels* ...6C **4**
Keynsham Gro. *Burn* ...3J **9**
Key Vw. *Dar* ...7G **27**
Khyber St. *Col* ...4F **5**
Kibble Cres. *Burn* ...6D **6**
Kibble Gro. *Brier* ...5E **6**
Kidder St. *B'brn* ...5G **19**
Kiddrow La. *Burn* ...3E **8**
Kielder Dri. *Burn* ...3K **9**
Killiard La. *B'brn* ...7B **12**
Killington St. *Burn* ...7D **6**
Kiln Clo. *Clith* ...3G **3**
Kiln Ho. Way. *Osw* ...5B **22**
Kilns, The. *Ross* ...7C **10**
Kiln St. *Nels* ...1E **6**
Kiln Ter. *Bacup* ...5F **31**
(off Holme St.)
Kimberley Clo. *Brclf* ...6G **7**
Kimberley St. *Bacup* ...6C **30**
Kimberley St. *Brclf* ...6G **7**
Kimble Bank. *Brier* ...5E **6**
Kimble Gro. *Brier* ...5E **6**
Kime St. *Burn* ...4H **9**
King Edward St. *Osw* ...5H **21**
King Edward Ter. *Barfd* ...6A **4**
Kingfisher Bank. ...6G **9**
Kingfisher Clo. *B'brn* ...4H **13**
Kingfisher Ct. *Osw* ...5K **21**
King La. *Clith* ...5E **2**
Kings Av. *Ross* ...4G **29**
King's Bri. Clo. *B'brn* ...4E **18**
King's Bri. St. *B'brn* ...4E **18**
Kingsbridge Wharf. *B'brn* ...4E **18**
Kingsbury Pl. *Burn* ...6E **6**
King's Causeway. *Brier* ...4E **6**
Kingsdale Av. *Burn* ...6C **6**
Kings Dri. *Hodd* ...4K **27**
Kings Dri. *Pad* ...4C **8**
King's Highway. *Acc* ...6G **17**
(in two parts)
King's Highway.
   Stone & Has ...5J **23**
Kingsland Gro. *Burn* ...6C **10**
Kingsland Rd. *Burn* ...7C **10**
Kingsley Av. *Pad* ...3D **8**
Kingsley Clo. *Chu* ...1A **22**
Kingsley St. *Nels* ...6C **4**
Kingsmead. *B'brn* ...4C **20**
King's Rd. *Acc* ...7C **16**
King's Rd. *Ross* ...5E **18**
Kingston Av. *Acc* ...4B **22**
Kingston Cres. *Ross* ...6A **28**
Kingston Pl. *Lwr D* ...6H **19**
King St. *Acc* ...2C **22**
King St. *Bacup* ...3H **31**
King St. *B'brn* ...1G **19**
King St. *Brclf* ...6G **7**
King St. *Brier* ...4B **6**
King St. *Chu* ...2K **21**
King St. *Clay M* ...5A **16**
King St. *Clith* ...5E **2**
King St. *Col* ...3H **5**
King St. *Gt Har* ...2H **15**
King St. *Has* ...1B **28**
King St. *Pad* ...2B **8**
King St. *Waterf* ...5A **30**
King St. Ter. *Brier* ...4B **6**
Kingsway. *Acc* ...6G **17**
Kingsway. *Burn* ...4B **10**
Kingsway. *Chu* ...7B **10**
Kingsway. *Gt Har* ...1A **16**
Kingsway. *Hap* ...7B **8**

Kingsway—Longsight Rd.

Kingsway. *Lwr D* 6K **19**
King William St. *B'brn* 7H **13**
Kinross Clo. *B'brn* 1K **19**
Kinross St. *Burn* 5J **9**
Kinross Wlk. B'brn *1K* ***19***
(off William Hopwood St.)
Kipling Pl. *Gt Har* 3G **15**
Kirby Rd. *B'brn* 4G **19**
Kirby Rd. *Nels* 1C **6**
Kirk Av. *Clith* 5C **2**
Kirkdale Av. *Ross* 4A **30**
Kirkdale Clo. *Dar* 7G **27**
Kirkfell Dri. *Burn* 2H **9**
Kirkgate. *Burn* 6B **10**
Kirkhill Av. *Has* 3C **28**
Kirk Hill Rd. *Has* 2C **28**
Kirk Ho. *Chu* 2K **21**
Kirkmoor Clo. *Clith* 4D **2**
Kirkmoor Rd. *Clith* 4D **2**
Kirk Rd. *Chu* 1K **21**
Kirkstone Av. *B'brn* 5B **18**
Kirk Vw. *Ross* 4C **30**
Knight Cres. *Lwr D* 7K **19**
Knighton Av. *B'brn* 4F **13**
Knightsbridge Av. *Col* 3E **4**
Knott Mt. *Col* 5F **5**
Knotts Dri. *Col* 5F **5**
Knotts La. *Burn* 4D **8**
Knotts La. *Col* 4F **5**
Knott St. *Dar* 4E **26**
Knowle La. *Dar* 2E **26**
Knowlesly Meadows. *Dar* 7G **27**
Knowlesly Rd. *Dar* 7F **27**
Knowles St. *Rish* 6G **15**
Knowl Gap Av. *Has* 4A **28**
Knowl Mdw. *Ross* 6A **28**
Knowlmere St. *Acc* 1C **22**
Knowsley Pk. Way. *Has* 5B **28**
Knowsley Rd. *B'brn & Wilp* 3B **14**
Knowsley Rd. *Has* 4B **28**
Knowsley Rd. Ind. Est. *Has* 4B **28**
Knowsley Rd. W. *Clay D* 2A **14**
Knowsley St. *Col* 4G **5**
Knunck Knowles Dri. *Clith* 4E **2**
Kyan St. *Burn* 7C **6**

L

Laburnham Cotts. *Good* 3G **25**
Laburnum Clo. *Burn* 6J **9**
Laburnum Cotts. *Burn* 2F **9**
Laburnum Dri. *Osw* 5A **22**
Laburnum Rd. *B'brn* 4K **13**
Laburnum Rd. *Ross* 6A **28**
Laburnum St. *Has* 2A **28**
Lacey Ct. *Has* 2B **28**
Lachman Rd. *Traw* 5J **5**
Ladbrooke Gro. *Burn* 7K **9**
Lady Av. *Lwr D* 7K **19**
Laithe St. *Burn* 6A **10**
Laithe St. *Col* 4F **5**
Lakeland Way. *Burn* 2G **9**
Lake Vw. Rd. *Col* 1G **5**
Lambert St. *Traw* 6K **5**
Lambeth Clo. *B'brn* 1K **19**
Lambeth St. *B'brn* 7K **13**
Lambeth St. *Col* 3K **5**
Lambton Gates. *Ross* 3J **29**
Lamlash Rd. *B'brn* 4C **20**
Lammack Rd. *B'brn* 3F **13**
Lanark St. *Burn* 6J **9**
Lancaster Av. *Acc* 1B **22**
Lancaster Av. *Has* 5A **28**
Lancaster Dri. *Clay M* 4A **16**
Lancaster Dri. *Clith* 6C **2**
Lancaster Dri. *Pad* 4C **8**
Lancaster Ga. *Nels* 2D **6**
Lancaster Pl. *B'brn* 7E **12**
Lancaster St. *B'brn* 1F **19**
Lancaster St. *Col* 3G **5**
Lancaster St. *Osw* 5H **21**
Lancing Pl. *B'brn* 2F **19**
Landless St. *Brier* 4B **6**
Landseer Clo. *Burn* 7K **9**
Lane End La. *Bacup* 4J **31**
Lane End Rd. *Bacup* 5J **31**
Lane Ends. *Nels* 3E **6**
Lane Head La. *Bacup* 2H **31**
Lane Ho. *Traw* 6K **5**
Lane Ho. Clo. *B'brn* 5E **18**
Laneshaw Clo. *Dar* 1C **26**
Laneside. *Alt* 1E **16**
Laneside Av. *Acc* 7C **16**
Laneside Clo. *Has* 4C **28**
Laneside Ct. *Ross* 3H **29**
Laneside Rd. *Has* 3C **28**
Langdale Av. *Clith* 6C **2**
Langdale Av. *Ross* 3E **28**
Langdale Clo. *Acc* 6E **16**
Langdale Clo. *B'brn* 5B **18**
Langdale Ri. *Col* 2J **5**
Langdale Rd. *B'brn* 6A **18**
Langdale Rd. *Pad* 1B **8**
Langden Brook Sq. *B'brn* 2K **19**
Langfield. *Wors* 4J **11**
Langford St. *Acc* 7F **23**
Langham Av. *Acc* 7C **16**
Langham Rd. *B'brn* 5G **13**
Langham St. *Burn* 4G **9**
Langholme St. *Nels* 2F **7**
Langho St. *B'brn* 4F **19**
Langroyd M. Col *1H* ***5***
(off Croft, The)
Langroyd Rd. *Col* 2H **5**
Langshaw Dri. *Clith* 7E **2**
Lang St. *Acc* 2B **22**
Langwyth Rd. *Burn* 5F **11**
Lansbury Pl. *Nels* 6C **4**
Lansdowne Clo. *Burn* 6K **9**
Lansdowne St. *B'brn* 2E **18**
Larch Clo. *B'brn* 5C **18**
Larch Clo. *Ross* 5F **29**
Larches, The. *B'brn* 5J **13**
Larch Rd. *Osw* 5A **22**
Larch St. *B'brn* 5K **13**
Larch St. *Burn* 3H **9**
Larch St. *Nels* 1G **7**
Largs Rd. *B'brn* 6B **20**
Larkhill. *B'brn* 7J **13**
Lark Hill. *Ross* 2G **29**
Larkhill Av. *Burn* 4D **6**
Larkspur Clo. *B'brn* 5A **18**
Lark St. *Burn* 3H **9**
Lark St. *Col* 2H **5**
Lark St. *Dar* 7F **27**
Latham St. *Burn* 1C **10**
Laund Clough Nature Reserve. 5F 23
Laund Gro. *Acc* 5F **23**
Laund Hey Vw. *Has* 4B **28**
Laund La. *Has* 2C **28**
Laund Rd. *Acc* 5E **22**
Laund St. *Ross* 1F **29**
Laurel Av. *Dar* 3F **27**
Laurel St. *Bacup* 2H **31**
Laurel St. *Burn* 6C **10**
Laurier Rd. *Burn* 7C **6**
(in two parts)
Lavender Hill. *Ross* 4F **29**
Lawley Rd. *B'brn* 7D **12**
Lawn St. *Burn* 2B **10**
Lawrence Av. *Burn* 6H **9**
(in two parts)
Lawrence St. *B'brn* 1F **19**
(in two parts)
Lawrence St. *Pad* 1C **8**
Lawrence St. *Ross* 1B **30**
Lawson St. *Ross* 4G **25**
Law St. *Ross* 4B **30**
Laxey Rd. *B'brn* 4H **19**
Lea Bank. *Ross* 3K **29**
Leach St. *B'brn* 3H **19**
Leach St. *Col* 4F **5**
Leacroft. *Lwr D* 7K **19**
Lea Dri. *B'brn* 7G **19**
Leamington Av. *Burn* 1D **10**
Leamington Rd. *B'brn* 6E **12**
Leamington St. *Nels* 2F **7**
Leaver St. *Burn* 5F **9**
Lebanon St. *Burn* 5D **10**
Lee Brook Clo. *Ross* 1G **29**
Leebrook Rd. *Ross* 1F **29**
Lee Ct. *Dar* 1C **26**
Leeds Clo. *B'brn* 1K **19**
Leeds Rd. *Nels* 1F **7**
(in two parts)
Lee Grn. St. Burn *2B* ***10***
(off North St.)
Lee Gro. *Burn* 6G **11**
Lee La. *Rish* 4F **15**
Lee Rd. *Bacup* 5G **31**
Lee Rd. *Nels* 6C **4**
Lee's St. *Bacup* 5K **31**
Lee St. *Acc* 2D **22**
Lee St. *Bacup* 3H **31**
Lee St. *Barfd* 5A **4**
Lee St. *Burn* 2B **10**
Lee St. *Ross* 1G **29**
Leeward Clo. *Lwr D* 7J **19**
Leicester Rd. *B'brn* 3B **20**
Leicester Wlk. *Has* 5B **28**
Leigh Pk. *Hap* 7B **8**
Lemonius St. *Acc* 4D **22**
Lenches Fold. *Col* 5G **5**
Lenches Rd. *Col* 5G **5**
Lench Rd. *Ross* 5K **29**
Lench St. *Ross* 5B **30**
Lennox St. *Wors* 4H **11**
Leonard St. Bacup *5E* ***30***
(off Booth Rd.)
Leonard St. Bacup *5D* ***30***
(off West Vw.)
Leonard St. *Nels* 2F **7**
Leonard Ter. *Waters* 2J **27**
Leopold Rd. *B'brn* 6E **12**
Leopold St. *Col* 4E **4**
Leopold Way. *B'brn* 5K **19**
Levant St. *Pad* 3B **8**
Leven Gro. *Dar* 1C **26**
Levens Clo. *B'brn* 5J **19**
Leven St. *Burn* 6C **10**
Lever St. *Ross* 3H **29**
Lewis St. *Gt Har* 2J **15**
Leyburn Clo. *Acc* 3F **23**
Leyburn Rd. *B'brn* 6E **18**
Leyland Clo. *Traw* 5J **5**
Leyland Rd. *Burn* 4C **10**
Leyland St. *Acc* 3A **22**
Ley St. *Acc* 6F **23**
Library St. *Chu* 2K **21**
Liddesdale Rd. *Nels* 6E **4**
Liddington Clo. *B'brn* 5K **19**
Lidgett. *Col* 3K **5**
Lightbown Cotts. Dar *3B* ***26***
(off Sunnyhurst La.)
Lightbown St. *Dar* 2E **26**
Lilac Av. *Has* 2B **28**
Lilac Gro. *Clith* 6C **2**
Lilac Gro. *Dar* 2F **27**
Lilac Rd. *B'brn* 4K **13**
Lilac St. *Col* 2J **5**
Lilac Ter. *Bacup* 5F **31**
Lilford Rd. *B'brn* 6G **13**
Lily St. *Bacup* 3H **31**
Lily St. *Dar* 4F **27**
Lily St. *Nels* 3G **7**
Limbrick. *B'brn* 6H **13**
Lime Av. *Osw* 6J **21**
Limefield Av. *Brier* 3D **6**
Limefield Ct. *B'brn* 7E **12**
Limefield St. *Acc* 3E **22**
Lime Rd. *Acc* 1C **22**
Lime Rd. *Has* 2C **28**
Limers La. *Gt Har* 2F **15**
Limes Av. *Dar* 5D **26**
Lime St. *B'brn* 6H **13**
Lime St. *Clith* 4F **3**
Lime St. *Col* 2H **5**
Lime St. *Gt Har* 1H **15**
Lime St. *Nels* 1D **6**
Lime Tree Gro. *Ross* 1G **29**
Limewood Clo. *Acc* 2E **22**
Lina St. *Acc* 2A **22**
Linby St. *Burn* 5C **10**
Lincoln Clo. *B'brn* 4A **20**
Lincoln Ct. *Chu* 1B **22**
Lincoln Pl. *Has* 2A **28**
Lincoln Rd. *B'brn* 4A **20**
Lincoln St. *Burn* 6B **10**
Lincoln St. *Has* 2A **28**
Lincoln Way. *Clith* 3G **3**
Lindadale Av. *Acc* 5B **22**
Lindadale Clo. *Acc* 5B **22**
Lindale Cres. *Burn* 7B **6**
Linden Av. *B'brn* 6G **13**
Linden Cres. *Dar* 3F **27**
Linden Dri. *Clith* 6F **3**
Linden Lea. *B'brn* 5C **18**
Linden Lea. *Raw* 5F **29**
Linden Rd. *Col* 3G **5**
Linden St. *Burn* 5C **10**
Lindisfarne Av. *B'brn* 4J **19**
Lindisfarne Clo. *Burn* 3K **9**
Lindley St. *B'brn* 3E **18**
Lindon Pk. Rd. *Has* 6C **28**
Lindred Rd. *Brier* 2B **6**
Lindsay Pk. *Burn* 5G **11**
Lindsay St. *Burn* 4B **10**
Lindsey Ho. *Chu* 1B **22**
Linedred La. *Brier* 2C **6**
Line St. *Bacup* 5G **31**
Lingfield Av. *Clith* 7E **2**
Lingfield Ct. *Fen* 5A **18**
Lingfield Way. *B'brn* 5A **18**
Lingmoor Dri. *Burn* 2F **9**
Linkside Av. *Nels* 1J **7**
Linton Dri. *Burn* 7J **9**
Linton Gdns. *Barfd* 5A **4**
Lion Ct. *Chu* 2K **21**
Lionel St. *Burn* 3H **9**
Lion St. *Chu* 1K **21**
Lisbon Dri. *Burn* 5K **9**
Lisbon Dri. *Dar* 4G **27**
Lister St. *Acc* 2B **22**
Lister St. *B'brn* 2H **19**
Littlemoor. *Clith* 7E **2**
Littlemoor Rd. *Clith* 7E **2**
Lit. Moor Vw. *Clith* 7E **2**
Lit. Peel St. *B'brn* 7G **13**
Lit. Queen St. *Col* 4F **5**
Little St. *Acc* 2B **22**
Lit. Toms La. *Burn* 6E **6**
Littondale Gdns. *B'brn* 6A **18**
Liverpool Rd. *Burn* 4F **9**
Livesey Branch Rd.
B'brn & Fen 5A **18**
Livesey Ct. *B'brn* 3F **19**
Livesey Fold. *Dar* 3D **26**
Livesey Hall Clo. *B'brn* 4B **18**
Livesey St. *Pad* 2B **8**
Livesey St. *Rish* 5F **15**
(in two parts)
Livingstone Rd. *Acc* 7C **16**
Livingstone Rd. *B'brn* 1E **18**
Livingstone St. *Brier* 4C **6**
Livingstone Wlk. *Brier* 3C **6**
Lloyd Clo. *Nels* 1F **7**
Lloyd St. *Bacup* 5E **30**
Lloyd St. *Dar* 2D **26**
Lloyd Wlk. *Nels* 2F **7**
Lock Ga. *Ross* 4C **28**
Lockside. *B'brn* 3G **19**
Lock St. *Osw* 4K **21**
Lockyer Av. *Burn* 4G **9**
Lodge La. *Bacup* 4H **31**
Lodgeside. *Clay M* 4A **16**
Lodge St. *Acc* 2D **22**
Lodge Ter. *Acc* 3K **21**
Logwood St. *B'brn* 5J **13**
Lois Pl. *B'brn* 7F **13**
Lomas La. *Ross* 4F **29**
Lomax Sq. *Gt Har* 2J **15**
Lomax St. *Dar* 3E **26**
Lomax St. *Gt Har* 2H **15**
Lomeshaye Bus. Village. *Nels* 1D **6**
Lomeshaye Ind. Est. *Nels* 1C **6**
(Churchill Way)
Lomeshaye Ind. Est. *Nels* 1B **6**
(Lindred Rd.)
Lomeshaye Pl. *Nels* 1D **6**
Lomeshaye Rd. *Nels* 1D **6**
Lomeshaye Way. *Nels* 1D **6**
Lomond Gdns. *B'brn* 4C **18**
London Rd. *B'brn* 6H **13**
London Ter. *Dar* 3F **27**
London Wlk. *B'brn* 6H **13**
Long Clo. *Clith* 3F **3**
Long Dike. *Ross & Acc* 7K **23**
Long Hey La. *Pick B* 4K **27**
Longholme Rd. *Raw* 3G **29**
Long Mdw. *Col* 3K **5**
Longridge Heath. *Brier* 5E **6**
Long Row. *Mel* 2E **12**
Longshaw La. *B'brn* 3G **19**
Longshaw St. *B'brn* 4G **19**
Longsight Av. *Acc* 7F **17**
Longsight Av. *Clith* 4F **3**
Longsight Rd.
Mel B & Clay D 1A **12**

A-Z Blackburn 45

Longton Clo. B'brn 3B 20
Longton Rd. Burn 2K 9
Longton St. B'brn 3A 20
Longworth Av. Burn 4E 10
Lonsdale Gdns. Barfd 5A 4
Lonsdale St. Acc 3A 22
Lonsdale St. B'brn 3H 9
Lonsdale St. Nels 1G 7
Lord Av. Bacup 5E 30
Lord's Cres. Lwr D 7K 19
Lord Sq. B'brn 7H 13
Lord St. Acc 2C 22
Lord St. Bacup 3H 31
Lord St. B'brn 7H 13
Lord St. Brier 4C 6
Lord St. Col 3F 5
Lord St. Craw 5F 25
Lord St. Dar 3E 26
Lord St. Gt Har 3H 15
Lord St. Osw 4K 21
Lord St. Raw 3G 29
Lord St. Rish 6G 15
Lord St. Mall. B'brn 7H 13
(off Lord Sq.)
Lord St. W. B'brn 7H 13
Lorne St. Dar 3D 26
Lorton Clo. Burn 2G 9
Lothersdale Clo. Burn 6E 6
Lottice La. B'brn & Osw 7E 20
Lotus St. Bacup 2H 31
(off Burnley Rd.)
Loughrigg Clo. Burn 3G 9
Loveclough Rd. Ross 2F 25
Lovely Hall La. Sale 1A 14
Lovers La. Has 1B 28
Lover's Wlk. Acc 5A 22
Low Bank. Burn 4D 8
Lwr. Antley St. Acc 3A 22
Lwr. Ashworth Clo. B'brn 1F 19
Lwr. Aspen La. Acc 3H 21
Lwr. Audley Ind. Est. B'brn ..1H 19
Lwr. Audley St. B'brn 1H 19
Lwr. Barnes St. Clay M 3K 15
Lwr. Barn St. Dar 6G 27
Lwr. Clough St. Barfd 6A 4
Lwr. Clowes St. Ross 5F 29
Lwr. Clowes Rd. Ross 5E 28
Lwr. Cockcroft. B'brn 7H 13
Lwr. Cribden Av. Ross 3D 28
Lwr. Cross St. Dar 4E 26
(in two parts)
Lwr. Eccleshill Rd. Dar 7K 19
(in two parts)
Lowerfields. Burn 4E 8
Lowerfold. Gt Har 1H 15
Lowerfold Rd. Gt Har 1H 15
Lowergate. Clith 5E 2
Lwr. Gate Rd. Acc 5G 17
Lwr. Hazel Clo. B'brn 1F 19
Lwr. Hollin Bank St. B'brn ...2G 19
Lowerhouse Cres. Burn 4F 9
Lowerhouse Fold. Burn 4E 8
Lowerhouse La. Burn 4E 8
Lower La. Has 1B 28
Lwr. Manor La. Burn 7A 6
Lwr. Mead Dri. Burn 7A 6
Lwr. Philips Rd. Whi I 7B 14
Lwr. Ridge Clo. Burn 4C 10
Lwr. Rosegrove La. Burn 5E 8
Lwr. School St. Col 4G 5
(off School St.)
Lwr. Tentre. Burn 5C 10
Lwr. Timber Hill La. Burn 7B 10
Lwr. Wilworth. B'brn 3H 13
Lwr. Wood Bank. Dar 3C 26
(off Higher Avondale Rd.)
Loweswater Cres. Burn 2G 9
Lowe Vw. Ross 4B 30
Low Hill. Dar 7E 26
Lowood Pl. B'brn 6D 12
Lowther Pl. B'brn 4K 13
Lowther St. Col 1H 5
Lowther St. Nels 1D 6
Lowthwaite Dri. Nels 3F 7
Loynd St. Gt Har 2H 15
Lubbock St. Burn 4H 9
Lucy St. Barfd 5A 4
Luke St. Bacup 5E 30
Lumb Holes La. Ross 6A 30
Lumb La. Ross 1B 30
Lumb Scarr. Bacup 3H 31

Lund St. B'brn 1F 19
Lune St. Col 4H 5
Lune St. Pad 2C 8
Lupin Clo. Acc 1B 22
Lupton Dri. Barfd 4A 4
Lupin Rd. Acc 1C 22
Lutner St. Burn 5B 10
Lych Ga. Wadd 1B 2
Lydgate. Burn 7F 7
Lydia St. Acc 4C 22
Lyndale Av. Has 3B 28
Lyndale Av. Wilp 1C 14
Lyndale Clo. Ross 5G 25
Lyndale Clo. Wilp 1C 14
Lyndale Rd. Hap 7B 8
Lyndhurst Av. B'brn 3D 20
Lyndhurst Gro. Gt Har 1K 15
Lyndhurst Rd. B'brn 3H 19
Lyndhurst Rd. Burn 5C 10
Lyndhurst Rd. Dar 2C 26
(in two parts)
Lyndon Av. Gt Har 1K 15
Lyndon Ct. Gt Har 1K 15
Lyndon Ho. Gt Har 1K 15
Lynfield Rd. Gt Har 1K 15
Lynthorpe Rd. B'brn 3H 19
Lynthorpe Rd. Nels 7D 4
Lynton Rd. Acc 4A 22
Lynwood Av. Clay M 4A 16
Lynwood Av. Dar 2C 26
Lynwood Clo. Clay M 3A 16
Lynwood Clo. Col 1G 5
Lynwood Clo. Dar 2C 26
Lynwood Rd. Acc 5F 17
Lynwood Rd. B'brn 6E 12
Lytham Rd. B'brn 5J 19
Lytham Rd. Burn 7D 6
Lytton St. Burn 3E 8

M

Mabel St. Col 3J 5
Macauley St. Burn 5H 9
Macleod St. Nels 1E 6
Maden Clo. Bacup 3H 31
Maden Rd. Bacup 3F 31
Magpie Clo. Burn 5H 9
Maiden St. Ross 6B 24
Maitland Pl. Ross 4G 29
Maitland St. Bacup 3H 31
Major St. Acc 4C 22
Major St. Ross 5G 25
Malham Av. Acc 4A 22
Malham Rd. Burn 6E 6
Malham Wend. Barfd 5A 4
Malkin Clo. Black 1B 4
Mallard Pl. Osw 5J 21
Malta St. Dar 5F 27
Malt St. Acc 1C 22
Malvern Av. B'brn 4G 19
Malvern Av. Osw 5K 21
Malvern Av. Pad 4C 8
Malvern Clo. Acc 1B 22
Malvern Rd. Nels 7C 4
Malvern Way. Ross 6A 28
Manchester Rd. Acc 3D 22
Manchester Rd. Dunn 7K 9
Manchester Rd. Hap & Pad 6B 8
Manchester Rd. Has 2B 28
Manchester Rd. Nels 2D 6
Mancknols St. Nels 2G 7
Mancknols Walton Cottage
  Homes, The. Nels 1J 7
(off Wimberley St.)
Manitoba Clo. B'brn 4E 12
Manner Sutton St. B'brn 7J 13
Manor Brook. 2D 22
Manor Pl. Chu 1A 22
Manor Rd. B'brn 7E 12
Manor Rd. Burn 3G 9
Manor Rd. Clith 6D 2
Manor Rd. Col 1H 5
Manor Rd. Dar 5D 26
Manor St. Acc 1D 22
Manor St. Bacup 4H 31
Manor St. Nels 2G 7

Mansergh St. Burn 7D 6
Mansfield Cres. Brier 3D 6
Mansfield Gro. Brier 3D 6
Mansion St. S. Acc 2E 22
Manxman Rd. B'brn 4H 19
Maple Av. Clith 6D 2
Maple Av. Has 2C 28
Maple Bank. Burn 3D 10
Maple Clo. Clay D 2A 14
Maple Cres. Rish 7G 15
Maple Dri. Osw 5A 22
Maple St. B'brn 5K 13
Maple St. Clay M 5A 16
Maple St. Gt Har 1J 15
Maple St. Rish 6G 15
Marabou Dri. Dar 2B 26
Marble St. Osw 4K 21
March St. Burn 2A 10
Margaret St. B'brn 4C 20
Margaret St. Osw 6H 21
Margaret St. Ross 1F 29
Maria Ct. Burn 6B 10
(off Glebe St.)
Maria St. Dar 7F 27
Maricourt Av. B'brn 3C 20
Marine Av. Burn 6H 9
Market Av. B'brn 7H 13
Market Pl. Clith 5E 2
Market Pl. Col 3H 5
Mkt. Promenade. Burn 4B 10
Market Sq. B'brn 4B 10
Market Sq. Nels 1E 6
Market St. Bacup 4H 31
Market St. Chu 3K 21
Market St. Col 3H 5
Market St. Dar 4E 26
Market St. Nels 1E 6
Market St. Ross 5A 30
Market St. La. B'brn 1H 19
Market Way. B'brn 7H 13
(off Blackburn Shop. Cen.)
Markham Rd. B'brn 2E 18
Markross St. Ross 3G 29
Mark St. Bacup 5E 30
Mark St. Burn 1C 10
Marlborough Rd. Acc 7C 16
Marlborough St. Burn 5A 10
Marles Ct. Burn 2C 10
(off Pheasantford Grn.)
Marlin St. Nels 6C 4
Marlowe Av. Acc 6F 23
Marlowe Av. Pad 3D 8
Marlowe Cres. Gt Har 3G 15
Marl Pits. Ross 2H 29
Marlton Rd. B'brn 3G 19
Marquis Clo. Lwr D 6J 19
Marsden Ct. Burn 6D 6
Marsden Cres. Nels 1H 7
Marsden Dri. Brier 3E 6
Marsden Gro. Brier 4D 6
Marsden Hall Rd. Nels 1H 7
Marsden Hall Rd. N. Nels 7D 4
Marsden Hall Rd. S. Nels 1H 7
Marsden Height Clo. Brier 4F 7
Marsden Pk. Golf Course. 1K 7
Marsden Pl. Nels 1H 7
Marsden Rd. Burn 6D 6
Marsden Sq. Has 1B 28
Marsden St. Acc 4C 22
Marsden St. B'brn 3E 18
Marsden St. Has 2A 28
Marshall Av. Acc 5G 17
Marsham Gro. Dar 4G 27
Marsh Ho. La. Dar 4F 27
Marsh St. B'brn 6H 13
Marsh Ter. Dar 3E 26
Martholme Av. Clay M 4B 16
Martin Cft. Rd. Has 7A 24
Martindale Clo. B'brn 6B 20
Martin Dri. Dar 7G 27
Martinfields. Burn 5D 6
Martinique Dri. Lwr D 7J 19
Marton St. Burn 1C 10
Marton Dri. Burn 7K 9
Marton Wlk. Dar 7F 27
Maryport Clo. B'brn 5J 19
Mary St. B'brn 1K 19
Mary St. Burn 5C 10
Mary St. Col 4F 5
Mary St. Dar 5F 27

Mary St. Rish 6G 15
Masefield Av. Pad 3D 8
Masefield Clo. Gt Har 3G 15
Mason St. Acc 2D 22
Mason St. Col 3G 5
Mason St. Osw 5J 21
Massey La. Brier 4B 6
Massey St. Brier 5B 6
Massey St. Burn 4B 10
(in two parts)
Mather Av. Acc 7C 16
Matlock Gro. Burn 7D 6
Matlock St. Dar 3C 26
Matthew Clo. Col 4H 5
Matthew St. B'brn 3E 18
Maudsley St. Acc 2D 22
Maudsley St. B'brn 7J 13
Maud St. Barfd 6A 4
Maurice St. Nels 1D 6
Mavis Rd. B'brn 7D 12
Maybury Av. Burn 3G 9
Mayfair Clo. Ross 6A 28
Mayfair Cres. Wilp 3B 14
Mayfair Rd. Burn 5F 11
Mayfair Rd. Nels 7D 4
Mayfield Av. Clith 6F 3
Mayfield Av. Has 4A 28
Mayfield Av. Osw 4K 21
Mayfield Flats. Dar 6F 27
Mayfield Gdns. Osw 4A 22
Mayfield Rd. Rams 4A 14
Mayfield St. B'brn 2H 19
Mayflower St. B'brn 3E 18
Mayson St. B'brn 1H 19
May St. Barfd 6A 4
May St. B'brn 1K 19
May St. Burn 6C 10
May St. Nels 6C 4
Mayville Rd. Brier 3C 6
Meadoway. Chu 1A 22
Meadow Bank. Acc 1D 22
Mdw. Bank Av. Burn 4C 6
Meadow Bank Rd. Nels 1E 6
Meadow Clo. Burn 5C 6
Meadow Clo. Hun 6G 17
Meadow Ct. Osw 4K 21
(off Haworth St.)
Meadowcroft. Lwr D 7K 19
Meadowcroft Clo. Raw 7G 25
Meadowfields. B'brn 6G 19
Meadow Gdns. Rish 6G 15
Meadow Ga. Dar 3F 27
Meadowhead. Rish 6G 15
Mdw. Head Clo. B'brn 4D 18
Meadowhead Dri. Rish 6H 15
Mdw. Head La. Dar 1A 26
Meadowlands. Clith 5C 2
Meadow Ri. B'brn 5D 18
Meadows Av. Bacup 1H 31
Meadows Av. Has 3C 28
Meadowside Av. Clay M 4K 15
Meadows, The. Burn 2J 9
Meadows, The. Col 2G 5
Meadows, The. Dar 1C 26
Meadows, The. Osw 5A 22
Meadow St. Acc 2D 22
Meadow St. Burn 4A 10
Meadow St. Dar 6F 27
Meadow St. Gt Har 3H 15
Meadow St. Pad 1B 8
Meadow Va. B'brn 7H 19
Meadow Vw. Clith 5C 2
Meadow Way. Bacup 3H 31
Mearley Brook Fold. Clith 6F 3
Mearley St. Clith 6E 2
Mearley Syke. Clith 5F 3
Medina Clo. Acc 3C 22
Meins Cft. B'brn 7D 12
Meins Rd. B'brn & Pleas 6A 12
Melbourne St. Clay M 5J 21
Melbourne St. Dar 7F 27
Melbourne St. Osw 6B 16
Melbourne St. Pad 3C 8
Melbourne St. Ross 4B 30
Melfort Clo. B'brn 4C 18
Melia Clo. Ross 3F 29
Melita St. Dar 5F 27
Melling Ct. Col 3F 5

Mellor Brow—Newton St.

Mellor Brow. *Mel* 1A **12**
Mellor Clo. *Burn* 7J **9**
Mellor La. *Mel* 2B **12**
Melrose Av. *Burn* 6J **9**
Melrose Av. *Osw* 5A **22**
Melrose St. *Dar* 3D **26**
Melville Av. *Dar* 6E **26**
Melville Dri. *B'brn* 7G **13**
Melville Gdns. *Dar* 5E **26**
Melville St. *Burn* 1D **10**
Melville St. *Dar* 5E **26**
Mercer Cres. *Has* 5A **28**
Mercer St. *Burn* 3E **8**
Mercer St. *Clay M* 4A **16**
Mercer St. *Gt Har* 2J **15**
Merchants Ho. B'brn 2J ***19***
(off Merchants Quay)
Merchants Landing. *B'brn* 2J **19**
Merchants Quay. *B'brn* 2J **19**
Merclesden Av. *Nels* 7E **4**
Mere Ct. *Burn* 6G **9**
Meredith St. *Nels* 2F **7**
Merlin Ct. *Osw* 5J **21**
Merlin Dri. *Osw* 5J **21**
Merlin Fold. *Burn* 3D **8**
Merlin Rd. *B'brn* 6E **12**
Mersey Av. *Dar* 2B **26**
Mersey St. *Bacup* 4J **31**
Mersey St. *Burn* 4F **9**
Merton St. *Burn* 3A **10**
Merton St. *Nels* 7A **4**
Messenger St. *Nels* 2G **7**
Meta St. *B'brn* 3H **19**
Metcalf Dri. *Alt* 1E **16**
Metcalfe St. *Burn* 5G **9**
Mettle Cote. *Bacup* 4J **31**
Mews, The. *Pad* 1B **8**
Middle Ga. Grn. *Ross* 3G **25**
Middlesex Av. *Burn* 3F **9**
Middle St. *Col* 4F **5**
Middleton Dri. *Barfd* 2B **4**
Midgley St. *Col* 4H **5**
Midland St. *Acc* 3D **22**
Midland St. *Nels* 7B **4**
Midsummer St. *B'brn* 7F **13**
Midville Pl. *Dar* 4E **26**
Milbrook Clo. *Burn* 5G **9**
Mile End Row. *B'brn* 6E **12**
Miles Av. *Bacup* 5F **31**
Milford St. *Col* 3F **5**
Milking La. *Lwr D* 7J **19**
(in two parts)
Millar Barn La. *Ross* 5A **30**
Millbrook St. *Lwr D* 6J **19**
Mill Entrance. *Clay M* 5A **16**
Miller Clo. *Osw* 3H **21**
Miller Fold Av. *Acc* 5C **22**
Mill Fld. *Clay M* 3A **16**
Mill Gap St. *Dar* 5E **26**
Mill Ga. *Ross* 2G **29**
Millgate Rd. *Ross* 2G **29**
Mill Grn. *Col* 4G **5**
Millham St. *B'brn* 6H **13**
Mill Hill. *Osw* 4J **21**
Mill Hill Bri. St. *B'brn* 3E **18**
Mill Hill La. *Hap* 5H **17**
Mill Hill St. *B'brn* 3E **18**
Mill La. *B'brn* 1H **19**
Mill La. *Gt Har* 1A **16**
Mill Row. *Ross* 7F **25**
Mills Fold. *Ross* 4A **30**
Mill St. *Acc* 2A **22**
Mill St. *Bacup* 2H **31**
Mill St. *Barfd* 4A **4**
Mill St. *Chu* 7F **23**
Mill St. *Clay M* 5A **16**
Mill St. *Dar* 6F **27**
Mill St. *Gt Har* 2H **15**
Mill St. *Has* 1B **28**
Mill St. *Nels* 7B **4**
Mill St. *Osw* 5J **21**
Mill St. *Pad* 2B **8**
Millthorne Av. *Clith* 6D **2**
Millwood Clo. *B'brn* 4D **18**
Milner Rd. *Dar* 1C **26**
Milner St. *Burn* 2B **10**
Milnshaw Gdns. *Acc* 1B **22**
Milnshaw La. *Acc* 2C **22**
Milton Av. *Clith* 4E **2**
Milton Clo. *Dar* 4G **27**
Milton Clo. *Gt Har* 3G **15**
Milton Clo. *Ross* 6A **28**
Milton Rd. *Col* 3G **5**
Milton St. *Acc* 2C **22**
Milton St. *Barfd* 4A **4**
Milton St. *B'brn* 7K **13**
Milton St. *Brclf* 6F **7**
Milton St. *Brier* 4C **6**
Milton St. *Clay M* 4A **16**
Milton St. *Nels* 7A **4**
Milton St. *Osw* 4K **21**
Milton St. *Pad* 3C **8**
Mincing La. *B'brn* 1H **19**
Minehead Av. *Burn* 7E **6**
Minnie Ter. *B'brn* 6F **13**
Minor St. *Ross* 5G **25**
Minster Cres. *Dar* 5G **27**
Mint Av. *Barfd* 4A **4**
Mire Ash Brow. *Mel* 3A **12**
Mire Ridge. *Col* 4K **5**
Mitchell St. *Burn* 4H **9**
Mitchell St. *Clith* 6D **2**
Mitchell St. *Col* 3G **5**
Mitella St. *Burn* 5D **10**
Mitre St. *Burn* 4K **9**
Mitton Av. *Barfd* 2C **4**
Mitton Av. *Ross* 1G **29**
Mitton Gro. *Burn* 5E **10**
Mitton St. *B'brn* 5J **13**
Mizpah St. *Burn* 5D **10**
Moleside Clo. *Acc* 2E **22**
Mollington Rd. *B'brn* 5E **12**
Molly Wood La. *Burn* 5E **8**
Monarch St. *Osw* 4K **21**
Mona Rd. *B'brn* 4H **19**
Monk Hall St. *Burn* 3B **10**
Monk St. *Acc* 2B **22**
Monk St. *Clith* 6D **2**
Monmouth Rd. *B'brn* 3B **20**
Monmouth St. Burn 4J ***9***
(off Shale St.)
Monmouth St. *Col* 3K **5**
Montague Clo. *B'brn* 1G **19**
Montague Rd. *Burn* 5K **9**
Montague St. *B'brn* 7G **13**
Montague St. *Brier* 4C **6**
Montague St. *Clith* 5D **2**
Montague St. *Col* 2H **5**
Montfieldhey. *Brier* 4B **6**
Montford Rd. *Brier* 3A **6**
Montgomery Clo. *Bax* 6F **23**
Montgomery Gro. *Burn* 3H **9**
Monton Rd. *Dar* 1C **26**
Montreal Rd. *B'brn* 4F **13**
Montrose St. *B'brn* 2F **19**
Montrose St. *Brier* 4C **6**
Montrose St. *Burn* 6A **10**
Moor Clo. *Dar* 5H **27**
Moorcroft. *Lwr D* 7K **19**
Moor End. *Clith* 6F **3**
Moore St. *Burn* 3E **8**
(in two parts)
Moore St. *Col* 3F **5**
Moore St. *Nels* 2G **7**
Moorfield Av. *Acc* 7G **17**
Moorfield Av. *Rams* 1H **13**
Moorfield Clo. *Acc* 4C **16**
Moorfield Dri. *Acc* 4C **16**
Moorfield Ind. Est. *Alt* 4C **16**
Moorfield Way. *Acc* 4C **16**
Moorgate. *Acc* 6C **22**
Moorgate Gdns. *B'brn* 4F **19**
Moorgate St. *B'brn* 4F **19**
Moorhead St. *Col* 3F **5**
Moorhouse Av. *Acc* 4B **22**
Moorhouse Clo. *Acc* 4B **22**
Moorhouse St. *Acc* 4B **22**
Moorhouse St. *Burn* 5H **9**
Moorings, The. *Burn* 3K **9**
Moorland Av. *B'brn* 6A **18**
Moorland Av. *Clith* 3F **3**
Moorland Av. *Dar* 3B **26**
Moorland Clo. *Barfd* 2C **4**
Moorland Cres. *Clith* 3F **3**
Moorland Dri. *Brier* 5E **6**
Moorland Ri. *Has* 3C **28**
Moorland Rd. *B'brn* 6F **19**
Moorland Rd. *Burn* 7K **9**
Moorland Rd. *Clith* 3F **3**
Moorlands Ter. *Bacup* 4J **31**
Moorlands Vw. *Ram* 7D **28**
Moorland Vw. *Nels* 3F **7**
Moor La. *Clith* 6E **2**
Moor La. *Dar* 2E **26**
Moor La. *Pad* 1B **8**
Moorside Av. *B'brn* 4C **20**
Moorside Av. *Brier* 5E **6**
Moorside Cres. *Bacup* 1J **31**
Moor St. *Clay M* 4A **16**
Moorthorpe Clo. *Dar* 7E **26**
Moor Vw. *Bacup* 1K **31**
Moorview Clo. *Burn* 7F **7**
Morecambe Rd. *B'brn* 4J **19**
Moreton St. *Acc* 2C **22**
Morley Av. *B'brn* 4D **18**
Morley St. *Burn* 6C **10**
Morley St. *Pad* 2B **8**
Morse St. *Burn* 5D **10**
Morton St. *B'brn* 7H **13**
Moscow Mill St. *Osw* 3K **21**
Moscow Pl. Osw 4K ***21***
(off Union Rd.)
Mosedale Dri. *Burn* 2G **9**
Moseley Clo. *Burn* 7B **10**
Moseley Rd. *Burn* 7B **10**
Mosley St. *B'brn* 3H **19**
Mosley St. *Nels* 1E **6**
Mossbank. *B'brn* 6K **13**
Moss Clo. *Has* 5A **28**
Mossdale. *B'brn* 6K **13**
Moss Fold Rd. *Dar* 1C **26**
Moss Ga. *B'brn* 6K **13**
Moss Hall Rd. *Acc* 7C **16**
Moss La. *Osw & B'brn* 5E **20**
Moss St. *B'brn* 6K **13**
Moss St. *Clith* 5D **2**
Moss St. *Gt Har* 3H **15**
Mostyn St. *Dar* 1C **26**
Moulding Clo. *B'brn* 1E **18**
Mountain La. *Acc* 4D **22**
Mount Av. *Ross* 5B **30**
Mt. Pleasant. Bacup 5E ***30***
(off Plantation St.)
Mt. Pleasant. *B'brn* 7J **13**
Mt. Pleasant. *Chat* 1K **3**
Mt. Pleasant. *Ross* 3E **28**
Mt. Pleasant. *Wors* 5H **11**
Mt. Pleasant St. *Burn* 5A **10**
Mt. Pleasant St. *Osw* 4K **21**
Mount Rd. *Burn* 6A **10**
Mt. St James. *B'brn* 4E **20**
Mount St. *Acc* 4C **22**
Mount St. *Barfd* 5A **4**
Mount St. *Brier* 4C **6**
Mount St. *Clay M* 5B **16**
Mount St. *Gt Har* 1H **15**
Mount St. *Ross* 3E **28**
Mount Ter. *Ross* 3G **29**
Mount, The. *Ross* 6B **30**
Mowbray Av. *B'brn* 3J **19**
Mowgrain Vw. *Bacup* 2H **31**
Mt Pleasant. Burn 4A ***10***
(off Bethesda St.)
Mulberry St. *B'brn* 3A **20**
Mulberry Wlk. *B'brn* 3A **20**
Murdock St. *B'brn* 1E **18**
Murray St. *Burn* 1C **10**
Musbury Cres. *Ross* 4G **29**
Musbury Vw. *Has* 4A **28**
Musden Av. *Ross* 6A **28**
Museum St. *B'brn* 7H **13**
Myrtle Av. *Burn* 6J **9**
Myrtle Bank Rd. *Bacup* 2H **31**
Myrtle Bank Rd. *B'brn* 5G **19**
Myrtle Gro. *Burn* 6G **11**
Myrtle Gro. *Has* 4A **28**
Mytton St. *Pad* 2B **8**
Mytton Vw. *Clith* 6C **2**

N

Nab La. *B'brn* 7G **13**
(in two parts)
Nab La. *Osw* 4G **21**
Nairne St. *Burn* 5J **9**
Nancy St. *Dar* 4F **27**
Nansen Rd. *B'brn* 2E **18**
Napier St. *Acc* 3D **22**
Napier St. *Nels* 3F **7**
Naples Av. *Burn* 6J **9**
Naples Rd. *Dar* 4G **27**
Narcissus Av. *Has* 5A **28**
Nares Rd. *B'brn* 2E **18**
Narvik Av. *Burn* 6G **9**
Nave Clo. *Dar* 5G **27**
Navigation Way. *B'brn* 2J **19**
Naze Ct. *Ross* 4A **30**
Naze Rd. *Ross* 4A **30**
Naze Vw. Av. *Ross* 3B **30**
Neath Clo. *B'brn* 5H **13**
Nelson Golf Course. 5F **7**
Nelson Rd. *Brclf* 4G **7**
Nelson Sq. *Burn* 5A **10**
Nelson St. *Acc* 3D **22**
Nelson St. *Bacup* 5K **31**
Nelson St. *Clith* 5B **2**
Nelson St. *Col* 3G **5**
Nelson St. *Dar* 3D **26**
Nelson St. *Gt Har* 1J **15**
Nelson Ter. Acc 2A ***22***
(off India St.)
Neptune St. *Burn* 4A **10**
Netherby St. *Burn* 6J **9**
Netherfield Clo. *Burn* 3J **9**
Netherfield Gdns. *Nels* 1F **7**
Netherfield Rd. *Nels* 2E **6**
Netherheys Clo. *Col* 3E **4**
Netherwood Rd. *Burn* 2D **10**
Netherwood St. *Burn* 7F **7**
Network 65 Bus. Pk. *Hap* 6E **8**
Newark St. *Acc* 3A **22**
New Bank Rd. *B'brn* 6E **12**
New Barn Clo. *Ross* 7A **28**
New Barn Ct. B'brn 3J ***19***
(off Yates Fold)
New Barn La. *Ross* 5G **29**
New Bath St. *Col* 3H **5**
Newbigging Av. *Ross* 3B **30**
New Brighton. *Ross* 1A **30**
New Brown St. *Nels* 7A **4**
New Bury Clo. *Osw* 5H **21**
Newby Clo. *Burn* 7K **9**
Newby Rd. *Acc* 7E **16**
Newcastle St. *B'brn* 2F **19**
New Chapel St. *B'brn* 3E **18**
Newchurch Clo. *B'brn* 3J **19**
New Chu. Clo. *Clay M* 4A **16**
New Chu. M. *Burn* 1C **10**
Newchurch Old Rd. *Bacup* 4F **31**
(in two parts)
Newchurch Rd. *Bacup* 5C **30**
Newchurch Rd. *Ross* 2G **29**
Newfield Dri. *B'brn* 5K **19**
Newfield Dri. *Nels* 1F **7**
New Garden St. *B'brn* 2H **19**
New Ground Ct. *Burn* 6D **6**
New Hall Hey Bus. Pk. *Ross* 4F **29**
New Hall Hey Rd.
Ross & Raw 4F **29**
New Hall St. *Burn* 1B **10**
Newhouse Rd. *Hun I* 7E **16**
New Ho. St. *Col* 3H **5**
Newington Av. *B'brn* 1J **13**
Newlands Av. *Clith* 6C **2**
Newlands Clo. *B'brn* 5B **18**
New La. *Osw* 6H **21**
New La. *W'gll* 7A **2**
New Line. *Bacup* 5H **31**
New Line Ind. Est. *Bacup* 5J **31**
Newman St. *Burn* 1C **10**
New Mkt. St. *B'brn* 7H **13**
New Mkt. St. *Clith* 5E **2**
New Mkt. St. *Col* 3G **5**
Newmeadow Clo. *B'brn* 5K **19**
New Mill St. *B'brn* 6J **13**
New Oxford St. *Col* 2H **5**
New Pk. St. *B'brn* 7G **13**
Newport St. *Nels* 7B **4**
New Rd. *Burn* 7A **10**
New Rd. *Ross* 3B **30**
New Row. *Alt* 1F **17**
New Scotland Rd. *Nels* 7B **4**
New St. *Col* 5E **4**
New St. *Has* 2B **28**
New St. *Nels* 7C **4**
New St. *Pad* 2A **8**
New Taylor Pde. *Brclf* 6G **7**
Newton Dri. *Acc* 5E **22**
Newton St. *B'brn* 3A **20**

Newton St.—Parramatta St.

Newton St. Burn 3H 9
Newton St. Clith 6D 2
Newton St. Dar 3E 26
Newton St. Osw 3G 21
Newtown St. Col 3H 5
(in two parts)
New Wellington Clo. B'brn 4F 19
New Wellington Gdns. B'brn 4F 19
New Wellington St. B'brn 4F 19
Nicholas St. Brclf 6F 7
Nicholas St. Burn 5B 10
Nicholas St. Col 4F 5
Nicholas St. Dar 4D 26
Nicholl St. Burn 2B 10
Nickey La. Mel 2C 12
Nightingale Cres. Burn 6H 9
Nile St. Nels 7A 4
(off Clayton Clo.)
Niton Clo. Has 4C 28
Noble St. Dar 5E 26
Noble St. Gt Har 3H 15
Noble St. Rish 6G 15
Noblett St. B'brn 7J 13
Nook La. B'brn 4C 18
Nook La. Osw 6F 21
Nook Ter. B'brn 4D 18
Nora St. Barfd 5A 4
Norbreck Clo. B'brn 5J 19
Norfolk Av. Burn 3G 9
Norfolk Av. Pad 4C 8
Norfolk Clo. Clay M 4A 16
Norfolk Gro. Chu 1B 22
Norfolk St. Acc 1E 22
Norfolk St. B'brn 3F 19
Norfolk St. Col 3H 5
Norfolk St. Dar 4F 27
Norfolk St. Nels 1E 6
Norfolk St. Rish 6F 15
Norham Clo. Burn 3K 9
Norman Rd. Osw 3H 21
Norman St. B'brn 2F 19
Norman St. Burn 3B 10
Norris St. Dar 4F 27
N. Bank Av. B'brn 3H 13
Northcliffe. Gt Har 1G 15
Northcote St. Dar 7F 27
Northcote St. Has 3B 28
Northfield Rd. Acc 4A 24
Northfield Rd. B'brn 5H 13
Northgate. B'brn 7H 13
North Pk. Av. Barfd 7A 4
North Rd. B'brn 4A 20
North Rd. Ross 3J 29
North St. Brclf 6G 7
North St. Burn 1B 10
North St. Clith 4F 3
North St. Col 2H 5
North St. Hap 5B 8
North St. Has 4C 28
North St. Nels 7A 4
North St. Pad 1B 8
North St. Raw 3G 29
North St. Ross 4A 30
N. Valley Rd. Col 3F 5
North Vw. Ross 4G 25
North Vw. Traw 6J 5
Northwood Clo. Burn 2J 9
Norton St. Hap 6B 8
Norwich St. B'brn 5J 13
Norwood Av. B'brn 3H 19
Norwood Av. Nels 6C 4
Notre Dame Gdns. B'brn 6J 13
Nottingham St. B'brn 1K 19
Nowell St. Gt Har 2H 15
Noyna St. Col 2H 5
Noyna Vw. Col 1H 5
Nursery Nook. E'hill 1H 27
Nuttall Av. Gt Har 3H 15
Nuttall St. Acc 7E 16
(Burnley Rd.)
Nuttall St. Acc 3D 22
(Mount St.)
Nuttall St. Bacup 2K 31
Nuttall St. B'brn 4G 19
Nuttall St. Burn 6C 10
Nuttall St. Ross 2H 29
Nuttall St. M. Acc 3D 22
(off Nuttall St.)
Nutter Rd. Acc 1D 22

O

Oak Av. Acc 4A 24
Oak Bank. Acc 5E 16
Oak Clo. Rish 7G 15
Oakdene Av. Acc 6F 17
Oaken Bank. Burn 6F 7
Oaken Clo. Bacup 2K 31
Oakenclough Rd. Bacup 2K 31
Oakeneaves Av. Burn 7J 9
Oakenhead Wood Old Rd. Ross 2D 28
Oakenhurst Rd. B'brn 1G 19
Oakfield Av. Acc 6F 17
Oakfield Av. Clay M 4K 15
Oakfield Cres. Osw 4A 22
Oakfield Rd. B'brn 6G 19
Oak Gro. Dar 3F 27
Oak Hill Clo. Acc 4D 22
Oakhurst Av. Acc 6F 17
Oaklands Av. Barfd 5A 4
Oaklands Dri. Ross 3E 28
Oakland St. Nels 1F 7
Oak La. Acc 3E 22
Oakley Rd. Ross 3F 29
Oakley St. Ross 4E 28
Oakmere Clo. B'brn 7G 19
Oak St. Acc 3D 22
Oak St. Bacup 2J 31
Oak St. B'brn 4J 13
Oak St. Brier 3C 6
Oak St. Burn 4H 9
Oak St. Clay M 5A 16
Oak St. Col 2H 5
Oak St. Dunn 1H 25
Oak St. Gt Har 1H 15
Oak St. Nels 7B 4
Oak St. Osw 5J 21
Oakwood Av. B'brn 3K 13
Oakwood Clo. Burn 6E 6
Oakwood Clo. Dar 1C 26
Oakwood Rd. Acc 5E 22
Oat St. Pad 3C 8
Oban Dri. B'brn 5B 20
Oban St. Burn 2D 10
Observatory Rd. B'brn 3K 19
O'er the Bridge. Hodd 4K 27
(off Hoddlesden Rd.)
Off Mt. Pleasant St. Osw 4K 21
(off Chapel St.)
Ogden Clo. Helm 6A 28
Ogden Dri. Helm 6A 28
O'Hagan Ct. Brier 3C 6
Old Bank La. B'brn 3K 19
(in two parts)
Old Bank St. B'brn 1H 19
Old Carr Mill St. Ross 7B 24
Old Farmside. B'brn 6G 19
Oldfield Av. Dar 2C 26
Old Gates Dri. B'brn 4C 18
Old Hall Dri. Hun 6G 17
Old Hall Sq. Wors 5H 11
Old Hall St. Burn 2B 10
Oldham St. Burn 6A 10
Old Kiln. Bacup 5F 31
Old Meadows Rd. Bacup 1H 31
Old Mill Dri. Col 4J 5
Old Mill St. B'brn 6J 13
Old Parsonage La. Pad 2A 8
Old Row. Ross 4E 28
Old School M. Stac 5E 30
Old Sta. Ct. Clith 5E 2
(off Station Rd.)
Old Station Ct. Clith 5E 2
(off Station Rd.)
Old St. Ross 4A 30
Olivant St. Burn 3H 9
Olive La. Dar 3E 26
Oliver St. Bacup 5E 30
Olive St. Bacup 5G 31
Olive Ter. Ross 7F 25
Olympia St. Burn 5D 10
Onchan Dri. Bacup 4K 31
Onchan Rd. B'brn 4H 19
Ontario Clo. B'brn 4D 12
Oozebooth Ter. B'brn 5H 13
Oozehead La. B'brn 7E 12
Opal St. B'brn 2H 13
Openshaw Dri. B'brn 3H 13
Oporto Clo. Burn 5K 9
Orange St. Acc 7C 16
Orchard Bri. Burn 4A 10
(off Active Way)
Orchard Clo. B'brn 7G 19
Orchard Dri. Osw 3A 22
Orchard Mill St. Dar 3D 26
Orchard St. Gt Har 3H 15
Orchard Ter. Traw 6J 5
Orchard, The. Burn 6H 9
(off Heather Bank)
Ordnance St. B'brn 7K 13
Oriole Clo. B'brn 6J 13
Orkney Clo. B'brn 5B 20
Ormerod Rd. Burn 4B 10
Ormerod St. Acc 4B 22
Ormerod St. Burn 5A 10
Ormerod St. Col 4F 5
Ormerod St. Has 5B 24
Ormerod St. Nels 1G 7
Ormerod St. Raw 3G 29
Ormerod St. Wors 6H 11
Ormerod Vw. Wors 5J 11
(off Ormerod St.)
Orpen Av. Burn 7A 10
Orpington Sq. Burn 6D 6
Orton Ct. Barfd 4A 4
Osborne Rd. B'brn 6E 12
Osborne Ter. Bacup 5F 31
Osborne Ter. Dar 3C 26
Osborne Ter. Raw 3E 28
Osborne Ter. Waterf 1B 30
Osborne Way. Has 4A 28
Oslo Rd. Burn 5G 9
Osprey Clo. B'brn 4G 13
Oswald St. Acc 2D 22
Oswald St. B'brn 6H 13
Oswald St. Burn 2A 10
Oswald St. Osw 5H 21
Oswald St. Rish 5H 15
Ottawa Clo. B'brn 4E 12
Otterburn Gro. Burn 4E 10
Otterburn Rd. B'brn 6F 19
Ottershaw Gdns. B'brn 4H 13
Ouseburn Rd. B'brn 5F 19
Outram La. B'brn 3H 13
Outwood Rd. Burn 6C 10
Owen Ct. Clay M 4A 16
Owen St. Acc 1C 22
Owen St. Burn 5F 9
Owen St. Dar 2E 26
Owlet Hall Rd. Dar 3C 26
Oxford Av. Clay M 4B 16
Oxford Clo. B'brn 1J 19
Oxford Clo. Pad 4C 8
Oxford Dri. B'brn 4D 20
Oxford Pl. Burn 5C 10
Oxford Rd. Burn 5C 10
Oxford Rd. Nels 6D 4
Oxford St. Acc 2C 22
Oxford St. Brier 4C 6
Oxford St. Col 3H 5
Oxford St. Dar 1D 26
Ox Hey. Clay M 3A 16
Oxhey Clo. Burn 4G 11

P

Paddock La. B'brn 4C 20
Paddock St. Osw 4K 21
Paddock, The. B'brn 4D 12
Paddock, The. Burn 6C 6
Paddock, The. Osw 4K 21
Padgate Pl. Burn 6G 9
Padiham Rd. Burn 3E 8
(in two parts)
Pagefield Cres. Clith 6G 3
Paignton Rd. B'brn 5G 13
Paisley St. Burn 5J 9
Palace Gdns. Burn 3G 9
Palace St. Burn 3H 9
Palatine Rd. B'brn 7F 13
Palatine Sq. Burn 5K 9
Pall Mall. B'brn 7B 12
Palmerston St. Pad 3C 8
Palmer St. B'brn 6G 13
Palm St. B'brn 5K 13
Palm St. Burn 5J 9
(off Burdett St.)
Pansy St. N. Acc 1C 22
Pansy St. S. Acc 1C 22
Parade, The. Has 5A 28
Paradise La. B'brn 1H 19
(off King St.)
Paradise St. Acc 3C 22
Paradise St. Barfd 3B 4
Paradise St. B'brn 1G 19
Paradise St. Burn 4A 10
Paradise St. Ross 3B 30
Paradise Ter. B'brn 1H 19
Paris. Rams 4A 14
Parish St. Pad 1B 8
Park Av. Barfd 1D 6
Park Av. B'brn 6G 13
Park Av. Burn 6K 9
Park Av. Chat 1K 3
Park Av. Clith 4E 2
Park Av. Gt Har 1J 15
Park Av. Has 4B 28
Park Bri. Rd. Burn 7E 10
Park Cres. Acc 4B 22
Park Cres. Bacup 5H 31
Park Cres. B'brn 6F 13
Park Cres. Has 4B 28
Parkdale Gdns. B'brn 7G 19
Park Dri. Brier 4D 6
Park Dri. Nels 2G 7
Parker Av. Clith 7E 2
Parker La. Burn 5B 10
Parker St. Acc 6F 23
(Hollins La.)
Parker St. Acc 7F 17
(South St.)
Parker St. Brclf 6G 7
Parker St. Burn 4B 10
(off Barnes St.)
Parker St. Burn 4B 10
(Kingsway, in two parts)
Parker St. Col 3F 5
Parker St. Nels 6C 4
Parker St. Rish 5G 15
Pk. Farm Rd. B'brn 6A 18
Parkinson Fold. Has 7C 28
Parkinson St. B'brn 3E 18
Parkinson St. Burn 6B 10
Parkinson St. Has 2A 28
Parkinson Ter. Traw 6J 5
Parklands. Has 4B 28
Parklands Way. B'brn 5E 18
Parkland Vw. Burn 7K 9
Park La. Brier 4D 6
Park La. Gt Har 1H 15
Park La. Osw 5K 21
Pk. Lee Rd. B'brn 4H 19
Park Pl. B'brn 2E 18
(off Spring La.)
Park Pl. Fen 6A 18
Park Rd. Acc 2B 22
Park Rd. Bacup 4H 31
Park Rd. B'brn 2H 19
Park Rd. Dar 7F 27
Park Rd. Gt Har 1J 15
Park Rd. Pad 3B 8
Park Rd. Rish 6H 15
Park Rd. Waterf 4B 30
Park Rd. Ind. Est. Bacup 4H 31
Park Side Rd. Nels 1J 7
Park St. Acc 2D 22
Park St. Barfd 4A 4
Park St. Clith 7E 2
Park St. Gt Har 2J 15
Park St. Has 2B 28
Park St. E. Barfd 4B 4
Park Ter. B'brn 5G 13
Park Vw. Brier 2C 6
(off Pk View. Clo.)
Park Vw. Chu 1B 22
Park Vw. Pad 2B 8
Park Vw. Ross 7G 25
Park Vw. Waterf 4B 30
Pk. View Clo. Brier 2C 6
Park Way. Col 2F 5
Parkwood Av. Burn 3J 9
Pk. Wood Dri. Ross 3E 28
Parkwood Rd. B'brn 4A 20
Parliament St. Burn 6B 10
Parliament St. Col 3H 5
Parliament St. Dar 4E 26
Parramatta St. Ross 3G 29

Parrock St. *Nels* 7B 4
Parrock St. *Ross* 5G 25
Parsonage Dri. *Brier* 4D 6
Parsonage Rd. *B'brn* 4B 14
Parsonage St. *Chu* 3K 21
Parsonage St. *Col* 4F 5
Partridge Dri. *Acc* 7G 23
Partridge Hill. *Pad* 1C 8
Partridge Hill St. *Pad* 2C 8
Partridge Wlk. *Burn* 5H 9
Pasture Clo. *Burn* 7K 9
Pasturegate. *Burn* 6J 9
Pasturegate Av. *Burn* 6J 9
Pasture La. *Barfd* 4A 4
Pastures, The. *B'brn* 4D 12
Paterson St. *B'brn* 2H 19
Patrick Cres. *Ross* 3J 29
Patten St. *B'brn* 3B 20
Patten St. *Col* 4G 5
Patterdale Av. *B'brn* 5B 20
Patterdale Av. *Osw* 3J 21
Patterdale Clo. *Burn* 5D 6
Paulhan St. *Burn* 7C 6
Pave La. *Traw* 6J 5
Paxton St. *Acc* 2C 22
Paythorne Av. *Burn* 5E 10
Peabody St. *Dar* 3E 26
Peace St. *Burn* 5J 9
Pearl St. *Acc* 3A 22
Pearl St. *B'brn* 3J 13
Pearson St. *B'brn* 1G 19
Peart St. *Burn* 7C 6
Peebles Gro. *Burn* 7J 9
Peelbank Rd. *Osw* 4G 21
Peel Clo. *B'brn* 5H 19
Peel Dri. *Bacup* 4J 31
Peel Gdns. *Col* 3F 5
Peel Mt. *B'brn* 4D 20
Peel Mt. Clo. *B'brn* 4E 20
Peel Pk. Av. *Acc* 1E 22
Peel Pk. Av. *Clith* 6F 3
Peel Pk. Clo. *Acc* 1E 22
Peel Pk. Clo. *Clith* 6F 3
Peel Pl. *Barfd* 2C 4
Peel Retail Pk. *B'brn* 1C 20
Peel Rd. *Col* 4E 4
Peel St. *Acc* 2D 22
Peel St. *B'brn* 3F 19
Peel St. *Clith* 5F 3
(in two parts)
Peel St. *Has* 2A 28
Peel St. *Osw* 5J 21
Peel St. *Pad* 2C 8
Peel St. *Raw* 3J 29
Pelham St. *B'brn* 6K 13
Pemberton St. *B'brn* 3H 13
Pembroke St. *Acc* 2E 22
Pembroke St. *Bacup* 4H 31
Pembroke St. *B'brn* 2H 19
Pembroke St. *Burn* 1C 10
Pendle Av. *Bacup* 2J 31
Pendle Av. *Clay M* 3A 16
Pendle Bri. *Burn* 6A 6
Pendle Clo. *Bacup* 3J 31
Pendle Clo. *Clith* 5F 3
Pendle Dri. *B'brn* 3J 19
Pendle Heritage Cen. 4B 4
Pendle Ho. *B'brn* 7J 13
Pendlehurst St. *Burn* 6K 9
Pendle Ind. Est. *Nels* 2G 7
Pendlemist Vw. *Col* 5F 5
Pendle Mt. *Clith* 5F 3
Pendle Rd. *Brier* 4B 6
Pendle Rd. *Clith* 5F 3
Pendle Rd. *Gt Har* 1K 15
Pendleside. *Brier* 1B 6
Pendle St. *Acc* 3B 22
Pendle St. *Barfd* 6A 4
Pendle St. *B'brn* 7K 13
Pendle St. *Nels* 7A 4
Pendle St. *Pad* 3C 8
(in two parts)
Pendleton Av. *Acc* 4A 22
Pendleton Av. *Ross* 1G 29
Pendle Trad. Est. *Chat* 1J 3
Pendle Vw. *Alt* 4B 16
Pendle Way. *Burn* 2J 9
Penistone St. *Burn* 4J 9
(off Shale St.)

Pennine Cres. *Brier* 4D 6
Pennine Ho. *Has* 2B 28
Pennine Rd. *Bacup* 4J 31
Pennine Way. *Brier* 4D 6
Penny Ho. La. *Acc* 1D 22
Penny St. *B'brn* 7H 13
Penrith Cres. *Col* 5E 4
Penrith Rd. *Col* 5D 4
Penshaw Clo. *B'brn* 3H 13
Pentland Ho. *Has* 2B 28
(off Pleasant St.)
Penzance St. *B'brn* 3E 18
Percival St. *Acc* 2A 22
Percival St. *B'brn* 5J 13
Percival St. *Dar* 2D 26
Percy St. *Acc* 2E 22
Percy St. *B'brn* 3E 18
Percy St. *Col* 2H 5
Percy St. *Nels* 2E 6
Percy St. *Osw* 3G 21
Peregrine Dri. *Dar* 2B 26
Peridot Clo. *B'brn* 2J 13
Peronne Cres. *B'brn* 3C 20
Perry St. *Dar* 3E 26
Persia St. *Acc* 2A 22
Perth St. *Acc* 3B 22
Perth St. *B'brn* 2F 19
Perth St. *Burn* 5J 9
Perth St. *Nels* 7C 4
Peter Birtwistle Clo. *Col* 3H 5
Peter Grime Row. *Acc* 5G 17
Peter St. *Acc* 3B 22
Peter St. *Barfd* 4A 4
Peter St. *B'brn* 6K 13
Peter St. *Col* 4H 5
Peter St. *Ross* 3G 29
Petre Cres. *Rish* 7G 15
Petrel Clo. *B'brn* 4G 13
Petre Rd. *Clay M* 6K 15
Pheasantford Grn. *Burn* 2C 10
Pheasantford St. *Burn* 2C 10
Philips Rd. *B'brn* 1A 20
(in two parts)
Philip St. *Dar* 4F 27
Phillips La. *Col* 4E 4
Phillipstown. *Ross* 1A 30
Phoenix Pk. *B'brn* 1A 20
Phoenix Way. *Burn* 5H 9
Piccadilly Rd. *Burn* 5K 9
Piccadilly Sq. *Burn* 5K 9
Piccadilly St. *Has* 2B 28
Pickering Fold. *B'brn* 6K 19
Pickering St. *Brier* 4C 6
Pickles St. *Burn* 3J 9
Pickup Fold. *Dar* 6G 27
Pickup Fold Rd. *Dar* 6G 27
Pickup Rd. *Rish* 7F 15
Pickup St. *Acc* 4A 22
(in two parts)
Pickup St. *Bacup* 3H 31
Pickup St. *B'brn* 7K 13
Pickup St. *Clay M* 4A 16
Picton St. *B'brn* 5E 18
Pierce Clo. *Pad* 1B 8
Piercy Higher Mt. *Ross* 2B 30
Piercy Mdw. *Ross* 2B 30
Piercy Mt. *Ross* 2B 30
(off Piercy Rd.)
Piercy Rd. *Ross* 2B 30
Piercy Ter. *Ross* 2B 30
(off Piercy Rd.)
Pilgrim St. *Nels* 3G 7
Pilkington Dri. *Clay M* 4B 16
Pilkington St. *B'brn* 1H 19
Pilling Av. *Acc* 6F 23
Pilling Barn La.
  Ross & Bacup 2D 30
Pilling St. *Has* 6B 24
Pilling St. *Ross* 5B 30
Pilmuir Rd. *B'brn* 3H 19
Pilot St. *Acc* 1C 22
Pimlico Ind. Area. *Clith* 2E 2
Pimlico Link Rd. *Clith* 2F 3
Pimlico Rd. *Clith* 4F 3
Pinder Clo. *Wadd* 1B 2
Pinder St. *Nels* 6C 4
Pine Clo. *Rish* 7G 15
Pine Cres. *Osw* 6A 22
Pine Gro. *Clith* 6D 2
Pine St. *Bacup* 4J 31

Pine St. *B'brn* 5K 13
Pine St. *Burn* 5C 10
Pine St. *Dar* 5F 27
Pine St. *Has* 2C 28
Pine St. *Nels* 1G 7
Pinewood. *B'brn* 5C 18
Pinewood Dri. *Acc* 1E 22
Pinfold. *Brier* 3B 4
Pinfold Pl. *Nels* 7E 4
Pink Pl. *B'brn* 2E 18
Pink St. *Burn* 4H 9
Pinner La. *Ross* 5F 25
Pinner Sq. *Ross* 5F 25
Piper Lea. *Ross* 4C 30
Pippin St. *Bacup* 4H 31
Pitt St. *Pad* 2C 8
Pitville St. *Dar* 2D 26
Place De Criel. *Nels* 1E 6
(off Manchester Rd.)
Plain Pl. *B'brn* 2H 19
Plane St. *Bacup* 1H 31
Plane St. *B'brn* 5K 13
Plane Tree Clo. *Burn* 7J 9
Plane Tree Hill. *Burn* 7E 6
(off Marsden Rd.)
Plane Tree Rd. *B'brn* 5K 13
Plantation Mill. *Bacup* 4H 31
Plantation Rd. *Acc* 2E 22
Plantation Rd. *B'brn* 4E 18
Plantation Sq. *Acc* 2E 22
Plantation St. *Acc* 3D 22
Plantation St. *Bacup* 5E 30
Plantation St. *Burn* 3B 10
Plantation St. *Nels* 7C 4
Plantation St. *Ross* 3H 29
Plant St. *Osw* 5J 21
Platt Clo. *Acc* 3B 22
Pleasant Pl. *Burn* 5A 10
Pleasant Vw. *Bacup* 6E 30
Pleasant Vw. *B'brn* 3K 19
Pleasant Vw. *Hodd* 4K 27
Pleasant Vw. *Ross* 4B 30
Pleasington Clo. *B'brn* 1E 18
Pleasington Gro. *Burn* 5E 10
Pleasington Rd. *B'brn* 7A 12
Pleasington St. *B'brn* 1E 18
Pleck Farm Av. *B'brn* 4H 13
Pleckgate Fold. *B'brn* 3G 13
Pleckgate Rd. *B'brn* 4H 13
Pleck Rd. *Acc* 2D 22
Plover St. *Acc* 4J 9
Plover St. *Burn* 5B 10
Plover Vw. *Burn* 4J 9
(off Plover St.)
Plumbe St. *Burn* 5B 10
Pocklington St. *Acc* 6E 22
Poets Rd. *Burn* 3E 8
Poland St. *Acc* 2A 22
Pole La. *Dar* 6G 27
Police St. *Dar* 4D 26
Pollard Row. *Fence* 1A 6
Pollard St. *Acc* 1D 22
Pollard St. *Burn* 5J 9
Pomfret St. *B'brn* 2G 19
Pomfret St. *Burn* 4K 9
Pont St. *Nels* 2E 6
Poole St. *B'brn* 3B 20
Poplar Av. *Gt Har* 1J 15
Poplar Clo. *Osw* 5A 22
Poplar Clo. *Rish* 7G 15
Poplar St. *B'brn* 5J 13
Poplar St. *Has* 2B 28
Poplar St. *Nels* 7C 4
Poplar Ter. *Ross* 6F 25
Portal Gro. *Burn* 4G 9
Porter St. *Acc* 2A 22
Portland St. *Acc* 2B 22
Portland St. *Barfd* 5A 4
Portland St. *B'brn* 2F 19
Portland St. *Col* 3J 5
Portland St. *Dar* 7F 27
Portland St. *Nels* 1E 6
Portree Cres. *B'brn* 5C 20
Portsmouth Av. *Burn* 7F 7
Post Office St. *Ross* 5G 25
(off Major St.)
Post Office Yd. *Col* 3H 5
(off Market Pl.)
Pot Ho. La. *Dar* 2G 27
Pot Ho. La. *Osw* 7K 21
Poulton Av. *Acc* 7B 16

Powell St. *Burn* 6K 9
Powell St. *Dar* 3E 26
Powys Clo. *Has* 4B 28
Prairie Cres. *Burn* 7C 6
Pratt St. *Burn* 1B 10
Premier Bus. Pk. *Gt Har* 1J 15
Prescott St. *Burn* 5D 10
Preston New Rd.
  Sam & Mel B 3A 12
(in two parts)
Preston St. *Dar* 2D 26
Prestwich St. *Burn* 6J 9
Priestfield Av. *Col* 3E 4
Priestley Nook. *Acc* 3D 22
(off Royds St.)
Primative Ter. *Ross* 5F 25
Primet Bri. *Col* 4F 5
Primet Bus. Cen. *Col* 4E 4
Primet Heights. *Col* 5E 4
(off Wackersall Rd.)
Primet Hill. *Col* 4F 5
Primet St. *Col* 4F 5
Primrose Bank. *Bacup* 5E 30
(off Tunstead Rd.)
Primrose Bank. *Bacup* 5D 30
(off Waterbarn La.)
Primrose Bank. *B'brn* 6J 13
Primrose Clo. *B'brn* 3E 18
Primrose Ct. *B'brn* 7J 13
(off Primrose Dri.)
Primrose Dri. *B'brn* 7J 13
Primrose Hill. *Col* 3J 5
Primrose Hill. *Mel* 1D 12
Primrose Rd. *Clith* 7D 2
Primrose St. *Acc* 4B 22
Primrose St. *Bacup* 5E 30
Primrose St. *Brier* 4C 6
(off Halifax Rd.)
Primrose St. *Burn* 1D 10
Primrose St. *Clith* 6D 2
Primrose St. *Dar* 5F 27
Primrose Ter. *B'brn* 3E 18
Primrose Ter. *Dar* 5F 27
Primrose Way. *Chu* 1K 21
Primula Dri. *Lwr D* 6K 19
Prince Lee Meadows. *Dar* 5F 27
Princess Av. *Clith* 4F 3
Princess Gdns. *B'brn* 6A 18
Princess St. *Acc* 2A 22
Princess St. *Bacup* 3H 31
Princess St. *B'brn* 3F 19
Princess St. *Chu* 2K 21
Princess St. *Col* 3F 5
Princess St. *Gt Har* 2J 15
Princess St. *Has* 3B 28
Princess St. *Nels* 2E 6
Princess St. *Pad* 2A 8
Prince's St. *Rish* 6G 15
Princes St. *Rish* 1G 19
Princess Way. *Burn* 3A 10
Prince St. *Burn* 5K 9
Prince St. *Dar* 4D 26
Pringle St. *B'brn* 2J 19
Prinny Hill Rd. *Has* 2A 28
Printers Fold. *Burn* 4D 8
Printshop La. *Dar* 7E 26
Prior's Clo. *B'brn* 6D 12
Priory Clo. *B'brn* 4D 20
Priory Clo. *Ross* 3A 30
Priory Ct. *Burn* 7C 10
Priory Dri. *Dar* 4G 27
Priory Grange. *Dar* 5G 27
Priory Pl. *Dar* 5G 27
Priory St. *Nels* 7C 4
Pritchard St. *B'brn* 3G 19
Pritchard St. *Burn* 6K 9
Private La. *Has* 5C 28
Procter St. *B'brn* 2J 19
Proctor Clo. *Brier* 4G 7
Proctor Cft. *Traw* 6J 5
Progress Av. *B'brn* 5K 13
Progress Rd. *Whit I* 5C 4
Progress St. *Dar* 4F 27
Prospect Av. *Dar* 3C 26
Prospect Hill. *Has* 3A 28
Prospect Hill. *Raw* 2G 29
(off Prospect Rd.)
Prospect Rd. *Ross* 2G 29
Prospect St. *Gt Har* 2J 15
Prospect St. *Ross* 4B 30

Prospect Ter. *Bacup* 6G **31**
Prospect Ter. *Barfd* 4A **4**
Prospect Ter. *Hun* 5F **17**
(off Enfield Rd.)
Prospect Ter. *Ross* 4B **30**
(off Prospect Clo.)
Prospect Ter. *Ross* 7F **25**
(off East St.)
Providence St. *B'brn* 4K **13**
Prunella Dri. *Lwr D* 6K **19**
Pump St. *B'brn* 1F **19**
Pump St. *Burn* 4K **9**
Pump St. *Clith* 5D **2**
Punstock La. *Dar* 5D **26**
Punstock Rd. *Dar* 4D **26**

Q

Quakerfields. *Dar* 3E **26**
Quaker La. *Dar* 3E **26**
Quarry Bank St. *Burn* 3H **9**
Quarry Farm Ct. *Chat* 1K **3**
Quarry Hill Nature Reserve. ..3G **7**
Quarry St. *Acc* 3D **22**
Quarry St. *Bacup* 3J **31**
Quarry St. *B'brn* 7J **13**
Quarry St. *Hap* 5K **17**
Quarry St. *Pad* 1C **8**
Quebec Rd. *B'brn* 4E **12**
Queen Anne St. *Has* 2A **28**
Queen Elizabeth Cres. *Acc* ..3D **22**
Queensberry Rd. *Burn* 5K **9**
Queensborough Rd. *Acc* 1C **22**
Queens Clo. *Clith* 6E **2**
Queen's Dri. *Osw* 5A **22**
Queensgate. *Nels* 2D **6**
Queen's Lancashire Way.
  Burn 4A **10**
Queen's Pk. *B'brn* 1K **19**
Queen's Pk. Rd. *Burn* 2C **10**
Queen's Rd. *Acc* 1C **22**
Queen's Rd. *B'brn* 5A **20**
Queens Rd. *Burn* 7C **6**
Queens Rd. *Clith* 6E **2**
Queens Rd. *Dar* 7F **27**
Queens Rd. W. *Chu* 7A **16**
Queen's Sq. *Hodd* 4K **27**
Queen's Sq. *Ross* 3G **29**
Queen's Ter. *Bacup* 5G **31**
Queen's Ter. *B'brn* 4E **18**
Queen's Ter. *Pad* 2B **8**
Queen's Ter. *Ross* 3G **29**
(off Queen St.)
Queen St. *Acc* 2D **22**
Queen St. *Bacup* 3H **31**
Queen St. *Barfd* 4A **4**
Queen St. *Brclf* 6G **7**
Queen St. *Burn* 5A **10**
Queen St. *Clay M* 4A **16**
Queen St. *Clith* 5C **2**
Queen St. *Col* 4F **5**
Queen St. *Dar* 3D **26**
Queen St. *Gt Har* 2H **15**
Queen St. *Hodd* 4K **27**
Queen St. *Nels* 7B **4**
Queen St. *Osw* 4K **21**
Queen St. *Pad* 2B **8**
Queen St. *Ross* 3G **29**
Queen St. *Stac* 5E **30**
Queens Wlk. *Gt Har* 2J **15**
Queensway. *B'brn* 6D **18**
Queensway. *Chu* 1A **22**
Queensway. *Clith* 6E **2**
Queensway. *Ross* 4A **30**
Queensway. *Wadd* 1B **2**
Queen Victoria Rd. *Burn* 1C **10**
(Briercliffe Rd.)
Queen Victoria Rd. *Burn* 3C **10**
(Ormerod Rd.)
Queen Victoria St. *B'brn* 3E **18**

R

Rabbit Wlk. *Burn* 7C **10**
Raby St. *Ross* 3G **29**
Radclyffe St. *Clith* 4E **2**
Radfield Av. *Dar* 5E **26**
Radfield Head. *Dar* 5D **26**

Radfield Rd. *Dar* 5D **26**
Radford Bank Gdns. *Dar* 5E **26**
Radford Gdns. *Dar* 6E **26**
Radford St. *Dar* 5E **26**
Radnor Av. *Burn* 3F **9**
Radnor Clo. *Osw* 4H **21**
Radnor St. *Acc* 1C **22**
Raeburn Av. *Burn* 7K **9**
Raedale Av. *Burn* 5C **6**
Raglan Rd. *Burn* 5K **9**
Raglan St. *Col* 4G **5**
Raglan St. *Nels* 7A **4**
Railgate. *Bacup* 5K **31**
Railton Av. *B'brn* 5D **18**
Railway Gro. *B'brn* 5K **13**
Railway Rd. *B'brn* 7H **13**
Railway Rd. *Dar* 4E **26**
Railway Rd. *Has* 1B **28**
Railway St. *Bacup* 5D **30**
Railway St. *Brier* 4C **6**
Railway St. *Nels* 3A **10**
Railway St. *Nels* 1F **7**
Railway Ter. *Brier* 4B **6**
Railway Ter. *Gt Har* 3H **15**
Railway Ter. *Ross* 4F **29**
Railway Vw. *Acc* 2C **22**
Railway Vw. *B'brn* 3E **18**
Railway Vw. *Brier* 3C **6**
(off Wesley St.)
Railway Vw. Av. *Clith* 4E **2**
Railway Vw. Rd. *Clith* 4E **2**
Rake Foot. *Has* 1B **28**
Rakehead La. *Bacup* 5D **30**
Rakes Bri. *Lwr D* 6K **19**
Rakes Ho. Rd. *Nels* 6B **4**
Raleigh St. *Pad* 3C **8**
Ralph St. *Acc* 7D **16**
Ramsbottom St. *Acc* 1C **22**
Ramsbottom St. *Ross* 5A **30**
Ramsey Av. *Bacup* 4J **31**
Ramsey Gro. *Burn* 7D **6**
Ramsey Rd. *B'brn* 4G **19**
Ramsgreave Av. *B'brn* 2G **13**
Ramsgreave Dri. *B'brn* 3F **13**
Ramsgreave Rd. *Rams* 1G **13**
Randall St. *Burn* 1C **10**
Randal St. *B'brn* 6H **13**
Randolph St. *B'brn* 1K **19**
Random Row. *Bacup* 5E **30**
Ranger St. *Acc* 3B **22**
Rankin Dri. *Hodd* 5J **27**
Rannoch Dri. *B'brn* 4C **18**
Ratcliffe Fold. *Has* 2B **28**
Ratcliffe St. *Dar* 4F **27**
Ratcliffe St. *Has* 2B **28**
Raven Av. *Ross* 6B **28**
Raven Cft. *Has* 5B **28**
Ravenglass Clo. *B'brn* 4K **19**
Ravenoak La. *Wors* 5J **11**
Raven Pk. *Has* 5B **28**
Raven Rd. *B'brn* 7E **12**
Ravenscroft Clo. *B'brn* 3K **13**
Ravens Gro. *Burn* 5D **6**
Raven St. *Nels* 7C **4**
Ravenswing Av. *B'brn* 5E **12**
Ravens Wood. *B'brn* 7E **12**
Ravenswood. *Gt Har* 1G **15**
Rawcliffe St. *Burn* 4B **10**
Rawlinson St. *Dar* 7F **27**
Raws Ct. *Burn* 4B **10**
(off Bank Pde.)
Rawson Av. *Acc* 4B **22**
Rawson St. *Burn* 1C **10**
Rawsthorne Av. *Has* 3B **28**
Rawstorne St. *B'brn* 1F **19**
Raw St. *Burn* 4B **10**
(off Bank Pde.)
Rawtenstall Rd. *Has* 4C **28**
Raygill Av. *Burn* 7J **9**
Raynor St. *B'brn* 7G **13**
Ray St. *Brier* 4B **6**
Reading Clo. *B'brn* 1K **19**
Read St. *Clay M* 6B **16**
Rectory Clo. *Dar* 5G **27**
Rectory Clo. *Ross* 4A **30**
Rectory Rd. *Burn* 3A **10**
Redearth Rd. *Dar* 4E **26**
Redgate Clo. *Burn* 7C **10**
Redlam. *B'brn* 2E **18**

Redlam Brow. *B'brn* 2F **19**
Red La. *Col* 2C **4**
Red Lees Av. *Burn* 6G **11**
Red Lees Rd. *Burn* 5F **11**
Red Lion St. *Burn* 5B **10**
Redman Rd. *Burn* 5C **6**
Redness Clo. *Nels* 3F **7**
Red Rake. *B'brn* 5F **13**
Red Rose Ct. *Clay M* 6K **15**
Redruth St. *Burn* 4J **9**
Redscar St. *Col* 5E **4**
Red Shell La. *Osw* 7G **21**
  (in two parts)
Red Spar Rd. *Burn* 7E **6**
Redvers Rd. *Dar* 1C **26**
Redvers St. *Burn* 1C **10**
Redwood Dri. *Ross* 5F **29**
Reedfield. *Burn* 5D **6**
Reedley Av. *Nels* 2G **7**
Reedley Dri. *Burn* 5C **6**
  (in two parts)
Reedley Gro. *Burn* 6C **6**
Reedley Mt. *Burn* 5C **6**
Reedley Rd. *Brier & Burn* ..5C **6**
Reeds Clo. *Ross* 6G **25**
Reedsholme Clo. *Ross* 6G **25**
Reeds La. *Ross* 6G **25**
  (in two parts)
Reed St. *Bacup* 2J **31**
Reed St. *Burn* 6B **10**
Reedyford Rd. *Nels* 6A **4**
Reeford Gro. *Clith* 6D **2**
Reeth Way. *Acc* 4A **22**
  (off Lynton Rd.)
Regent Av. *Col* 2H **5**
Regent Clo. *Pad* 3B **8**
Regent Pl. *Nels* 6B **4**
Regent Rd. *Chu* 1A **22**
Regent St. *Bacup* 3J **31**
Regent St. *B'brn* 7H **13**
Regent St. *Brier* 4C **6**
Regent St. *Has* 2A **28**
Regent St. *Nels & Col* 7B **4**
Regent St. *Wadd* 1B **2**
Regents Vw. *B'brn* 3H **13**
Reginald St. *Col* 3E **4**
Rendel St. *Burn* 3H **9**
Rennie St. *Burn* 5D **10**
Renshaw St. *Burn* 1C **10**
Reservoir St. *Burn* 6A **10**
Reservoir St. *Dar* 4D **26**
Revidge Rd. *B'brn* 6E **12**
Rewe Clo. *B'brn* 5F **19**
Rexington Bldgs. *Burn* 5H **9**
Reynolds St. *Burn* 7K **9**
Rhoda St. *Nels* 1G **7**
Rhoden Rd. *Osw* 6J **21**
Rhodes Av. *B'brn* 4G **13**
Rhodes Av. *Ross* 6A **28**
Rhuddlan Clo. *Has* 4B **28**
Rhyddings St. *Osw* 4K **21**
Rhyl Av. *B'brn* 5H **13**
Ribble Av. *Burn* 7D **6**
Ribble Av. *Dar* 1C **26**
Ribble Av. *Gt Har* 1K **15**
Ribble Bus. Pk. *B'brn* 7A **14**
Ribble Ho. *B'brn* 7J **13**
  (off Primrose Bank)
Ribble La. *Chat* 1K **3**
Ribblesdale Av. *Acc* 7C **16**
Ribblesdale Av. *Clith* 4E **2**
Ribblesdale Av. *Wilp* 1C **14**
Ribblesdale Pl. *Barfd* 3B **4**
Ribblesdale Pl. *B'brn* 7F **13**
Ribblesdale St. *Burn* 2C **10**
Ribble St. *Bacup* 5J **31**
Ribble St. *B'brn* 6H **13**
Ribble St. *Pad* 2C **8**
Ribbleton Dri. *Acc* 7C **16**
Ribble Way. *Clith* 5C **2**
Ribchester Av. *Burn* 5E **10**
Ribchester Rd. *Clay D* 2A **14**
  (in two parts)
Ribchester Way. *Brier* 5E **6**
Richard St. *B'brn* 1G **19**
Richard St. *Brier* 4C **6**
Richard St. *Burn* 5C **10**
Richmond Av. *Acc* 3C **22**
Richmond Av. *Burn* 6G **11**
Richmond Av. *Has* 4C **28**

Richmond Cres. *B'brn* 3D **20**
Richmond Hill. *B'brn* 7H **13**
Richmond Hill St. *Acc* 3B **22**
Richmond Ind. Est. *Acc* 3C **22**
Richmond Pk. *Dar* 3E **26**
Richmond Rd. *Acc* 4A **22**
Richmond Rd. *Nels* 1D **6**
Richmonds Ct. *Col* 3H **5**
  (off New Ho. St.)
Richmond St. *Acc* 3B **22**
Richmond St. *Burn* 5K **9**
Richmond Ter. *B'brn* 7H **13**
Richmond Ter. *Clith* 6D **2**
Richmond Ter. *Dar* 3E **26**
Rickard Rd. *Nels* 3F **7**
Riddings Av. *Burn* 4G **11**
Ridehalgh St. *Col* 5E **4**
Ridge Av. *Burn* 3D **10**
Ridge Ct. *Burn* 4D **10**
Ridge Rd. *Burn* 4C **10**
Ridge Row. *Burn* 4E **10**
Ridge, The. *Nels* 3F **7**
Ridgeway. *Barfd* 5A **4**
Ridgeway. *Gt Har* 1G **15**
Ridgeway Av. *B'brn* 5K **19**
Ridgeways. *Has* 3C **28**
Ridgeway, The. *Nels* 2E **6**
Riding Barn St. *Chu* 2A **22**
Ridings, The. *Burn* 2J **9**
Riding St. *Burn* 5K **9**
Rifle St. *Has* 3B **28**
Rigby St. *Col* 4F **5**
Rigby St. *Nels* 1E **6**
Rigg St. *Nels* 1F **7**
Riley St. *Acc* 4C **22**
Riley St. *Bacup* 1H **31**
Riley St. *Brier* 4C **6**
Riley St. *Burn* 6C **10**
Rimington Av. *Acc* 5B **22**
Rimington Av. *Burn* 5E **10**
Rimington Av. *Col* 2F **5**
Rimington Clo. *B'brn* 3J **19**
Rimington Pl. *Nels* 7E **4**
Rings St. *Love* 2G **25**
Ringstone Cres. *Nels* 1J **7**
Ringwood Clo. *Acc* 6C **16**
Ripon Rd. *Osw* 3H **21**
Ripon St. *B'brn* 1K **19**
Ripon St. *Nels* 2E **6**
Risedale Gro. *B'brn* 6D **18**
Rishton Golf Course. 1G **21**
Rishton Rd. *Clay M* 4K **15**
Rising Bri. Rd. *Acc & Has* ..5A **24**
River Dri. *Pad* 2C **8**
River Lea Gdns. *Clith* 5F **3**
Riverside. *Clith* 5B **2**
Riverside Mill. *Col* 4E **4**
Riverside Wlk. *Helm* 6A **28**
River St. *Bacup* 4H **31**
River St. *B'brn* 1J **19**
River St. *Col* 4G **5**
River St. *Dar* 3D **26**
River St. *Traw* 5K **5**
Riversway Dri. *Lwr D* 7J **19**
River Vw. *Barfd* 5A **4**
  (off River Way)
River Way. *Barfd* 5A **4**
Rivington St. *B'brn* 4A **20**
Roberts St. *Nels* 1G **7**
Roberts St. *Raw* 2G **29**
Robert St. *Acc* 1D **22**
Robert St. *B'brn* 2H **19**
Robert St. *Col* 3H **5**
Robert St. *Dar* 3D **26**
Robert St. *Gt Har* 1J **15**
Robert St. *Osw* 5J **21**
Robert St. *Waterf* 3B **30**
Robin Bank Rd. *Dar* 3E **26**
Robin Ho. La. *Brclf* 6K **7**
Robinson La. *Brier* 5A **6**
Robinson St. *B'brn* 5K **13**
Robinson St. *Burn* 1B **10**
Robinson St. *Chat* 1K **3**
Robinson St. *Col* 3F **5**
Robson St. *Brier* 3C **6**
Rochdale Rd. *Bacup* 4J **31**
Rochester Dri. *Burn* 6D **6**
Rock Bri. Fold. *Ross* 1A **30**
Rockcliffe Av. *Bacup* 4G **31**
Rockcliffe Dri. *Bacup* 4G **31**

Rockcliffe Rd. *Bacup* 4H **31**	Rosewood Ct. *Burn* 5F **9**
Rockcliffe St. *B'brn* 3H **19**	(off Owen St.)
Rockfield Rd. *Acc* 2E **22**	Rossall Clo. *Pad* 4C **8**
Rockfield St. *B'brn* 2H **19**	Rossall Ter. *B'brn* 4H **19**
Rock Hall Rd. *Has* 1B **28**	Rossendale Av. *Burn* 7J **9**
Rock La. *Burn* 7C **10**	**Rossendale Golf Course.** 6B **28**
Rock La. *Traw* 6K **5**	**Rossendale Mus.** 3E **28**
(Church St.)	Rossendale Rd. *Burn* 5G **9**
Rock La. *Traw* 5K **5**	Rossendale Rd. Ind. Est.
(Keighley Rd.)	*Burn* 6G **9**
Rockliffe. *Ross* 2G **29**	Rosser Ct. *Nels* 1F **7**
Rockliffe La. *Bacup* 4J **31**	Rossetti Av. *Burn* 7A **10**
Rock St. *Clith* 5E **2**	Ross St. *Brier* 4C **6**
Rock St. *Has* 2B **28**	Ross St. *Dar* 7E **26**
Rock Ter. *Ross* 5G **25**	Rostron's Bldgs. *Ross* 4K **29**
Rock Vw. *Ross* 5A **30**	(off Bacup Rd.)
Rockville. *Barfd* 3B **4**	Rothesay Rd. *B'brn* 6B **20**
Rockwater Bird Conservation Cen.	Rothesay Rd. *Brier* 3D **6**
. . . . .7K **11**	Rothwell Av. *Acc* 4D **22**
Rockwood Clo. *Burn* 6F **7**	Rough Hey. *Acc* 6A **22**
Rodney St. *B'brn* 2F **19**	Roughlee Gro. *Burn* 5E **10**
Roebuck Clo. *B'brn* 2G **19**	Rough Lee Rd. *Acc* 4D **22**
Roe Greave Rd. *Osw* 5J **21**	Roughlee St. *Barfd* 6A **4**
Roe Lee Pk. *B'brn* 2J **13**	Roundel St. *Burn* 7C **6**
Rolleston Rd. *B'brn* 1E **18**	Roundhill La. *Has* 6A **24**
Roman Rd. *B'brn* 3K **19**	Roundhill Vw. *Acc* 4A **24**
(in two parts)	Roundwood Av. *Burn* 5B **6**
Roman Rd. *Hodd* 6J **27**	Rowan Av. *Osw* 6J **21**
Roman Rd. W. Ind. Est. *B'brn* . .7K **19**	Rowan Clo. *B'brn* 3K **13**
Roman Way. *Clith* 5F **3**	Rowan Gro. *Burn* 4D **10**
Rome Av. *Burn* 6H **9**	Rowan Tree Clo. *Acc* 1F **23**
Romford St. *Burn* 3H **9**	Rowen Pk. *B'brn* 4E **12**
Romney Av. *Barfd* 5A **4**	Rowland Av. *Nels* 1H **7**
Romney Av. *Nels* 7K **9**	Rowland St. *Acc* 3B **22**
Romney St. *Nels* 2E **6**	Royal Ct. *Brclf* 6G **7**
Romney Wlk. *B'brn* 4B **20**	Royal Oak Av. *B'brn* 3H **13**
Ronald St. *B'brn* 3B **20**	Royds Av. *Acc* 4D **22**
Ronald St. *Burn* 5F **9**	Royds Rd. *Bacup* 6C **30**
Ronaldsway. *Nels* 6E **4**	Royds St. *Acc* 3D **22**
Ronaldsway Clo. *Bacup* 4J **31**	Royle Rd. *Burn* 3A **10**
Roney St. *B'brn* 7F **13**	(in three parts)
Rook Hill Rd. *Bacup* 5D **30**	Royshaw Av. *B'brn* 4H **13**
Rook St. *Col* 3G **5**	Royshaw Clo. *B'brn* 4H **13**
Rook St. *Nels* 7A **4**	Ruby St. *B'brn* 2J **13**
Rooley Moor Rd. *Bacup* 6D **30**	Rudd St. *Has* 2A **28**
Rooley Vw. *Bacup* 4G **31**	Rudyard Dri. *Dar* 5H **27**
Roseacre Clo. Ross 1B **30**	Rugby Av. *Acc* 7D **16**
(off Foxhill Dri.)	Rupert St. *Nels* 2D **6**
Roseacre Clo. Ross 4K **29**	Rushbed Dri. *Ross* 6G **25**
(off Bacup Rd.)	Rushes Farm Clo. *Osw* 5H **21**
Rose Av. *Burn* 6K **9**	Rushey Clo. *Raw* 6G **25**
Rosebank. *Clay M* 4B **16**	Rushton Clo. *Nels* 6E **4**
Rose Bank. *Ross* 2G **29**	Rushton St. *Bacup* 5G **31**
Rose Bank St. *Bacup* 2H **31**	Rushton St. *Barfd* 5A **4**
Rosebay Av. *B'brn* 5A **18**	Rushton St. *Gt Har* 3G **15**
Roseberry St. *Burn* 7C **6**	Rushworth St. *Burn* 1C **10**
Rose Cotts. *Brclf* 7H **7**	Rushworth St. E. *Burn* 1C **10**
Rosedale St. Ross 7F **25**	Rushy Fld. *Clay M* 2A **16**
(off Holmes, The)	Ruskin Av. *Col* 2G **5**
Rosegrove La. *Burn* 5F **9**	Ruskin Av. *Osw* 3H **21**
Rose Hill. B'brn 7K **13**	Ruskin Av. *Pad* 3D **8**
(off Higher Barn St.)	Ruskin Gro. *Hap* 6B **8**
Rose Hill Av. *B'brn* 1K **19**	Ruskin Pl. *Nels* 6C **4**
Rosehill Av. *Nels* 7K **9**	Ruskin St. *Burn* 7B **6**
Rosehill Av. *Nels* 7C **4**	Russell Av. *Col* 2H **5**
Rosehill Mt. *Nels* 6K **9**	Russell Ct. *Burn* 6C **10**
Rosehill Rd. *Burn* 6K **9**	Russell Pl. *Gt Har* 2G **15**
Rosehill Rd. *Col* 6D **4**	Russell St. *Acc* 3D **22**
Rose Hill Rd. *Pleas* 4A **18**	Russell St. *Bacup* 1H **31**
Rose Hill St. *Bacup* 3H **31**	Russell St. *B'brn* 2H **19**
Rose Hill St. *Dar* 5F **27**	Russell St. *Nels* 1E **6**
Rose Hill St. *Ross* 3G **25**	Russell Ter. *Pad* 3C **8**
Roseland Av. *Brier* 3D **6**	Russia St. *Acc* 2A **22**
Rosemount. *Bacup* 1J **31**	Ruthin Clo. *B'brn* 5H **13**
Rosemount. *Ross* 4B **30**	Rutland Av. *B'brn* 4D **20**
Rosemount Av. *Burn* 6K **9**	Rutland Av. *Burn* 4F **9**
Rosendale Clo. *Bacup* 2K **31**	Rutland Clo. *Clay M* 4A **16**
Rosendale Cres. *Bacup* 2J **31**	Rutland Pl. *Pad* 3C **8**
Rose Pl. *Acc* 4C **22**	Rutland St. *Acc* 3A **22**
Rose St. *Acc* 4C **22**	Rutland St. *B'brn* 2E **18**
Rose St. *Bacup* 3H **31**	Rutland St. *Col* 3J **5**
Rose St. *B'brn* 2H **19**	Rutland St. *Nels* 7B **4**
Rose St. *Dar* 4F **27**	Rutland Wlk. *Has* 5A **28**
Rose St. *Ross* 3A **30**	Ryburn Av. *B'brn* 5D **12**
Rose Va. St. *Ross* 3H **29**	Rydal Av. *Dar* 5E **26**
Roseway. *Brier* 2B **6**	Rydal Clo. *Acc* 6E **16**
Rosewood Av. *B'brn* 3H **13**	Rydal Clo. *Burn* 5D **6**
Rosewood Av. *Burn* 7K **9**	Rydal Clo. *Pad* 1B **8**
Rosewood Av. *Has* 2C **28**	Rydal Pl. *Col* 3K **5**
Rosewood Bus. Pk. *B'brn* 4H **13**	

Rydal Rd. *B'brn* 5K **13**	St James's La. *Burn* 4B **10**
Rydal Rd. *Has* 5C **28**	(off St James Row)
Rydal St. *Burn* 7B **6**	*St James's Pl. B'brn* 5H **13**
Ryde Clo. *Has* 4C **28**	(off St James's Rd.)
Ryden Rd. *B'brn* 2A **14**	St James Sq. *Bacup* 2H **31**
Ryefield Av. *Has* 3B **28**	St James's Rd. *B'brn* 5H **13**
Ryefield Av. W. *Has* 3A **28**	St James's Row. *Burn* 4B **10**
Ryefield Pl. *Has* 3B **28**	St James's St. *Burn* 4A **10**
Rye Gdns. *B'brn* 7G **19**	(in two parts)
Rye Gro. *Pad* 3C **8**	St James St. *Acc* 3C **22**
Rylands St. *Burn* 1C **10**	St James St. *Bacup* 3H **31**
	St James St. *B'brn* 4F **19**
S	St James St. *Brier* 4C **6**
	St James St. *Clith* 6E **2**
Sabden Wlk. *B'brn* 3J **19**	St James' St. *Raw* 2G **29**
Saccary La. *Mel* 1D **12**	St James' St. *Waterf* 5A **30**
Sackville Gdns. *Brier* 4B **6**	St John's. *B'brn* 6G **13**
Sackville St. *Brier* 4C **6**	St John's Av. *Dar* 5F **27**
Sackville St. *Burn* 5A **10**	St John's Clo. *Acc* 6F **23**
Sackville St. *Nels* 3G **7**	St John's Clo. *Craw* 5G **25**
Saddlers M. *Clith* 5E **2**	St John's Ct. *Bacup* 2H **31**
Sadler St. *Chu* 3K **21**	*St Johns Ct. Burn* 4H **9**
Sagar Holme Ter. *Ross* 1A **30**	(off Gannow La.)
Sagar St. *Nels* 1F **7**	St Johns Pl. *Nels* 1H **7**
Sahara Fold. B'brn 5K **13**	St John's Rd. *Burn* 4H **9**
(off Warmden Gdns.)	St John's Rd. *Pad* 4B **8**
St Aidans Av. *B'brn* 4F **19**	St John's St. *Dar* 5F **27**
(in two parts)	St John's St. *Gt Har* 3H **15**
St Aidan's Av. *Dar* 5F **27**	St John's St. *Ross* 5B **30**
St Aidan's Clo. *B'brn* 4F **19**	St John St. *Bacup* 2H **31**
St Alban's St. *B'brn* 6J **13**	St Kitts Clo. *Lwr D* 7H **19**
St Alban's Rd. *Dar* 2C **26**	St Lawrence Av. *B'brn* 4E **12**
St Albans Rd. *Rish* 7F **15**	St Lawrence St. *Gt Har* 2H **15**
St Andrews Clo. *Col* 5F **5**	*St Leger Ct. Acc* 3D **22**
St Andrews Clo. *Osw* 4J **21**	(off Plantation La.)
St Andrews Ct. *Osw* 5J **21**	*St Leger Ct. Acc* 3D **22**
St Andrew's Pl. *B'brn* 6G **13**	(off Midland St.)
St Andrew's St. *B'brn* 6G **13**	St Leonard's St. *Pad* 1B **8**
St Andrew's St. *Burn* 1C **10**	St Lucia Clo. *Lwr D* 7J **19**
St Annes Clo. *B'brn* 2J **19**	St Margaret's Ct. *B'brn* 3A **20**
St Anne's Clo. Chu 3K **21**	St Margaret's Gdns. *Hap* 6B **8**
(off Blackpool St.)	St Margaret's Way. *B'brn* 3A **20**
St Anne's Cres. *Ross* 2B **30**	St Mark's Pl. *B'brn* 1E **18**
St Anne's St. *Pad* 3B **8**	St Mark's Rd. *B'brn* 1E **18**
St Ann's Ct. *Clith* 5B **2**	St Martin's Dri. *B'brn* 5A **18**
St Anns Sq. *Clith* 5C **2**	St Mary's Clo. *B'brn* 3A **20**
St Barnabas St. *B'brn* 7F **13**	St Mary's Ct. *Clay M* 5A **16**
St Barnabas St. *Dar* 7F **27**	St Mary's Ct. *Mel* 2B **12**
St Bede's Pk. *Dar* 1C **26**	St Mary's Ct. *Raw* 3F **29**
St Bee's Clo. *B'brn* 4J **19**	St Mary's Gdns. *Mel* 2B **12**
St Cecilia St. *Gt Har* 2J **15**	St Mary's Ga. *Burn* 5C **10**
(in two parts)	St Mary's Pl. *Ross* 3F **29**
St Charles Rd. *Rish* 6F **15**	St Mary's St. *Clith* 4E **2**
St Clements Clo. *B'brn* 4A **20**	St Mary's St. *Nels* 1D **6**
St Clements St. *Barfd* 5A **4**	St Mary's Ter. *Ross* 3G **29**
St Clement St. *B'brn* 3A **20**	St Mary's Way. *Ross* 3G **29**
St Crispin Way. *Has* 3A **28**	St Mary's Wharf. *B'brn* 2J **19**
St Cuthbert's Clo. *Dar* 2C **26**	*St Matthew's Ct. Burn* 5K **9**
St Cuthbert St. *Burn* 7C **6**	(off Harriet St.)
St David's Av. *B'brn* 6B **18**	*St Matthew's Ct. Burn* 5J **9**
St David's Wood. *Acc* 1E **22**	(off Colin St.)
St Denys Cft. *Clith* 4E **2**	St Matthew St. *Burn* 5K **9**
St Edmund St. *Gt Har* 2J **15**	St Michael's Clo. *B'brn* 6B **18**
St Frances Clo. *B'brn* 2J **19**	(in two parts)
St Francis Rd. *B'brn* 3D **18**	St Michael's Ct. *B'brn* 6J **13**
St Gabriel's Av. *B'brn* 4J **19**	St Michael's St. *B'brn* 5J **13**
St George's Av. *B'brn* 4E **18**	St Nicholas Rd. *Chu* 1A **22**
St Georges Clo. *Col* 5F **5**	St Oswald's Clo. *B'brn* 4D **20**
St George's Rd. *Nels* 2G **7**	St Oswald's Rd. *B'brn* 4D **20**
St Georges Ter. Dar 3D **26**	St Paul's Av. *B'brn* 7G **13**
(off Harwood St.)	St Pauls Clo. *Clith* 5C **2**
St Georges Ter. *Ross* 7C **30**	St Pauls Ct. *Burn* 5A **10**
St Giles St. *B'brn* 1B **8**	*St Paul's Ct. Osw* 4K **21**
St Giles Ter. Pad 1B **8**	(off Union Rd.)
(off East St.)	St Paul's Rd. *Nels* 2E **6**
St Helens Clo. *Osw* 5A **22**	St Paul's Rd. *Rish* 6F **15**
St Helier Clo. *B'brn* 5E **18**	St Paul's St. *B'brn* 7G **13**
St Hubert's Rd. *Gt Har* 3H **15**	St Paul's St. *Clith* 5C **2**
St Hubert's St. *Gt Har* 2J **15**	St Paul's St. *Osw* 4K **21**
St Ives Rd. *B'brn* 4C **20**	St Pauls Ter. *Clith* 5C **2**
St James Clo. *Chu* 1K **21**	St Paul's Ter. *Hodd* 3J **27**
St James Clo. *Has* 2B **28**	St Peter's Av. *Has* 3B **28**
St James Ct. *B'brn* 3H **15**	St Peter's Clo. *Clay D* 2A **14**
St James Cres. *Dar* 3F **27**	St Peter's Clo. *Dar* 5F **27**
St James M. *Chu* 1K **21**	St Peter's Pl. *Has* 3B **28**
St James Pl. *Pad* 2C **8**	St Peter's Rd. *Ross* 3A **30**
St James' Rd. *Chu* 1K **21**	St Peter St. *Burn* 1G **19**
St James Row. *Ross* 2G **29**	St Peter St. *Rish* 6F **15**
	St Philip's St. *B'brn* 2E **18**
	St Philip St. *Burn* 1B **10**

St Phillips St. *Nels* 7B **4**
St Saviours Ct. *Bacup* 4H **31**
(off Park Rd.)
St Silas's Rd. *B'brn* 7E **12**
St Stephen's Av. *B'brn* 5K **13**
St Stephen's Rd. *B'brn* 5K **13**
St Stephen's St. *Burn* 6C **10**
St Stephen's Way. *Col* 2J **5**
St Thomas Clo. *Ross* 6A **28**
St Thomas's Rd. *Ross* 5G **25**
St Thomas St. *B'brn* 4A **20**
St Vincent Clo. *Lwr D* 7J **19**
Salem St. *Has* 2B **28**
Salesbury Vw. *Wilp* 4B **14**
Salford. *B'brn* 7H **13**
Salisbury Rd. *Dar* 2C **26**
Salisbury St. *Col* 3H **5**
Salisbury St. *Gt Har* 1J **15**
Salisbury St. *Has* 2B **28**
Saltburn St. *Burn* 4G **9**
Salterford La. *Cliv* 7H **11**
Salthill Ind. Est. *Clith* 3G **3**
Salthill Rd. *Clith* 4F **3**
Salthill Vw. *Clith* 4F **3**
Salus St. *Burn* 1C **10**
Sand Beds La. *Ross* 7G **29**
Sandfield Rd. *Bacup* 4J **31**
Sandhill St. *Dar* 7F **27**
Sandhurst St. *Burn* 4C **10**
Sandiway Dri. *Brclf* 6G **7**
Sandon St. *B'brn* 2F **19**
Sandon St. *Dar* 3F **27**
Sandon Ter. *B'brn* 2F **19**
Sandown Rd. *Has* 3C **28**
Sandpiper Clo. *B'brn* 6J **13**
Sandpiper Sq. *Burn* 5H **9**
Sandringham Clo. *B'brn* 3H **13**
Sandringham Gro. *Has* 4A **28**
Sandringham Rd. *Dar* 1C **26**
Sands Clo. *Rish* 5G **15**
Sands Rd. *Rish* 5G **15**
Sandwich Clo. *B'brn* 4B **20**
Sandy Bank Ter. *Ross* 4K **29**
Sandybeds Clo. *Acc* 6E **22**
Sandygate. *Burn* 4K **9**
Sandy La. *Acc* 3D **22**
(in two parts)
Sandy La. *Barfd* 6A **4**
Sandy La. *Dar & Lwr D* 7H **19**
Sangara Dri. *Lwr D* 7J **19**
Sansbury Cres. *Nels* 6D **4**
Sapphire St. *B'brn* 3J **13**
Sarah St. *Bacup* 5K **31**
Sarah St. *Dar* 4F **27**
Saunder Bank. *Burn* 5A **10**
Saunder Height La. *Ross* 2A **30**
Saunders Clo. *Ross* 5G **25**
Saunders Rd. *B'brn* 7F **13**
Savoy St. *Acc* 3A **22**
Sawley Av. *Acc* 1E **22**
Sawley Clo. *Dar* 5G **27**
Sawley Dri. *Gt Har* 1K **15**
Sawrey Ct. *Clay M* 5K **15**
Saxifield St. *Burn* 6F **7**
Saxon Clo. *Osw* 3H **21**
Saxon St. *Burn* 3B **10**
Scafell Clo. *Burn* 2H **9**
Scaitcliffe St. *Acc* 2C **22**
Scarborough Rd. *B'brn* 4K **19**
Scarlett St. *Burn* 5K **9**
Scarr La. *B'brn* 5C **12**
(in two parts)
Scarr St. *Bacup* 2H **31**
Scar St. *B'brn* 2E **18**
Scarth La. *Hap* 6A **8**
Schofield Clo. *Ross* 3F **29**
Schofield Rd. *Ross* 3F **29**
Schofield St. *Dar* 3D **26**
Schofield St. *Ross* 7A **28**
Schofield St. *Waterf* 5A **30**
Scholefield Av. *Nels* 3F **7**
Scholefield La. *Nels* 4F **7**
Scholes St. *Dar* 4D **26**
School Ho. Fold. *Hap* 7B **8**
School Ho. La. *Acc* 7C **22**
School La. *Burn* 4B **10**
School La. *Guide* 7C **20**
School St. *Acc* 2C **22**
School St. *Bacup* 5D **30**
School St. *Col* 4G **5**

School St. *Dar* 4E **26**
School St. *Good* 4G **25**
School St. *Gt Har* 3H **15**
School St. *Nels* 1D **6**
School St. *Rish* 6G **15**
School St. *Whit B* 1B **30**
Scotland Bank Ter. *B'brn* 5E **18**
Scotland Rd. *Nels* 6A **4**
Scotshaw Brook Ind. Est.
  B'brn 6H **19**
Scott Av. *Acc* 6F **23**
Scott Clo. *Osw* 3J **21**
Scott Pk. Rd. *Burn* 6K **9**
Scott's Ter. *Burn* 4J **9**
Scott St. *Burn* 3E **8**
Scott St. *Clay M* 4A **16**
Scott St. *Nels* 7A **4**
Scout Rd. *Ross* 2B **30**
Seascale Clo. *Burn* 4K **19**
Seaton Ct. *B'brn* 5J **19**
Second Av. *Chu* 7B **16**
Sedburgh Clo. *Acc* 3E **22**
Sedburgh St. *Burn* 7D **6**
Seedall Av. *Clith* 5D **2**
Sefton Av. *Burn* 5K **9**
Sefton Clo. *Clay M* 4B **16**
Sefton Clo. *Dar* 7G **27**
Sefton St. *Brier* 4C **6**
Sefton St. *Col* 3J **5**
Sefton St. *Nels* 1F **7**
Sefton Ter. *Burn* 5K **9**
Segar St. *Gt Har* 2H **15**
Selborne M. *B'brn* 2E **18**
(off Selborne St.)
Selborne St. *B'brn* 2E **18**
Selby Clo. *Acc* 5F **23**
Selby St. *Col* 3F **5**
Selby St. *Nels* 2F **7**
Seldon St. *Col* 4G **5**
Seldon St. *Nels* 7B **4**
Selkirk Clo. *B'brn* 1K **19**
Selkirk St. *Burn* 6J **9**
Selous Rd. *B'brn* 2E **18**
Serpentine Rd. *Burn* 6A **10**
Sett End Rd. *B'brn* 7B **20**
Settle Ter. *Burn* 7D **6**
Seven Trees Av. *B'brn* 4K **13**
Shackleton St. *Burn* 2C **10**
Shadsworth Clo. *B'brn* 4B **20**
Shadsworth Ind. Est. *B'brn* ..7B **20**
Shadsworth Ind. Pk. *B'brn* ..6B **20**
Shadsworth Rd. *B'brn* 7B **20**
Shaftesbury Av. *Burn* 6A **10**
Shaftesbury Av. *Dar* 2C **26**
Shaftesbury Av. *Gt Har* 1K **15**
Shakeshaft St. *Burn* 1K **19**
Shakespeare Av. *Gt Har* 3G **15**
Shakespeare St. *Pad* 3C **8**
(in two parts)
Shakespeare Way. *B'brn* 2F **19**
Shale St. *Burn* 4J **9**
Shannon Sq. *Burn* 7D **6**
Shap Clo. *Acc* 5F **23**
Shap Clo. *Barfd* 4A **4**
Shap Gro. *Burn* 6B **6**
Sharples St. *Acc* 3A **22**
Sharples St. *Burn* 2G **19**
Sharp St. *Barfd* 5A **4**
Sharp St. *Burn* 1C **10**
Shawbridge Ct. *Clith* 5F **3**
Shaw Bri. St. *Clith* 5F **3**
Shawbrook Clo. *Rish* 7F **15**
Shaw Clo. *B'brn* 7F **13**
Shaw Clough Rd. *Ross* 2B **30**
Shaw Clough St. *Ross* 2B **30**
Shawfield. *Ross* 4F **29**
Shaw St. *B'brn* 7G **13**
Shaw St. *Col* 4F **5**
Shaw St. *Has* 6B **24**
Shays Dri. *Clith* 6F **3**
Shear Bank Clo. *B'brn* 6G **13**
Shear Bank Gdns. *B'brn* 6G **13**
Shear Bank Rd. *B'brn* 5G **13**
Shear Brow. *B'brn* 5G **13**
Shearwater Dri. *B'brn* 6J **13**
Sheddon Gro. *Burn* 5F **11**
Shed St. *Col* 4F **5**
Shed St. *Burn* 5J **21**
Sheep Grn. *Has* 2B **28**
Shelfield Rd. *Nels* 7E **4**

Shelley Dri. *Acc* 6F **23**
Shelley Gdns. *Gt Har* 3G **15**
Shelley Gro. *Dar* 4G **27**
Shepherd St. *Bacup* 2H **31**
Shepherd St. *Dar* 6E **26**
Sherbourne Rd. *Acc* 5F **23**
Sheridan St. *Burn* 7F **7**
(off Stanbury Dri.)
Sheridan St. *Nels* 6C **4**
Sherwood Ct. *Burn* 5D **10**
Sherwood Rd. *B'brn* 4A **20**
Sherwood Way. *Acc* 6B **16**
Shetland Clo. *B'brn* 5B **20**
Shetland Clo. *Wilp* 1B **14**
Ship All. *Burn* 5B **10**
(off Parker La.)
Shireburn Av. *Clith* 6C **2**
Shires, The. *B'brn* 7G **19**
Shop La. *Acc* 3E **22**
Shore Av. *Burn* 7G **7**
Shorey Bank. *Burn* 3B **10**
Shorrock La. *B'brn* 5E **18**
Shorrock St. *Dar* 5E **26**
Short Clough Clo. *Ross* 6G **25**
Short Clough La. *Ross* 6G **25**
Shortenbrook Dri. *Alt* 1F **17**
Shortenbrook Way. *Alt* 1F **17**
Short St. *Bacup* 5D **30**
Short St. *Col* 4G **5**
Showfield. *Wors* 4J **11**
Showley Brook Clo. *Wilp* ...4B **14**
Showley Ct. *Clay D* 2A **14**
Shropshire Dri. *Wilp* 2B **14**
Shuttle Clo. *Acc* 2B **22**
(off Dale St.)
Shuttleworth St. *Burn* 7C **6**
Shuttleworth St. *Pad* 2B **8**
Shuttleworth St. *Rish* 5G **15**
Siddow's Av. *Clith* 6C **2**
Sidebeet La. *Rish* 7D **14**
Sidings, The. *Bacup* 5J **31**
Sidings, The. *Dar* 6F **27**
Siding St. *Bacup* 5E **30**
Sidmouth Av. *Has* 3C **28**
Silbury Clo. *B'brn* 5K **19**
Silloth Clo. *B'brn* 4J **19**
Silverdale Clo. *Burn* 5J **19**
Silverdale Clo. *Burn* 6D **6**
Silverdale Clo. *Clay M* 5K **15**
Simmonds Way. *Brier* 2C **6**
Simmons St. *B'brn* 7G **13**
Simpson St. *Hap* 4H **7**
Simpson St. *Osw* 5J **21**
Size Ho. Rd. *Has* 3B **28**
Size Ho. Village. *Has* 3C **28**
Skelshaw Clo. *B'brn* 2K **19**
Skelton St. *Col* 3H **5**
Skiddaw Clo. *Burn* 1H **9**
Skiddaw St. *B'brn* 7K **13**
Skipton New Rd. *Col* 1H **5**
Skipton Old Rd. *Col* 2K **5**
Skipton Rd. *Col* 1H **5**
Skipton Rd. *Traw* 5J **5**
Skye Cres. *B'brn* 5B **20**
Slack Booth. *Traw* 7K **5**
Slack Royd. *Traw* 7K **5**
Slade La. *Pad* 1B **8**
(in two parts)
Slaidburn Av. *Burn* 6E **10**
Slaidburn Av. *Ross* 1G **29**
Slaidburn Dri. *Acc* 4B **22**
Slater Av. *Col* 2G **5**
Slater St. *B'brn* 4F **19**
Sliven Clod Rd. *Ross* 1E **24**
Smalley St. *Burn* 6C **10**
(in two parts)
Smalley Thorn Brow. *Gt Har* ..2E **14**
Smalley Way. *B'brn* 3H **19**
Smallshaw Ind. Est. *Burn* ...5H **9**
Smallshaw La. *Burn* 4G **9**
(in two parts)
Smirthwaite St. *Burn* 5J **9**
Smith St. *Burn* 4A **10**
Smith St. *Col* 4F **5**
Smith St. *Nels* 1F **7**
Smith St. *Wors* 5J **11**
Smithy Bri. St. *Osw* 5J **21**
Smithy Brow. *Has* 1B **28**
(off High St.)
Smithy Brow Ct. *Has* 1B **28**

Smithfield Av. *Burn* 4G **11**
Smithy La. *Col* 1E **4**
Smithy St. *Has* 2B **28**
(off Ratcliffe St.)
Snaefell Rd. *B'brn* 4H **19**
Snape St. *Dar* 2D **26**
Snell Gro. *Col* 2J **5**
Sniddle Hill La. *Dar* 5C **26**
Snowden Av. *B'brn* 5H **13**
Snowden St. *Burn* 4G **9**
Snowdrop Clo. *Has* 5A **28**
Snow St. *B'brn* 6J **13**
Solway Av. *B'brn* 4C **18**
Somerford Clo. *Burn* 3J **9**
Somerset Av. *Clith* 3F **3**
Somerset Av. *Dar* 2D **26**
Somerset Av. *Wilp* 2B **14**
Somerset Clo. *Osw* 5A **22**
Somerset Gro. *Chu* 1A **22**
Somerset Pl. *Nels* 7D **4**
Somerset Rd. *Rish* 6E **14**
Somerset St. *Burn* 7B **10**
Somerset Wlk. *Has* 5B **28**
Soudan St. *Burn* 7C **6**
Sough La. *Guide* 6E **20**
Sough Rd. *Dar* 5F **27**
Southcliffe. *Gt Har* 1G **15**
Southcliffe Av. *Burn* 3H **9**
South Dri. *Pad* 2C **8**
Southern Av. *Burn* 3H **9**
Southey St. *Burn* 4K **9**
Southfield La. *S'fld & Col* ...2K **7**
Southfield Sq. *Nels* 1G **7**
Southfield St. *Nels* 1F **7**
S. Shore St. *Chu* 3K **21**
S. Shore St. *Has* 2A **28**
South St. *Acc* 7F **17**
(Burnley Rd.)
South St. *Acc* 3D **22**
(Nuttall St.)
South St. *Bacup* 5D **30**
(Brandwood Rd.)
South St. *Bacup* 3H **31**
(St James St.)
South St. *Burn* 4B **10**
South St. *Dar* 4E **26**
South St. *Has* 4C **28**
South St. *Newc* 4A **30**
South St. *Raw* 2G **29**
S. Valley Dri. *Col* 5F **5**
South Vw. *Gt Har* 2H **15**
South Vw. *Has* 2B **28**
South Vw. *Nels* 2E **6**
Southwark. *Burn* 4K **9**
(off Woodbine Rd.)
Southwood Dri. *Acc* 5F **23**
Southworth St. *B'brn* 3G **19**
Sow Clough Rd. *Bacup* 4F **31**
Sowerby St. *Pad* 2B **8**
Spa Gth. *Clith* 5F **3**
Sparth Av. *Clay M* 4A **16**
Sparth Rd. *Clay M* 4K **15**
Spa St. *Burn* 3K **9**
Spa St. *Pad* 2C **8**
Speedwell St. *B'brn* 3E **18**
Speke St. *B'brn* 3E **18**
Spencer St. *Acc* 2E **22**
Spencer St. *Bacup* 5E **30**
Spencer St. *Burn* 1B **10**
Spencer St. *Ross* 4G **25**
Spenser Clo. *Wors* 6K **11**
Spenser Gro. *Gt Har* 2G **15**
Spenser St. *Pad* 3C **8**
Spindle Berry Ct. *Acc* 4D **22**
Spinney, The. *B'brn* 4D **12**
Spinney, The. *Burn* 2J **9**
Spire Clo. *Dar* 5H **27**
Spout Ho. La. *Acc* 6G **17**
Spread Eagle St. *Osw* 3H **21**
Spring Av. *Gt Har* 1H **15**
Springbank. *Barfd* 3B **4**
Springbank Gdns. *Good* 2F **25**
Spring Bank Ter. *B'brn* 3F **19**
Spring Brook Ho. *Clay M* ...5A **16**
(off Canal St.)
Spring Ct. *Col* 3G **5**
(off Derby St.)
Springfield Av. *Acc* 4A **22**
Springfield Av. *Bacup* 2J **31**
Springfield Av. *B'brn* 4B **18**

Springfield Bank. Burn 5B 10
Springfield Ct. Bacup 2J 31
(off Springfield Av.)
Springfield Dri. Ross 4A 30
Springfield Flats. Dar 5E 26
Springfield Rd. Burn 6B 10
(in two parts)
Springfield Rd. Gt Har 3G 15
Springfield Rd. Nels 3F 7
Springfield Rd. Ross 2H 29
Springfield St. B'brn 2E 18
Springfield St. Dar 5E 26
Springfield St. Osw 5J 21
Springfield Ter. B'brn 4D 18
Spring Gdns. Acc 3D 22
Spring Gdns. Bacup 2J 31
Spring Gdns. Dar 5E 26
Spring Gdns. Ross 5G 25
(off Lord St.)
Spring Gdns. Ross 7B 30
(Springside)
Spring Gdns. Wadd 1B 2
Spring Gdns. Rd. Col 4G 5
Spring Gdns. St. Ross 5B 30
Spring Gdns. Ter. Pad 1B 8
Spring Hall. Acc 2A 16
Spring Hill. B'brn 7H 13
(off Lord Sq.)
Springhill. Ross 3J 29
Springhill Av. Bacup 5F 31
Spring Hill Rd. Acc 4A 22
Spring Hill Rd. Burn 5A 10
Springhill Vs. Bacup 5E 30
Spring La. B'brn 2E 18
(in two parts)
Spring La. Col 3G 5
Spring La. Has 1B 28
Spring Meadows. Dar 6H 27
Spring Pl. Col 3G 5
Springside. Ross 7B 30
Spring St. Acc 4A 22
Spring St. Bacup 4H 31
Spring St. Nels 2D 6
Spring St. Osw 4K 21
Spring St. Rish 5G 15
Spring St. Ross 4G 25
Spring Ter. Bacup 5F 31
Spring Ter. Ross 2F 25
Spring Ter. S. Ross 3E 28
Springthorpe St. Dar 7F 27
Springvale. 4A 22
Springvale Bus. Pk. Dar 7F 27
Spring Va. Rd. Dar 6F 27
Spring Vw. B'brn 7F 13
Spring Yd. Col 3G 5
Spruce Ct. Acc 7F 17
Sprucewood Clo. Acc 2E 22
Square, The. Wadd 1B 2
Square, The. Wors 5J 11
(off Water St.)
Squire Rd. Nels 1G 7
Squirrels Clo. Acc 7F 17
Stables Clo. Ross 6G 25
Stables, The. Hap 5B 8
Stackhouses, The. Burn 4B 10
(off Bank Pde.)
Stack La. Bacup 5K 31
Staffa Cres. B'brn 4C 20
Stafford St. Burn 3B 10
Stafford St. Dar 1D 26
Stafford St. Nels 1G 7
Staghills Rd. Ross 3K 29
Stainton Dri. Burn 2K 9
Stakes Hall Pl. B'brn 3F 19
Stamford Pl. Clith 4F 3
Stanbury Clo. Burn 7F 7
Stanbury Dri. Burn 7F 7
Stancliffe St. B'brn 2E 18
Stancliffe St. Ind. Est. B'brn ...2F 18
Standen Hall Clo. Burn 6F 7
Standen Hall Dri. Burn 7E 6
Standen Rd. Clith 6F 3
Standen Rd. Bungalows. Clith ...6F 3
Standish St. Burn 4B 10
Standroyd Dri. Col 3K 5
Standroyd Rd. Col 3K 5
Stanford Gdns. B'brn 4K 19
Stanhill La. Osw 4G 21
Stanhill Rd. B'brn & Osw ...4D 20

Stanhill St. Osw 5H 21
Stanhope St. Burn 3A 10
Stanhope St. Dar 3E 26
Stanley Ct. Acc 1E 22
Stanley Dri. Dar 7F 27
Stanley Ga. Mel 2B 12
Stanley Mt. Bacup 2H 31
Stanley Range. B'brn 3E 18
Stanley St. Acc 2D 22
Stanley St. Bacup 1H 31
Stanley St. B'brn 6K 13
Stanley St. Brier 4C 6
Stanley St. Burn 5A 10
Stanley St. Col 3G 5
Stanley St. Nels 1E 6
Stanley St. Osw 5J 21
Stansfeld St. B'brn 2F 19
Stansfield Clo. Barfd 4A 4
Stansfield Rd. Ross 5A 30
Stansfield St. Bacup 5E 30
Stansfield St. Burn 5G 9
Stansfield St. Dar 5E 26
Stansfield St. Nels 1F 7
Stanthorpe Wlk. Burn 1B 10
Stanworth Rd. Nels 1E 6
Stanworth St. Wors 5J 11
Star Bank. Bacup 6F 31
Starkie St. B'brn 7J 13
Starkie St. Burn 5K 9
Starkie St. Dar 5F 27
Starkie St. Pad 2B 8
Star St. Acc 3A 22
Star St. Dar 4F 27
Station Clo. Rish 7F 15
Station Clo. Wilp 4B 14
Station Rd. Acc 5F 17
Station Rd. Burn 3B 10
Station Rd. Clith 5E 2
Station Rd. Gt Har 2J 15
Station Rd. Has 1B 28
Station Rd. Helm 6A 28
Station Rd. Pad 2B 8
Station Rd. Rish 7F 15
Sted Ter. B'brn 6G 13
Steer St. Burn 1C 10
Steiner's La. Chu 1K 21
(off York St.)
Steiner St. Acc 2B 22
Stephenson Dri. Burn 3G 9
Stephen St. B'brn 3E 18
Stevenson St. E. Acc 3B 22
Stevenson St. W. Acc 4A 22
Stewart St. B'brn 5G 19
Stewart St. Burn 6C 10
Stirling Clo. Clith 7C 2
Stirling Ct. Brclf 5J 7
Stirling Dri. B'brn 1J 19
Stirling St. B'brn 4E 18
Stockbridge Dri. Pad 2D 8
Stockbridge Rd. Pad 2C 8
Stockclough La. Fen 6A 18
Stockholm St. Burn 5G 9
Stockwood Clo. B'brn 4D 12
Stone Bri. La. Osw 5J 21
Stonebridge Ter. Col 3H 5
Stone Cft. Barfd 2B 4
Stone Edge Rd. Barfd 2B 4
Stone Hill Dri. B'brn 3K 13
Stoneholme Ind. Est. Ross ...4G 25
Stoneholme Rd. Ross 4G 25
Stone Holme Ter. Ross 4G 25
Stonemoor Bottom. Pad ...4B 8
Stone St. Bacup 6D 30
Stone St. Ross 3A 28
(Hutch Bank Rd.)
Stone St. Ross 5B 30
(Townsend St.)
Stoneybutts. B'brn 7H 13
(off Lord Sq.)
Stoneycroft. Wors 5H 11
Stoneyhurst Height. Brier ...5E 6
Stoney St. Burn 6C 10
Stonyhurst Av. Burn 5E 10
Stonyhurst Clo. B'brn 1G 19
Stonyhurst Clo. Pad 4D 8
Stonyhurst Rd. B'brn 1G 19
Stoops Fold. Mel 1B 12
Stoop St. Burn 5H 9
Stopes Brow. Lwr D 6K 19
Stopford Ct. Clay M 4A 16

Store St. Has 2B 28
Store St. Lwr D 6K 19
Stott St. Nels 1E 6
Stourton St. Rish 5F 15
Stout St. B'brn 1G 19
Straits. Osw 4K 21
Strange St. Burn 6C 10
Stratford Way. Acc 1B 22
Stratford Way. Col 3J 5
Strathclyde Rd. B'brn 1K 19
Strawberry Bank. B'brn 7G 13
Streatly Wlk. B'brn 5K 19
Stroyan St. Burn 5D 10
Stuart Av. Bacup 5F 31
Stuart Clo. Dar 4E 26
Stuart St. Acc 1C 22
Stubbylee La. Bacup 5H 31
Stunstead Rd. Traw 5K 5
Sudell Clo. Dar 4G 27
Sudell Cross. B'brn 7H 13
(off Limebrick)
Sudell Nook. Guide 7B 20
Sudell Rd. Dar 4E 26
Sudellside St. Dar 4F 27
Suffolk Av. B'brn 3F 19
Suffolk St. B'brn 3F 19
Sulby Rd. B'brn 4K 19
Sullivan Dri. B'brn 4K 19
Sultan St. Acc 2D 22
Summer Brook. Nels 2D 6
Summer St. Nels 2D 6
Summerton Wlk. Dar 3E 26
(off Allerton Clo.)
Summerville Wlk. B'brn 7G 13
Sumner St. B'brn 2G 19
(in two parts)
Suncliffe Rd. Brier 5E 6
Sunderland St. Burn 4G 9
Sunnindale Av. Ross 4C 30
Sunningdale Gdns. Burn 6E 6
Sunnybank. Ross 4G 25
Sunnybank Clo. Ross 7A 28
Sunnybank Dri. Osw 6H 21
Sunny Bank Rd. B'brn 4G 19
Sunny Bank Rd. Helm 7A 28
Sunnybank St. Dar 4K 21
Sunnybank St. Has 2A 28
Sunny Bower Clo. B'brn ...6A 14
Sunny Bower Rd. B'brn ...6A 14
Sunnyfield La. Hodd 4K 27
Sunnyhill Clo. Dar 3B 26
Sunnyhurst Clo. Dar 3B 26
Sunnyhurst La. Dar 3B 26
Sunnyhurst Rd. B'brn 1G 19
Sunnyhurst Wood & Vis. Cen.
......3B 26
Sunny Lea St. Ross 7F 25
Sunnymere Dri. Dar 3C 26
Sunnyside Av. Cher T 5B 18
Sunnyside Av. Wilp 1C 14
Sunnyside Clo. Ross 6G 25
Sun St. Col 3H 5
Sun St. Nels 1D 6
Sun St. Osw 4K 21
Super St. Clay M 3K 15
Surrey Av. Burn 3G 9
Surrey Av. Dar 2D 26
Surrey Rd. B'brn 3C 20
Surrey Rd. Nels 6A 4
Surrey St. Acc 1E 22
Sussex Clo. Chu 1A 22
Sussex Dri. B'brn 1K 19
Sussex Dri. Has 5E 28
Sussex Rd. Rish 6E 14
Sussex St. Burn 6C 10
Sussex St. Nels 7B 4
Sussex Wlk. B'brn 1K 19
Sutcliffe St. Bacup 5K 31
Sutcliffe St. Brclf 6G 7
Sutcliffe St. B'brn 4A 10
Sutherland Clo. Wilp 1C 14
Sutherland St. Col 4F 5
Sutton Av. Burn 7E 6
Sutton Cres. Hun 6G 17
Sutton St. B'brn 5A 10
Swainbank St. Burn 5C 10
Swaine St. Nels 1D 6
Swaledale Av. Burn 5C 6
Swallow Dri. B'brn 6H 13
Swallowfields. B'brn 4G 13

Swallow Pk. Burn 5H 9
Swanage Rd. Burn 1D 10
Swan Courtyard. Clith 5E 2
Swan Farm Clo. Lwr D 6J 19
Swanfield Ct. Col 3K 5
Swanfield Ter. Col 3K 5
Swan Mdw. Clith 4D 2
Swan Pl. Col 3H 5
(off Market St.)
Swan St. B'brn 2H 19
Swan St. Dar 7F 27
Sweet Clough Dri. Burn ...4E 8
Swift Clo. B'brn 7J 13
Swinburne Clo. Acc 6F 23
Swinden Hall Rd. Nels 6B 4
Swinden La. Col 6D 4
Swindon St. Burn 5J 9
Swinless St. Burn 1C 10
Swinshaw Clo. Ross 2G 25
Swiss St. Acc 2A 22
Sycamore Av. Burn 3F 9
Sycamore Clo. B'brn 4J 13
Sycamore Clo. Burn 4H 9
Sycamore Clo. Rish 7G 15
Sycamore Cres. Clay M 2B 16
Sycamore Cres. Ross 4F 29
Sycamore Gro. Acc 5F 23
Sycamore Gro. Dar 3F 27
Sycamore Rd. B'brn 4J 13
Sydney St. Acc 2D 22
Sydney St. Burn 4A 10
Sydney St. Clay M 6B 16
Sydney St. Dar 6F 27
Sydney St. Hodd 4K 27
Sydney Ter. Traw 5K 5
Sykefield. Brier 4B 6
Syke Side Dri. Alt 1F 17
Syke St. Has 4C 28

T

Tabor St. Burn 3J 9
Tadema Gro. Burn 7A 10
Talbot Av. Clay M 5A 16
Talbot Clo. Clith 6F 3
Talbot Clo. Ross 5E 28
Talbot Dri. Brclf 7G 7
Talbot Rd. Acc 7B 16
Talbot St. Brclf 6G 7
Talbot St. Burn 4C 10
Talbot St. Col 2G 5
Talbot St. Rish 6H 15
Tanner St. Burn 4A 10
Tanpits Rd. Chu 2K 21
Tapestry St. B'brn 4G 19
Tarbert Cres. B'brn 4C 20
Tarleton Av. Burn 6C 10
Tarleton St. Burn 6C 10
Tarn Av. Clay M 3A 16
Tarn Brook Clo. Hun 6G 17
Tarvin Clo. Brclf 6G 7
Tasker St. Acc 2D 22
Tattersall Sq. Ross 2B 30
Tattersall St. B'brn 1H 19
Tattersall St. Osw 4J 21
Tattersall St. Pad 2C 8
Tattersall St. Ross 6B 24
Tatton St. Col 5E 4
Taunton Rd. B'brn 7E 12
Tavistock St. Nels 1G 7
Taylor Av. Ross 3B 30
Taylor Clo. B'brn 2G 19
Taylor Holme Ind. Est.
Bacup 5D 30
Taylor St. B'brn 2G 19
Taylor St. Brier 3C 6
Taylor St. Burn 3B 10
Taylor St. Clith 5F 3
Taylor St. Dar 5E 26
Taylor St. Ross 2G 29
(Greenfield St.)
Taylor St. Ross 6B 24
(Pilling St.)
Taylor St. W. Acc 2C 22
Tay St. Burn 5J 9
Teal Clo. B'brn 4G 13
Tedder Av. Burn 4G 9
Telford St. Burn 3H 9
Temple Clo. B'brn 4A 20

Temple Ct.—Victor St.

Temple Ct. B'brn 7H 13
Temple Dri. B'brn 4A 20
Temple St. Burn 5C 10
Temple St. Col 2H 5
Temple St. Nels 1G 7
Templeton Clo. Dar 3E 26
Tenby Clo. B'brn 5H 13
Tennis St. Burn 2B 10
Tennyson Av. Osw 4H 21
Tennyson Av. Pad 3D 8
Tennyson Pl. Gt Har 3G 15
Tennyson Rd. Col 3F 5
Tennyson St. Brclf 6G 7
Tennyson St. Burn 5J 9
Tennyson St. Hap 6B 8
Tenterfield St. Ross 5B 30
Tenterheads. Ross 6B 30
Terry St. Nels 6D 4
Tetbury Clo. B'brn 5B 18
Tewkesbury Clo. Acc 5F 23
Tewksbury St. B'brn 4E 18
Thames Av. Burn 6D 6
Thirlmere Av. Burn 7B 6
Thirlmere Av. Col 2J 5
Thirlmere Av. Has 5C 28
Thirlmere Av. Pad 1B 8
Thirlmere Clo. Acc 6E 16
Thirlmere Clo. B'brn 6J 13
Thirlmere Dri. Dar 3G 27
Thirlmere Rd. Burn 5F 11
Thirlmere Way. Ross 3G 25
Thistlemount Av. Ross 4B 30
Thistle St. Bacup 3H 31
Thomas St. B'brn 1G 19
Thomas St. Burn 5B 10
Thomas St. Col 4F 5
Thomas St. Has 2A 28
Thomas St. Nels 4B 6
(Clitheroe Rd.)
Thomas St. Nels 2F 7
(Duerden St.)
Thomas St. Osw 5J 21
Thompson St. B'brn 1F 19
Thompson St. Dar 6F 27
Thompson St. Pad 2B 8
Thompson St. Ind. Est.
B'brn 1F 19
(off Thompson St.)
Thorn Bank. Bacup 3J 31
Thornber Clo. Burn 1D 10
Thornber St. B'brn 2F 19
Thorncliffe Dri. Dar 5H 27
Thorn Clo. Bacup 3J 31
Thorn Cres. Bacup 3J 31
Thorn Dri. Bacup 3J 31
Thorne St. Nels 6D 4
Thorneybank Ind. Est. Hap 5K 17
Thorneybank St. Burn 5A 10
Thorneyholme Rd. Acc 1D 22
Thornfield Av. Ross 4A 30
Thorn Gdns. Bacup 3J 31
Thorn Gro. Col 2J 5
Thornhill Av. Rish 7F 15
Thorn Hill Clo. B'brn 7K 13
Thornhill St. Burn 4F 9
Thornley Av. B'brn 2B 20
Thorn St. Bacup 3J 31
Thorn St. Burn 2B 10
Thorn St. Clith 5D 2
Thorn St. Gt Har 1J 15
Thorn St. Ross 7F 25
Thornton Clo. Acc 7B 16
Thornton Clo. B'brn 5J 19
Thornton Cres. Burn 5F 11
Thornton Rd. Burn 5F 11
Thornwood Clo. B'brn 3H 13
Throstle Clo. Burn 3B 10
Throstle St. B'brn 1F 19
Throstle St. Nels 7B 4
Throup Pl. Nels 6B 4
Thursby Pl. Nels 6C 4
Thursby Rd. Burn 1C 10
Thursby Rd. Nels 6C 4
Thursby Sq. Burn 2B 10
Thursby St. Burn 1C 10
Thursden Av. Brclf 6G 7
Thursden Pl. Nels 7E 4
Thursfield Rd. Burn 5C 10
Thurston St. Burn 4C 10
Thwaites Av. Mel 2B 12
Thwaites Rd. Osw 5H 21
Thwaites St. Osw 5H 21
Tiber Av. Burn 6H 9
Timber St. Acc 3D 22
Timber St. Bacup 4H 31
Timber St. Brier 3C 6
Tinedale Vw. Pad 1C 8
Tintern Clo. Acc 6F 23
Tintern Cres. B'brn 7A 14
Tippet Clo. B'brn 4K 19
Tiverton Dri. B'brn 5F 19
Tiverton Dri. Brclf 6G 7
Tockholes Rd. Dar 3C 26
Todd Carr Rd. Ross 4B 30
Todd Hall Rd. Has 2A 28
Toddy Fold. B'brn 3H 13
Todmorden Old Rd. Bacup 2J 31
Todmorden Rd. Bacup 2J 31
Todmorden Rd. Brclf 6H 7
Todmorden Rd. Burn 5C 10
Toll Bar Bus. Pk. Bacup 5E 30
Tom La. Ross 3B 30
Tong La. Bacup 2J 31
Tontine St. B'brn 7H 13
Topaz St. B'brn 2J 13
Top Barn La. Ross 4K 29
Top o' th' Cft. B'brn 5G 19
Tor End Rd. Ross 7A 28
Toronto Rd. B'brn 4F 13
Torquay Av. Burn 7D 6
Torridon Clo. B'brn 4C 18
Torver Clo. Burn 2G 9
Tor Vw. Ross 4G 29
Tor Vw. Rd. Has 4C 28
Tottenham Rd. Lwr D 6J 19
Tottleworth Rd. B'brn 4H 15
Tourist Info. Cen. 2D 22
(Accrington)
Tourist Info. Cen. 7H 13
(Blackburn)
Tourist Info. Cen. 5A 10
(Burnley)
Tourist Info. Cen. 1E 6
(Nelson)
Tourist Info. Cen. 3G 29
(off Kay St., Rawtenstall)
Tower Hill. Clith 4F 3
Tower Rd. B'brn 3A 18
Tower Rd. Dar 5F 27
Tower St. Bacup 3H 31
Tower St. Osw 3G 21
Tower Vw. Dar 4G 27
Towneley Av. Acc 5G 17
Towneley Golf Course. 6D 10
Towneley Hall. 7D 10
(Art Gallery & Mus.)
Towneley 9 Hole Golf Course.
6E 10
Towneley St. Burn 1C 10
Townfield Av. Burn 4G 11
Towngate. Gt Har 2H 15
(off Church St.)
Town Hall Sq. Gt Har 2H 15
(off Blackburn Rd.)
Town Hall St. B'brn 7H 13
Town Hall St. Gt Har 2H 15
(off Curate St.)
Town Hill Bank. Pad 1C 8
Town Ho. Rd. Nels 1J 7
Townley St. Brclf 6G 7
Townley St. Brier 4C 6
Townley St. Col 2H 5
Townsend St. Has 2A 28
Townsend St. Waterf 5B 30
Townsley St. Nels 3F 7
Town Vw. B'brn 1J 19
Town Wlk. B'brn 1J 19
(off Town Vw.)
Trafalgar St. Burn 4K 9
Trans Britannia Enterprise Cen.
Burn 7G 9
Travis St. Burn 2B 10
Trawden Clo. Acc 4D 22
Trawden Hill. Traw 6K 5
(off Colne Rd.)
Tremellen St. Acc 2B 22
Trent Rd. Nels 1H 7
(in two parts)
Tresco Clo. B'brn 4E 18
Trevor Clo. B'brn 5H 13
Trinity Clo. Pad 4C 8
Trinity Ct. B'brn 6J 13
Trinity St. Bacup 5E 30
Trinity St. B'brn 7J 13
Trinity St. Osw 5J 21
Trinity Towers. Burn 4K 9
(off Accrington Rd.)
Troon Av. B'brn 5B 20
Trout Beck. Clay M 3A 16
Troutbeck Clo. Burn 2G 9
Trout St. Burn 2B 10
(off Grey St.)
Troy St. B'brn 5J 13
(in two parts)
Tucker Hill. Clith 4E 2
Tudor Clo. Dar 3E 26
Tunnel St. Burn 4J 9
Tunnel St. Dar 6G 27
Tunstall Dri. Acc 6C 16
Tunstead Cres. Bacup 4E 30
Tunstead La. Bacup 4C 30
(in two parts)
Tunstead Mill Ter. Bacup 5D 30
(off Newchurch Rd.)
Tunstead Rd. Bacup 5E 30
Tunstill Fold. Fence 1A 6
Tunstill Sq. Brier 4C 6
Tunstill St. Burn 1C 10
Turf St. Burn 5B 10
Turkey St. Acc 1E 22
Turncroft Rd. Dar 5F 27
Turner Rd. Nels 1C 6
Turner St. Bacup 5E 30
Turner St. B'brn 1F 19
Turner St. Clith 6E 2
Turney Crook M. Col 3G 5
Turn La. Dar 4C 26
Turnpike. Ross 4A 30
Turnpike Gro. Osw 3G 21
Turton Gro. Burn 4D 10
Turton Hollow Rd. Ross 4G 25
Tuscan Av. Burn 5H 9
Twitter La. Bas E & Wadd 3A 2
Two Gates Dri. Dar 3F 27
Two Gates Wlk. Dar 4F 27
Tynwald Rd. B'brn 4H 19
Tythebarn St. Dar 4F 27

U

Uldale Clo. Nels 3F 7
Ullswater Av. Acc 6E 16
Ullswater Clo. B'brn 6J 13
Ullswater Clo. Rish 6F 15
Ullswater Rd. Burn 5G 11
Ullswater Way. Ross 3G 25
Ulpha Clo. Burn 2G 9
Ulster St. Burn 5J 9
Ulverston Clo. B'brn 4K 19
Ulverston Dri. Rish 6F 15
Underbank Clo. Bacup 2H 31
Underbank Cotts. Acc 5A 24
Underbank Rd. Ris B 5A 24
Underbank Rd. Ross 2A 28
Underbank Way. Has 2A 28
Under Billinge La. B'brn 1B 18
Underley St. Burn 6D 6
Union Ct. Bacup 5E 30
(off Old School M.)
Union Rd. Osw 5J 21
Union Rd. Ross 3D 28
Union Sq. Bacup 3H 31
(off Union St.)
Union St. Acc 2C 22
Union St. Bacup 5E 30
(Church St.)
Union St. Bacup 3H 31
(Market St.)
Union St. B'brn 2H 19
Union St. Brier 4C 6
Union St. Clith 5C 2
Union St. Col 3H 5
Union St. Dar 4E 26
Union St. Has 2A 28
Union St. Raw 2G 29
Union Ter. Raw 3J 29
Unity St. B'brn 3H 19
Unity St. Dar 4F 27
Unity Way. Raw 2F 29
Unsworth St. Bacup 6F 31
Up Brooks. Clith 4F 3
(in two parts)
Up Brooks Ind. Est. Clith 4G 3
Up. Ashmount. Ross 4J 29
Up. Cliffe. Gt Har 1H 15

V

Vale Ct. Hun 6G 17
Va. Rock Gdns. Hodd 4K 27
Vale St. Bacup 2J 31
Vale St. B'brn 3H 19
Vale St. Dar 4D 26
Vale St. Has 1B 28
Vale St. Nels 1G 7
Vale Ter. Ross 2B 30
Valley Centre, The. Ross 3G 29
Valley Clo. Nels 7D 4
Valley Dri. Pad 2C 8
Valley Gdns. Hap 6E 8
Valley Rd. Wilp 3B 14
Valley St. Burn 6G 9
Valli Ga. B'brn 1A 20
Vancouver Cres. B'brn 4F 13
Vardon Rd. B'brn 2E 18
Varley St. Col 2H 5
Varley St. Dar 4E 26
Vaughan St. Nels 2G 7
Vauxhall St. B'brn 2E 18
Veevers St. Brier 4B 6
Veevers St. Burn 4A 10
(off Calder St.)
Veevers St. Pad 2C 8
Venables Av. Col 2J 5
Venice Av. Burn 6H 9
Venice St. Burn 5J 9
Ventnor Rd. Has 4C 28
Venture Ct. Alt 2E 16
Venture St. Bacup 2J 31
Verax St. Bacup 4H 31
Vernon St. B'brn 1H 19
Vernon St. Dar 4F 27
Vernon St. Nels 2F 7
Verona Av. Burn 5H 9
(off Florence Av.)
Veronica St. Dar 1C 26
Vicarage Av. Pad 2A 8
Vicarage Dri. Dar 5G 27
Vicarage La. Acc 7F 23
Vicarage La. Wilp 2A 14
Vicarage Rd. Nels 2E 6
Vicar St. B'brn 7J 13
Vicar St. Gt Har 3H 15
Victoria Apartments. Pad 1B 8
(off Habergham St.)
Victoria Av. Bax 6E 22
Victoria Av. B'brn 4B 18
Victoria Av. Brier 3C 6
Victoria Bldgs. Waters 2J 27
Victoria Bus. & Ind. Cen.
Acc 3C 22
Victoria Ct. B'brn 7H 13
(off Blackburn Shop. Cen.)
Victoria Ct. Chat 1K 3
Victoria Ct. Pad 3D 8
Victoria Dri. Has 3A 28
Victoria Gdns. Barfd 6A 4
Victoria Ho. B'brn 5A 20
Victoria Pde. Ross 5A 30
Victoria Rd. Pad 2C 8
Victoria St. Acc 3C 22
Victoria St. Bacup 5F 31
Victoria St. Barfd 5A 4
Victoria St. B'brn 7H 13
Victoria St. Burn 5A 10
Victoria St. Chu 2K 21
Victoria St. Clay M 5A 16
Victoria St. Clith 6D 2
Victoria St. Dar 4E 26
Victoria St. Gt Har 2J 15
Victoria St. Has 2A 28
Victoria St. Nels 1D 6
Victoria St. Osw 5J 21
Victoria St. Raw 4J 29
Victoria St. Rish 6G 15
Victoria St. Ross 5A 30
Victoria Way. Raw 3J 29
Victor St. Clay M 4A 16

54 A-Z Blackburn

Victory Cen., The. *Nels* 1F **7**
Victory Clo. *Nels* 1F **7**
View Rd. *Dar* 1C **26**
Viking Pl. *Burn* 3B **10**
Villiers St. *Nels* 5H **9**
Villiers St. *Pad* 3C **8**
Vincent Ct. *B'brn* 5G **19**
Vincent Rd. *Nels* 1G **7**
Vincent St. *B'brn* 5G **19**
Vincent St. *Col* 2J **5**
Vincit St. *Burn* 2C **10**
Vine St. *Acc* 2B **22**
Vine St. *Brier* 4C **6**
Vine St. *Osw* 5H **21**
Violet St. *Burn* 1B **10**
Viscount Av. *Lwr D* 7K **19**
Vivary Way. *Col* 4E **4**
Vulcan St. *Burn* 4A **10**
Vulcan St. *Nels* 7C **4**

W

Wackersall Rd. *Col* 5E **4**
Waddington Av. *Burn* 4E **10**
Waddington Hospital. *Wadd* . .1B **2**
Waddington Rd. *Acc* 1E **22**
Waddington Rd. *Clith* 3D **2**
Waddington Rd. *W Brad* 1D **2**
Waddington St. *Pad* 2C **8**
Waddow Grn. *Clith* 5C **2**
Waddow Gro. *Wadd* 1C **2**
Waddow Vw. *Wadd* 1B **2**
Wade St. *Pad* 1C **8**
Waidshouse Clo. *Nels* 3F **7**
Waidshouse Rd. *Nels* 3F **7**
Wain Ct. *B'brn* 1E **18**
Waingate Clo. *Ross* 2H **29**
Waingate La. *Ross* 2H **29**
Waingate Rd. *Ross* 2H **29**
Walden Rd. *B'brn* 4B **14**
Wales Rd. *Ross* 4B **30**
Wales St. *Ross* 3B **30**
Wales Ter. *Ross* 4B **30**
Walker Av. *Acc* 4B **22**
Walker St. *B'brn* 1J **19**
Walker St. *Clith* 5F **3**
Wallhurst Clo. *Wors* 5J **11**
(in two parts)
Wallstreams La. *Wors* 5J **11**
Wall St. *Ross* 3A **30**
Walmesley Ct. *Clay M* 6A **16**
Walmsley Av. *Rish* 7F **15**
Walmsley Clo. *Chu* 2K **21**
Walmsley St. *Dar* 3F **27**
Walmsley St. *Gt Har* 2H **15**
Walmsley St. *Rish* 6G **15**
Walney Gdns. *B'brn* 4J **19**
Walnut Av. *Has* 2C **28**
Walnut St. *Bacup* 2H **31**
Walnut St. *B'brn* 5J **13**
Walpole St. *B'brn* 1J **19**
Walpole St. *Burn* 1C **10**
Walsden Gro. *Burn* 4D **10**
Walshaw La. *Burn* 7E **6**
Walshaw St. *Burn* 2C **10**
Walsh St. *Acc* 2B **22**
Walter St. *Acc* 1K **19**
Walter St. *Brier* 5C **6**
Walter St. *Dar* 7F **27**
Walter St. *Hun* 5F **17**
Walter St. *Osw* 5J **21**
Waltham Clo. *Acc* 5F **23**
Walton Clo. *Bacup* 4J **31**
Walton Cottage Homes. *Nels* . .7D **4**
(off Broadway Pl.)
Walton Cres. *B'brn* 4K **19**
Walton Dri. *Alt* 1F **17**
Walton La. *Nels* 6C **4**
Walton St. *Acc* 6B **16**
Walton St. *Barfd* 4B **4**
Walton St. *Col* 3G **5**
(in two parts)
Walton St. *Nels* 7B **4**
Walverden Cres. *Nels* 1G **7**
Walverden Rd. *Brclf* 5J **7**
Walverden Rd. *Brier* 4E **6**
Walverden Ter. *Nels* 2G **7**
Wansfell Rd. *Clith* 6C **2**

Warburton Bldgs. *Has* 4A **28**
Warburton St. *Has* 4A **28**
Warcock La. *Bacup* 2K **31**
Ward Av. *Osw* 5H **21**
Wardle St. *Bacup* 5F **31**
Ward St. *Burn* 4K **9**
Ward St. *Gt Har* 2H **15**
Ward St. *Nels* 1F **7**
Wareham Clo. *Acc* 6C **16**
Wareham St. *B'brn* 5K **13**
Warings, The. *Nels* 3F **7**
Warkworth Ter. Bacup 2J **31**
(off Venture St.)
Warmden Av. *Acc* 5F **23**
Warmden Gdns. *B'brn* 5K **13**
Warner St. *Acc* 3D **22**
Warner St. *Has* 2B **28**
Warrenside Clo. *B'brn* 4C **14**
Warrington St. *B'brn* 4K **13**
Warth Old Rd. *Ross* 5A **30**
Warwick Av. *Acc* 1B **22**
Warwick Av. *Clay M* 4A **16**
(in two parts)
Warwick Av. *Dar* 2C **26**
Warwick Clo. *Chu* 1A **22**
Warwick Dri. *Brier* 4E **6**
Warwick Dri. *Clith* 3F **3**
Warwick Dri. *Pad* 3C **8**
Warwick St. *Chu* 1A **22**
Warwick St. *Has* 2B **28**
Warwick St. *Nels* 2F **7**
Wasdale Av. *B'brn* 5B **20**
Wasdale Clo. *Pad* 1B **8**
Washington St. *Acc* 2D **22**
Waterbarn St. *Burn* 1C **10**
Waterfall Ind. Est. *B'brn* 3F **19**
(off Dimmock St.)
Waterfield Av. *Dar* 7F **27**
Waterford St. *Nels* 7C **4**
Waterloo. *Acc* 1C **22**
Waterloo Clo. *B'brn* 5E **18**
Waterloo Rd. *Burn* 5E **10**
(in two parts)
Waterloo Rd. *Clith* 5F **3**
Waterloo St. *Clay M* 6B **16**
Water Meadows. *B'brn* 6G **19**
Waters Edge. *B'brn* 2J **19**
Waterside Ind. Est. *Col* 4H **5**
Waterside M. *Pad* 2B **8**
Waterside Rd. *Col* 4G **5**
Waterside Rd. *Has* 3A **28**
Waterside Ter. Bacup 2H **31**
(off Myrtle Bank Rd.)
Waterside Ter. *Waters* 2J **27**
Water St. *Acc* 2D **22**
(in two parts)
Water St. *Barfd* 4A **4**
Water St. *Clay M* 2A **16**
Water St. *Col* 3H **5**
Water St. *Craw* 4G **25**
Water St. *Gt Har* 2H **15**
Water St. *Hap* 6B **8**
Water St. *Nels* 1F **7**
Water St. *Wors* 5J **11**
Watery La. *Dar* 7F **27**
Watford St. *B'brn* 6H **13**
Watkins Clo. *Brier* 5D **6**
Watling Clo. *B'brn* 5K **19**
Watson St. *B'brn* 3E **18**
Watson St. *Osw* 5K **21**
Watt St. *Burn* 3H **9**
Wavell Clo. *Acc* 7G **23**
Wavell St. *Burn* 4H **9**
Waverlede Bus. Pk. *Gt Har* . . .3G **15**
Waverledge Rd. *Gt Har* 3G **15**
Waverledge St. *Gt Har* 3H **15**
Waverley Clo. *Brier* 5E **6**
Waverley Pl. *B'brn* 7E **12**
Waverley Rd. *Acc* 5F **23**
Waverley Rd. *Int* 4D **20**
Waverley Rd. *Rams* 4A **14**
Waverley St. *Burn* 4K **9**
Weatherhill Cres. *Brier* 4F **7**
Weavers' Triangle Vis. Cen.
. . . . .5A **10**
Webber Ct. *Burn* 7F **9**
Weber St. *Ross* 4K **29**
Wedgewood Rd. *Acc* 6G **17**

Weir St. *B'brn* 1H **19**
Welbeck Av. *B'brn* 7A **14**
Weldon St. *Burn* 5K **9**
Well Ct. *Clith* 4F **3**
(off Causeway Cft.)
Wellesley St. *Burn* 4E **8**
Wellfield. *Clay M* 5B **16**
Wellfield Dri. *Burn* 2H **9**
Wellfield Rd. *B'brn* 6F **13**
Well Fold. *Clith* 5F **3**
Wellgate. *Clith* 5E **2**
Wellington Ct. *Acc* 3D **22**
Wellington Ct. *Burn* 5C **10**
Wellington Fold. *Dar* 4E **26**
Wellington Rd. *B'brn* 2F **19**
Wellington St. *Acc* 3D **22**
Wellington St. *B'brn* 6G **13**
Wellington St. *Clay M* 5A **16**
Wellington St. *Gt Har* 3H **15**
Wellington St. *Nels* 7A **4**
Wells St. *Has* 2B **28**
Well St. *Pad* 1A **8**
Well St. *Rish* 5G **15**
Well St. *Waterf* 2B **30**
Well Ter. *Clith* 4F **3**
Wenning St. *Nels* 2G **7**
Wensley Clo. *Burn* 7K **9**
Wensley Dri. *Acc* 2E **22**
Wensley Rd. *B'brn* 1E **18**
Wesleyan Row. *Clith* 5F **3**
Wesley Gro. *Burn* 3J **9**
Wesley Pl. *Bacup* 4G **31**
Wesley St. *B'brn* 5J **13**
Wesley St. *Brier* 3C **6**
Wesley St. *Chu* 2A **22**
Wesley St. *Osw* 3K **21**
Wesley St. *Pad* 2C **8**
Wessex Clo. *Acc* 7F **17**
Westbourne. *Ross* 5A **28**
Westbourne Av. *Burn* 6J **9**
Westbourne Av. S. *Burn* 7K **9**
W. Bradford Rd. *Clith* 1F **3**
W. Bradford Rd. *Wadd* 1B **2**
Westbury Clo. *Burn* 7F **7**
Westbury Gdns. *B'brn* 4B **20**
Westcliffe. *Gt Har* 1G **15**
Westcliffe Wlk. *Nels* 2E **6**
Westcote St. *Dar* 7F **27**
West Cres. *Acc* 7C **16**
W. End Bus. Pk. *Osw* 3G **21**
Western Av. *Burn* 6K **9**
Western Ct. *Bacup* 5E **30**
Western Rd. *Bacup* 5E **30**
Westfield. *Nels* 7A **4**
West Gdns. *Bacup* 5D **30**
(off West Vw.)
Westgate. *Burn* 4K **9**
Westgate Trad. Cen. *Burn* 4A **10**
(off Wiseman St.)
West Hill. *Barfd* 4A **4**
Westland Av. *Dar* 5D **26**
W. Leigh Rd. *B'brn* 4F **13**
Westminster Clo. *Acc* 5F **23**
Westminster Rd. *Dar* 2C **26**
Westmorland Rd. *Burn* 5J **9**
Westmorland St. *Nels* 1D **6**
West Pk. Rd. *B'brn* 6H **13**
West St. *Burn* 2D **10**
West St. *Col* 4H **5**
West St. *Gt Har* 3H **15**
West St. *Nels* 7A **4**
West St. *Pad* 2A **8**
West St. *Ross* 5A **30**
West Vw. *B'brn* 1E **18**
West Vw. *Clith* 6D **2**
West Vw. *Has* 1B **28**
West Vw. *Helm* 6A **28**
West Vw. *Osw* 4K **21**
West Vw. *Stac* 5D **30**
West Vw. Waterf 4B **30**
(off Pleasant Vw.)
W. View Pl. *B'brn* 6E **12**
W. View Rd. *Ross* 1B **30**
(in two parts)
W. View Ter. *Pad* 3B **8**
Westway. *Burn* 4J **9**
Westwell St. *Dar* 1C **26**
Westwell St. *Gt Har* 2H **15**
Westwood Av. *Rish* 6F **15**

Westwood Ct. *B'brn* 6K **13**
Westwood Rd. *B'brn* 4A **20**
Westwood Rd. *Burn* 2H **9**
Westwood St. *Acc* 1C **22**
Whalley Banks. *B'brn* 1G **19**
Whalley Banks Trad. Est.
B'brn 1G **19**
Whalley Cres. *Dar* 4F **27**
Whalley Dri. *Ross* 1G **29**
Whalley New Rd.
B'brn & Rams 1H **13**
Whalley Old Rd. *B'brn* 6J **13**
Whalley Range. *B'brn* 6H **13**
Whalley Rd. *Clay M & Acc* . . .6B **16**
Whalley Rd. *Clith* 7D **2**
Whalley Rd. *Read & S'stne* . . .1A **8**
Whalley Rd. *Wilp* 4B **14**
Whalley St. *B'brn* 6H **13**
Whalley St. *Burn* 1B **10**
Whalley St. *Clith* 5D **2**
Whalley Ter. *Live* 7E **18**
Wham Brook Clo. *Osw* 3G **21**
Wharfedale Av. *Burn* 5C **6**
Wharfedale Clo. *B'brn* 6A **18**
Wharf St. *B'brn* 7J **13**
Wharf St. *Rish* 6H **15**
Wheatfield St. *Rish* 5G **15**
Wheatholme St. *Ross* 3H **29**
Wheatley Clo. *Burn* 3J **9**
Wheatley La. Rd. *Barfd* 5A **4**
Wheat St. *Acc* 2B **22**
Wheat St. *Pad* 3C **8**
Whewell Row. *Osw* 3H **21**
Whinberry Av. *Ross* 4G **29**
Whinberry Vw. *Ross* 3H **29**
Whinfield Pl. *B'brn* 6D **12**
Whinfield St. *Clay M* 6B **16**
Whinney Hill Rd.
Acc & Hun I 6B **16**
Whinney La. *Mel & B'brn* 2D **12**
Whipp Av. *Clith* 6D **2**
Whitaker St. *Acc* 1C **22**
Whitby Dri. *B'brn* 4J **19**
White Acre Rd. *Acc* 6G **23**
White Ash Est. *Osw* 4H **21**
White Ash La. *Osw* 5J **21**
Whitebirk Dri. *B'brn* 7A **14**
Whitebirk Ind. Est. *B'brn* 6B **14**
(in two parts)
Whitebirk Rd. *B'brn* 2C **20**
White Bull St. Burn 4H **9**
(off Keith St.)
Whitecroft Av. *Has* 3B **28**
Whitecroft Clo. *Has* 3B **28**
Whitecroft La. *Mel* 2B **12**
Whitecroft Meadows. *Has* 3B **28**
White Cft. Rd. *Acc* 7G **21**
Whitecroft Vw. *Acc* 6F **23**
Whitefield St. *Hap* 6B **8**
Whitefield Ter. Burn 6C **10**
(off Somerset St.)
Whitegate Clo. *Pad* 3D **8**
Whitegate Gdns. *Pad* 3D **8**
White Gro. *Col* 2F **5**
Whitehall Rd. *B'brn* 5E **12**
Whitehall Rd. *Dar* 7F **27**
Whitehall St. *Nels* 1G **7**
Whitehaven Clo. *B'brn* 4K **19**
Whitehaven St. *Burn* 5J **9**
Whitehead St. *B'brn* 7F **13**
Whitehead St. *Ross* 2G **29**
Whitehough Pl. *Nels* 7E **4**
White Lee Av. *Traw* 6K **5**
Whiteley Av. *B'brn* 4D **18**
Whiteley St. *Has* 4C **28**
Whitendale Cres. *B'brn* 2J **19**
White Rd. *B'brn* 6E **12**
White St. *Burn* 4G **9**
White St. *Col* 5E **4**
Whitewalls Clo. *Col* 5D **4**
Whitewalls Ind. Est. *Col* 5C **4**
Whitewell Dri. *Clith* 6C **2**
Whitewell Pl. B'brn 6J **13**
(off Ribble St.)
Whitewell Rd. *Acc* 7E **16**
Whitewell Va. Ross 3B **30**
(off Burnley Rd.)
Whittaker Clo. *Burn* 2G **9**
Whittaker St. *B'brn* 7F **13**

Whittam Ct. *Wors* 4J **11**
   (off Showfield)
Whittam St. *Burn* 5A **10**
Whittle Clo. *Clith* 4F **3**
Whittles St. *Bacup* 5K **31**
Whittle St. *Has* 3A **28**
Whittle St. *Raw* 2G **29**
Whittycroft Av. *Barfd* 2B **4**
Whittycroft Dri. *Barfd* 2B **4**
Wicken Gro. *Ross* 4G **25**
Wickliffe St. *Nels* 7B **4**
Wickworth St. *Nels* 2G **7**
Widow Hill Ct. *Burn* 1E **10**
Widow Hill Rd. *Burn* 1D **10**
Wilfield St. *Burn* 4K **9**
Wilfred St. *Acc* 4D **22**
Wilkie Av. *Burn* 7A **10**
Wilkin Bri. *Clith* 5E **2**
Wilkinson St. *Burn* 6E **6**
Wilkinson St. *Has* 1B **28**
Wilkinson St. *Nels* 5A **4**
Wilkin Sq. *Clith* 5E **2**
Willaston Av. *Black* 1B **4**
William Griffiths Ct. *B'brn* 3E **18**
   (off Mill Hill Bri. St.)
William Herbert St. *B'brn* 6J **13**
William Hopwood St. *B'brn* 1K **19**
Williams Pl. *Nels* 1G **7**
Williams Rd. *Burn* 1C **10**
William St. *Acc* 1D **22**
William St. *Bacup* 5K **31**
William St. *B'brn* 3H **19**
William St. *Brier* 3C **6**
William St. *Clay M* 6B **16**
William St. *Col* 4H **5**
William St. *Dar* 4E **26**
William St. *Nels* 1F **7**
Willis Rd. *B'brn* 3C **18**
Willis St. *Burn* 5K **9**
Willoughby St. *B'brn* 6H **13**
Willow Av. *Ross* 1G **29**
Willow Bank. *Dar* 7E **26**
Willow Bank La. *Dar* 4D **26**
Willow Brook. *Acc* 2C **22**
Willow Clo. *Clay M* 4K **15**
Willow Mt. *B'brn* 1J **13**
Willow Pk. *Osw* 6H **21**
Willows La. *Acc* 3B **22**
Willow St. *Acc* 2C **22**
Willow St. *B'brn* 5K **13**
Willow St. *Burn* 4K **9**
Willow St. *Clay M* 4K **15**
Willow St. *Dar* 4D **26**
Willow St. *Gt Har* 3H **15**
Willow St. *Has* 2B **28**
Willow St. *Ross* 5A **30**
Willow Tree Av. *Ross* 3E **28**
Willow Trees Dri. *B'brn* 4F **13**
Wilmore Clo. *Col* 3F **5**
Wilpshire Banks. *Wilp* 4B **14**
Wilpshire Golf Course. 3C **14**
Wilson St. *B'brn* 3G **19**
Wilson St. *Clith* 6D **2**
Wilton St. *Barfd* 5A **4**
Wilton St. *Brier* 4C **6**
Wilton St. *Burn* 1C **10**
Wiltshire Av. *Burn* 3G **9**
Wiltshire Dri. *Has* 5B **28**
Wilworth Cres. *B'brn* 3H **13**
Wimberley Banks. *B'brn* 5J **13**
   (off Wimberley St.)
Wimberley Gdns. *B'brn* 6H **13**
Wimberley Pl. *B'brn* 6H **13**

Wimberley St. *B'brn* 6H **13**
Winchester Av. *Acc* 1D **22**
Winchester Rd. *Pad* 4C **8**
Winchester St. *B'brn* 2K **19**
Winckley Rd. *Clay M* 5A **16**
Windermere Av. *Acc* 6E **16**
Windermere Av. *Burn* 7B **6**
Windermere Av. *Clith* 6C **2**
Windermere Av. *Col* 2J **5**
Windermere Clo. *B'brn* 6J **13**
Windermere Dri. *Dar* 2G **27**
Windermere Dri. *Rish* 6F **15**
Windermere Rd. *Bacup* 2J **31**
Windermere Rd. *Pad* 1B **8**
Windsor Av. *Chu* 7B **16**
Windsor Av. *Clith* 6C **2**
Windsor Av. *Helm* 4A **28**
Windsor Av. *Ross* 4A **30**
Windsor Clo. *B'brn* 5A **20**
Windsor Rd. *B'brn* 3D **20**
   (Blackburn Rd.)
Windsor Rd. *B'brn* 6E **12**
   (Revidge Rd.)
Windsor Rd. *Dar* 2D **26**
Windsor Rd. *Gt Har* 2J **15**
Windsor St. *Acc* 2D **22**
Windsor St. *Burn* 4H **9**
Windsor St. *Col* 3H **5**
Windsor St. *Nels* 2G **7**
Windy Bank. *Col* 3H **5**
Winmarleigh St. *B'brn* 4B **20**
Winmarleigh Wlk. *B'brn* 4A **20**
Winnipeg Clo. *B'brn* 4E **12**
Winsford Wlk. *Burn* 5G **9**
Winster Ct. *Clay M* 5K **15**
Winston Rd. *B'brn* 5G **13**
Winterburn Rd. *B'brn* 6F **19**
Winterley Dri. *Acc* 6F **17**
Winterton Rd. *Dar* 3E **26**
Winward Clo. *Lwr D* 7J **19**
Wiseman St. *Burn* 4K **9**
Wisteria Dri. *Lwr D* 6K **19**
Wiswell Clo. *Burn* 7F **7**
Wiswell Clo. *Ross* 1G **29**
Withers St. *B'brn* 1J **19**
Within Gro. *Acc* 6E **16**
Witney Av. *B'brn* 5B **18**
Wittlewood Dri. *Acc* 6C **16**
Witton Country Pk. & Vis. Cen.
   .2C **18**
Witton Pde. *B'brn* 2F **19**
Woburn Clo. *Acc* 5F **23**
Wolfenden Grn. *Ross* 5B **30**
Wolseley St. *B'brn* 4G **19**
Woodale Laithe. *Barfd* 5A **4**
Wood Bank. *Ross* 7A **28**
Woodbank Av. *Dar* 3C **26**
Woodbine Gdns. *Burn* 3G **9**
Woodbine Rd. *B'brn* 6E **12**
Woodbine Rd. *Burn* 4H **9**
Woodburn Clo. *B'brn* 4D **12**
Woodbury Av. *B'brn* 3G **19**
Wood Clough Flats. *Brier* 4B **6**
Woodcourt Av. *Burn* 7J **9**
Woodcrest. *Wilp* 3B **14**
Woodcroft Av. *Ross* 7F **25**
Woodcroft St. *Ross* 7F **25**
Wood End. *Burn* 6A **6**
Woodfield Av. *Acc* 5E **22**
Woodfield Ter. *Brier* 4D **6**
Woodfold Pl. *B'brn* 7E **12**
Woodgates Rd. *B'brn* 7B **12**
Woodgrove Rd. *Burn* 7C **10**

Woodhead Clo. *Ross* 4C **30**
Woodhouse St. *Burn* 6C **10**
Woodland Av. *Bacup* 1H **31**
Woodland Dri. *Clay M* 2A **16**
Woodland Mt. *Bacup* 5E **30**
Woodland Pl. *Lwr D* 6J **19**
Woodlands Av. *B'brn* 4B **18**
Woodlands Gro. *Dar* 3B **26**
Woodlands Gro. *Pad* 2A **8**
Woodlands Rd. *Nels* 1G **7**
Woodland Ter. *Bacup* 1H **31**
Woodland Vw. *Bacup* 1H **31**
Woodland Vw. *Gt Har* 1H **15**
Wood Lea Bank. *Ross* 5B **30**
   (off Wood Lea Rd.)
Woodlea Gdns. *Brier* 4E **6**
Woodlea Rd. *B'brn* 4A **20**
Wood Lea Rd. *Ross* 5A **30**
Woodley Av. *Acc* 4D **22**
Wood Nook. *Ross* 5G **25**
Woodpecker Hill. *Burn* 5H **9**
   (off Nightingale Cres.)
Woodplumpton Rd. *Burn* 7A **10**
Woodsend Clo. *B'brn* 5K **19**
Woodside. *Has* 3C **28**
Woodside Av. *Rish* 7E **14**
Woodside Clo. *Acc* 6G **17**
Woodside Cres. *Ross* 4K **29**
Woodside Gro. *B'brn* 5D **18**
Woodside Rd. *Acc* 7F **17**
   (Bolton Av., in two parts)
Woodside Rd. *Acc* 6G **17**
   (Sutton Cres.)
Woodside Ter. *Nels* 1D **6**
Woodside Way. *Clay M* 3A **16**
Woodsley St. *Burn* 5G **9**
Woodstock Cres. *B'brn* 5B **18**
Wood St. *Brier* 4C **6**
Wood St. *Burn* 2B **10**
Wood St. *Col* 4H **5**
Wood St. *Dar* 3D **26**
   (Alexandra Rd.)
Wood St. *Dar* 4D **26**
   (Vale Rd.)
Wood St. *Gt Har* 2K **15**
Wood St. *Hap* 6B **8**
Wood St. *Osw* 3K **21**
Wood Ter. *Chat* 1K **3**
Woodvale. *Dar* 4D **26**
Wood Vw. *B'brn* 4C **18**
Woodville Rd. *B'brn* 5K **13**
Woodville Rd. *Brier* 3C **6**
Woodville Ter. *Dar* 7F **27**
Wooley La. *Acc* 5G **23**
Woolwich St. *B'brn* 3A **20**
Woone La. *Clith* 7D **2**
Worcester Av. *Acc* 1B **22**
Worcester Rd. *B'brn* 3B **20**
Wordsworth Av. *Pad* 3D **8**
Wordsworth Clo. *Osw* 4H **21**
Wordsworth Dri. *Gt Har* 2G **15**
Wordsworth Gdns. *Dar* 4F **27**
Wordsworth Rd. *Acc* 5B **22**
Wordsworth Rd. *Col* 3G **5**
Wordsworth St. *Brclf* 7G **7**
Wordsworth St. *Burn* 4H **9**
Wordsworth St. *Hap* 6B **8**
Worksey Ct. *Osw* 4K **21**
Worsley St. *Acc* 4E **22**
Worsley St. *Ris B* 5A **24**
Worston Clo. *Acc* 4A **22**
Worston Clo. *Ross* 1G **29**
Worston La. *Gt Har* 1K **15**

Worston Pl. *B'brn* 7E **12**
Worston Rd. *Chat* 2J **3**
Worswick Cres. *Ross* 3G **29**
Wraith St. *Dar* 5E **26**
Wren St. *Burn* 4H **9**
Wren St. *Nels* 1G **7**
Wroxham Clo. *Burn* 7E **6**
Wycollar Clo. *Acc* 4D **22**
Wycollar Dri. *B'brn* 6D **12**
Wycollar Rd. *B'brn* 6D **12**
Wycoller Av. *Burn* 5E **10**
Wyfordby Av. *B'brn* 5C **12**
Wynotham St. *Burn* 7C **6**
Wyre Cres. *Dar* 2B **26**
Wyresdale Av. *Acc* 7B **16**
Wyre St. *Pad* 2C **8**
Wytham St. *Pad* 3C **8**
Wythburn Av. *B'brn* 5B **18**
Wythburn Clo. *Burn* 2G **9**

Y

Yare St. *Ross* 5B **30**
Yarmouth Av. *Has* 3C **28**
Yarm Pl. *Burn* 4B **10**
Yarraville St. *Ross* 3G **29**
Yates Fold. *B'brn* 3J **19**
Yerburgh Rd. *Mel* 2B **12**
Yewbarrow Clo. *Burn* 1H **9**
Yewlands Dri. *Burn* 6C **6**
Yew St. *B'brn* 5K **13**
Yew Tree Clo. *Clay D* 2A **14**
Yew Tree Dri. *B'brn* 4C **12**
Yew Tree Dri. *Osw* 5A **22**
Yew Tree Gro. *Ross* 5F **29**
York Av. *Has* 5A **28**
York Clo. *Clay M* 4A **16**
York Cres. *B'brn* 1J **13**
Yorke St. *Burn* 5A **10**
York Pl. *Acc* 1C **22**
York Rd. *Brier* 4C **6**
Yorkshire St. *Acc* 4D **22**
Yorkshire St. *Bacup* 2H **31**
Yorkshire St. *Burn* 4B **10**
   (in two parts)
Yorkshire St. *Hun* 5F **17**
Yorkshire St. *Nels* 1F **7**
York St. *Acc* 1C **22**
York St. *B'brn* 2H **19**
York St. *Chu* 2K **21**
York St. *Clith* 4F **3**
York St. *Col* 3H **5**
York St. *Gt Har* 2J **15**
York St. *Nels* 1G **7**
York St. *Osw* 5H **21**
York St. *Rish* 6G **15**
York St. *Ross* 5G **25**
York Ter. *B'brn* 5A **18**
York Vw. *Live* 7E **18**
Young St. *B'brn* 3E **18**

Z

Zebudah St. *B'brn* 3F **19**
Zechariah Brow. *B'brn* 1E **12**
Zion Rd. *B'brn* 4K **13**
Zion St. *Bacup* 2J **31**
Zion St. *Col* 4G **5**

Every possible care has been taken to ensure that, to the best of our knowledge, the information contained in this atlas is accurate at the date of publication. However, we cannot warrant that our work is entirely error free and whilst we would be grateful to learn of any inaccuracies, we do not accept any responsibility for loss or damage resulting from reliance on information contained within this publication.

The representation on the maps of a road, track or footpath is no evidence of the existence of a right of way.

The Grid on this map is the National Grid taken from Ordnance Survey mapping with the permission of the Controller of Her Majesty's Stationery Office.

Copyright of Geographers' A-Z Map Company Ltd.

No reproduction by any method whatsoever of any part of this publication is permitted without the prior consent of the copyright owners.